"*In Suicide: The Basics*, the author, Matias Gay, presents his roadmap to some basics on suicide. The word basics in the Oxford English Dictionary (OED) is defined as central, essential, fundamental, important, principal; but also, as elementary. This book is 'consistently useful to newcomers' (beginners/learners). It is not for the veteran suicidologists; it is rather written for those who aspire to become an expert in suicide prevention. It will launch your journey to help you understand suicide and life better, to help in suicide prevention and life promotion, and to reflect on yourself."

Antoon A. Leenaars, PhD, *Psychologist; Founding/First Editor-in-Chief,* Archives of Suicide Research

"*Suicide: The Basics* is a compelling and insightful work. Matias Gay offers a thoughtful exploration of suicide prevention, presenting the subject with clarity, depth, and compassion. Drawing on his extensive experience as both a researcher and clinician, he captures the core of effective suicide prevention, empathy. This text skillfully integrates theory and practice, serving as an essential educational resource for those who wish to prevent and learn more about suicidal behavior."

Igor Galynker, *Clinical Professor of Psychiatry, Icahn School of Medicine at Mount Sinai, NY, USA*

SUICIDE

Suicide: The Basics is a concise, accessible, and evidence-informed introduction to the study, prevention, and lived experience of suicide.

Written for students and readers approaching the topic for the first time, this book explains key areas in suicidology such as theories, risk and protective factors, and suicidal crisis processes. Rather than reducing suicide to diagnoses or statistics, it explains how suicidal crises develop through pain, meaning, relationships, and moments of feeling trapped. Bridging science and humanity, it shows not just *what* suicide is, but *how* it unfolds and *where* intervention can make a real difference. By considering methods of assessment, treatments, and community and policy strategies that help, the author explores how age, culture, and identity shape both vulnerability and recovery. He provides a compassionate and straightforward overview of suicide with short sections, illustrative tables, end-of-chapter summaries, and annotated reading lists.

By including practical ways to find help, support others, and pursue further study, this book will appeal to students of counseling, nursing, philosophy, psychology, public health, social work, and sociology, as well as readers with a general interest in the topic of mental well-being and suicide prevention.

Matias Gay is a suicidology researcher, clinician, and educator whose work advances narrative identity, acute risk assessment, and compassionate, person-centered suicide prevention.

The Basics

The Basics is a highly successful series of accessible guidebooks which provide an overview of the fundamental principles of a subject area in a jargon-free and undaunting format.

Intended for students approaching a subject for the first time, the books both introduce the essentials of a subject and provide an ideal springboard for further study. With over 50 titles spanning subjects from artificial intelligence (AI) to women's studies, *The Basics* are an ideal starting point for students seeking to understand a subject area.

Each text comes with recommendations for further study and gradually introduces the complexities and nuances within a subject.

GLOBAL COMICS
FREDERICK LUIS ALDAMA

CONTEMPORARY INDIA
REKHA DATTA

POLYGAMY
BRUCE WHITEHOUSE AND WILLIAM JANKOWIAK

SUICIDE
MATIAS GAY

ROMANTICISM
ELIZABETH A. FAY

LEADERSHIP
MORGEN WITZEL

HUMAN-COMPUTER INTERACTION
ALAN DIX

ECOLOGY
PHILIP JAMES

TRANSGENDER PHILOSOPHY
MATTHEW J. CULL

CULTURAL GEOGRAPHIES
ANDREW LAPWORTH AND TOM ROBERTS

For more information about this series, please visit: www.routledge.com/The-Basics/book-series/B

SUICIDE

THE BASICS

Matias Gay

Routledge
Taylor & Francis Group
NEW YORK AND LONDON

Designed cover image: © Matias Gay

First published 2027
by Routledge
605 Third Avenue, New York, NY 10158

and by Routledge
4 Park Square, Milton Park, Abingdon, Oxon, OX14 4RN

Routledge is an imprint of the Taylor & Francis Group, an informa business

Library of Congress Cataloging-in-Publication Data
Names: Gay, Matias author
Title: Suicide: the basics / Matias Gay.
Description: New York, NY: Routledge, 2027. |
Series: The basics | Includes bibliographical references and index. |.
Identifiers: LCCN 2026020808 (print) | LCCN 2026020809 (ebook) |
ISBN 9781041283119 hardback | ISBN 9781041278443 paperback |
ISBN 9781003758792 ebook
Subjects: LCSH: Suicide | Suicide—Prevention
Classification: LCC HV6545 .G394 2027 (print) | LCC HV6545 (ebook)
LC record available at https://lccn.loc.gov/2026020808
LC ebook record available at https://lccn.loc.gov/2026020809

ISBN: 978-1-041-28311-9 (hbk)
ISBN: 978-1-041-27844-3 (pbk)
ISBN: 978-1-003-75879-2 (ebk)

DOI: 10.4324/9781003758792

Typeset in Bembo
by codeMantra

CONTENTS

A Note on Care and Safety ix
Acknowledgments x
Preface xii

1 **Suicide in Definition and History** 1

2 **The Architecture of Suicide: Core Models Explained** 16

3 **Clues and Measures: Risk Factors, Warning Signs, and Tools** 41

4 **Roots of Vulnerability** 57

5 **Turning Points: Triggers Across a Life** 73

6 **Suicidal Schemas: Narrative Pathways of Risk** 92

7 **Crisis at the Core: Acute Suicidal States** 109

8 **After the Storm: Suicide, Attempts, and Their Aftermath** 123

9 **Support as Prevention: Working Together in Suicide Care** 142

10 **Making Meaning: Bringing It All Together** 155

References 165
Global Suicide Prevention and Crisis Support 185
Appendix 187
Index 199

A NOTE ON CARE AND SAFETY

This book has been written and edited with the intention of education, reflection, and understanding. It is not meant to replace professional medical advice, treatment, or support. The themes discussed here may touch on sensitive experiences and emotions. If at any point you feel overwhelmed, sad, or unsafe, please know that you do not have to carry those feelings alone.

If you are in North America and are experiencing thoughts of suicide or are in crisis, you can dial or text 9-8-8 at any time to be connected with immediate support. If you are outside of North America, please reach out to your local crisis or emergency number.

In addition to professional resources, you might also consider:

- Talking with a trusted friend, peer, or family member who can listen and be present with you.
- Creating or revisiting a safety plan—a personal guide that outlines your warning signs, coping strategies, reasons for living, and the people and places you can turn to in difficult moments.
- Keeping crisis numbers, supportive contacts, and grounding activities close at hand so you can reach for them if sadness or distress intensifies.

Most importantly, please remember: needing help is never a weakness. It is a sign of being human. Your life matters, and there are people who want to hear your story and stand beside you.

ACKNOWLEDGMENTS

This book exists because of many people, moments, and quiet forms of support along the way. First, I would like to thank the editor and team at the Routledge Mental Health department for reaching out and inviting this collaboration. I am deeply grateful for the opportunity, the trust placed in this work, and the space to develop ideas that sit at the intersection of suicidology, narrative, and meaning.

I would like to extend sincere thanks to Dr. Igor Galynker. His work profoundly reshaped how I understand suicide, not as a static state or isolated act but as a dynamic and evolving process unfolding over time. His scholarship introduced me to Narrative Identity Theory, particularly the work of Dan McAdams, which has since become the core theoretical foundation of my thinking, writing, and clinical approach.

To my dear friend and mentor, Dr. Antoon Leenaars, thank you for your unwavering support, guidance, and the countless meaning-making moments that emerged in between our conversations about suicide. Your generosity, wisdom, and humanity continue to shape how I think about people, pain, and purpose.

I am also deeply grateful to my friend, colleague, and mentor, Normand. Thank you for the validation, reflection, and patience you have offered me, especially during my longer rants and spiraling ideas. Most importantly, thank you for keeping me grounded when my thinking drifted too far ahead of itself.

To my dogs, Mozart and Freud, thank you for your quiet presence, occasional chaos, and intermittent barking at the crows. In your own subtle and indirect way, you reminded me to pause, breathe, and keep going.

And finally, and most importantly, to my love, Katie. You see my passion in this work, hold more patience and space than I ever thought possible, and have been my partner in crime since the very beginning of my suicidology journey. This book carries your support on every page.

PREFACE

If you've picked up this book, you've likely wrestled with a question that has echoed through philosophy, religion, law, culture, and personal lives across human history:

WHY DOES SUICIDE HAPPEN?

As a teenager in the mid-2000s, I often heard the phrase: "We know a lot about suicide, but we just don't know why people die by suicide." Nearly two decades later, working in emergency mental health with youth and families, I found myself asking that same question. I had worked with suicidal adults before, but meeting young people in crisis struck me differently—their pain was raw, amplified by the anguish of their families, and shadowed by the sense that their entire lives still lay ahead. There seemed to be so much more room for change, for possibility, and for help.

At the same time, I saw youth presenting with crises that, from the outside, might seem trivial—conflict over having their internet access restricted, for example—yet the intensity of their suicidal despair was no less real. This wide spectrum of experience fueled my curiosity: how do we distinguish between fleeting distress and near-lethal risk? Surely, there must be a better way to understand suicidality's many forms.

My search led me to Dr. Igor Galynker's *Suicide Crisis Syndrome* (SCS), a validated screening tool that predicts near-term suicidal behavior. As I immersed myself in his work, I discovered the broader *Narrative Crisis Model* (NCM), which reframed suicidality not as a fixed state but as a dynamic process that unfolds and shifts over time. That realization changed everything for me.

What began as a goal of reading 30 books on suicide soon expanded into a library of more than 230. The deeper I went, the larger the puzzle became. I came to see that while research and theory on suicide are flourishing, their translation into practice—and into meaningful reductions in suicide deaths—remains one of our greatest challenges. Clinicians and families alike often feel lost: too many are sent home from care feeling as though "nothing was done," while those admitted may not receive treatment directly tailored to suicidality, since it is not itself considered a psychiatric illness.

And yet, suicidality is not static. It has elements, phases, and vulnerabilities that shift over time. If we learn to recognize and work with these, we can better assess, monitor, and support those at risk.

That is the goal of this book. You will not find a single definitive answer to why people die by suicide. Instead, you will encounter ways of understanding individual vulnerabilities, contexts, and opportunities for help. Suicide prevention is an art as much as it is a science, requiring sensitivity, humility, and a willingness to listen deeply to each person's story before applying our tools. Through this integrative approach, we can help people make sense of their experiences, feel less alone, and discover the time and space they may not realize they still have.

While this book shares evidence-based knowledge, its aim is not to be prescriptive. The material is meant to be adaptive—offering frameworks, reflections, and practices that you can adapt to your context and the people you serve. Whether working with someone experiencing passive suicidal thoughts or an individual at imminent risk, the hope is that you come away with greater confidence, nuance, and compassion.

This book includes material that is both evidentially robust and consistently useful to newcomers: clear definitions, concise explanatory frameworks, near-term clinical signals, developmental and social determinants, protective processes, and practices that improve safety and connection. We do not attempt an exhaustive survey of diagnoses, advanced statistical methods, or protocol manuals; those are well served elsewhere. Throughout, we indicate where evidence is strong and where it is limited, and we attend to cultural variation in how distress, help-seeking, and recovery are understood. The aim is to offer principles that can be translated with kindness, humility, and respect for difference, rather than a single script for everyone.

Above all, my wish is that this book helps you not only understand those who struggle with suicidality but also reflect on yourself—why this work matters to you, why you picked up this book, and how kindness shapes the way we encounter others.

Because at its core, suicide prevention begins—and always continues—with kindness.

1

SUICIDE IN DEFINITION AND HISTORY

WHAT COUNTS AS SUICIDE?

At first glance, *suicide* appears deceptively simple: the act of ending one's own life. Yet, beneath that surface lies a long history of debate over meaning, intent, and context. Even the word itself carries history. The term *suicide* entered the English language in the mid-seventeenth century, adapted from the Latin *sui* (of

DOI: 10.4324/9781003758792-1

oneself) and *caedere* (to kill). Its introduction reflected a shift away from older expressions such as "self-murder" or "self-slaughter," which carried overt moral judgment, toward a more clinical and descriptive term.

Definitional debates continue to this day. Edwin Shneidman, widely considered the founder of modern suicidology, offered perhaps the most influential clinical definition: *suicide is a conscious act of self-induced annihilation, best understood as a multidimensional malaise in a needful individual who defines an issue for which the suicide is perceived as the best solution* (Shneidman, 1985). This formulation placed suicide not only in the realm of psychiatry but also within psychology, philosophy, and the human search for meaning. Shneidman emphasized that suicide is never reducible to a single cause; it is always the convergence of inner pain, personality, and circumstance.

This framing was not abstract for him. In the 1950s, while working at the Veterans Administration in Los Angeles, Shneidman and Norman Farberow established the Los Angeles Suicide Prevention Center, the first facility of its kind in the United States. The Center pioneered crisis lines, outreach, and systematic study of suicidal behavior (Farberow & Shneidman, 1961). In its earliest days, Shneidman famously discovered two boxes of suicide notes stored at the LA County Coroner's Office. Reading them cover to cover, he realized that suicide notes were invaluable psychological documents, offering direct insight into the mental states of those who died. This discovery became foundational to suicidology, shaping the clinical, research, and humanistic approaches that followed.

Families, clinicians, and researchers still confront the same definitional ambiguity Shneidman wrestled with. One individual may carefully plan their death over weeks; another may act impulsively in a moment of crisis; a third may engage in self-harm that was never meant to be lethal yet still results in death. The common denominator of "intent" remains central to definitions, but intent itself is rarely straightforward. Many who survive describe wanting to die and wanting to live at the same time, caught in the tension of ambivalence.

To bring order to this complexity, contemporary nomenclature emphasizes that suicide is a *self-inflicted death with at least some intent to die* (O'Carroll et al., 1996; Silverman et al., 2007a, 2007b). This framework also acknowledges the gray zones—undetermined, mixed, or masked intent—that matter deeply for clinical practice, legal classification, and public health surveillance.

Language here is not trivial. Terminology shapes how deaths are recorded, which behaviors are coded in surveillance systems, what gets counted in prevention programs, and how families experience the recognition—or denial—of their loved one's suffering. In this way, terminology is not simply semantics; it is *ethics, care, and practice* (Shneidman, 1993; Silverman et al., 2007a).

INTENT, SELF-HARM, AND RELATED TERMS

Intent lies at the heart of most definitions of suicide, but it is rarely straightforward. For many individuals, intent is not absolute but conflicted. Survivors of attempts often describe a state of *ambivalence*—the simultaneous pull between wanting to live and wanting to escape suffering. This tension is a defining feature of suicidality, reminding us that suicide is seldom the product of a single, fixed wish but a shifting balance of despair, hope, and perceived possibility.

To capture this complexity, clinicians and researchers have developed instruments that assess suicidal thoughts and behaviors along a **continuum** rather than as all-or-nothing states. The *Scale for Suicide Ideation* (Beck et al., 1979) measures severity and persistence of suicidal thinking, while the *Columbia–Suicide Severity Rating Scale* (Posner et al., 2011) assesses ideation, intent, and behavior across gradations of risk. Both underscore that suicide is best understood dimensionally, with levels of ideation and intent that fluctuate over time.

Equally important is the distinction between suicidal behavior and **nonsuicidal self-injury (NSSI)**. NSSI refers to deliberate self-harm without intent to die, often used as a way of regulating overwhelming affect, communicating distress, or restoring a sense of control (Nock, 2009). While conceptually distinct from suicide attempts, NSSI and suicidal behavior frequently co-occur, and both signal profound psychological pain and vulnerability.

Diagnostic and classification systems have moved toward recognizing these nuances. The Diagnostic and Statistical Manual of Mental Disorders, Fifth Edition, Text Revision lists *Suicidal*

Behavior Disorder and *Nonsuicidal Self-Injury* under conditions for further study, highlighting their clinical importance while maintaining their distinction (American Psychiatric Association, 2022). Similarly, the International Classification of Diseases, Eleventh Revision differentiates intentional self-harm from cases of undetermined intent, aiming to improve global consistency in clinical documentation, death certification, and public health surveillance (World Health Organization, 2019).

Taken together, these approaches stress that suicide-related behaviors cannot be reduced to a single category or motive. Instead, they must be situated along a spectrum of intent, meaning, and function—each requiring sensitive recognition in order to guide care.

COMMON CLASSIFICATIONS (WORKING DEFINITIONS)

- **Suicidal ideation**: thoughts of wanting to die, which range from passive wishes for life to end ("I wish I wouldn't wake up") to active thoughts involving planning and intent (Silverman et al., 2007b; Posner et al., 2011).
- **Suicide attempt**: an act of self-injurious behavior carried out with at least some intent to die, regardless of the medical lethality of the method used (Silverman et al., 2007b).
- **Death by suicide**: a self-inflicted death where there is evidence—direct or indirect—of intent to die (O'Carroll et al., 1996; Silverman et al., 2007a).
- **NSSI**: deliberate harm to one's own body without intent to die, often functioning as a means of emotional regulation, communication of distress, or self-punishment (Nock, 2009; American Psychiatric Association, 2022).

These categories provide a necessary framework, but they are not perfect. Human suffering does not always fit neatly into definitions. A person's behavior may hold layers of meaning, motives may shift even within a single episode, and "intent" itself can be ambiguous. Yet shared language offers something vital: it allows clinicians, researchers, and families to communicate more clearly, align care practices, and generate more accurate data for prevention (Silverman et al., 2007a, 2007b).

WHY LANGUAGE MATTERS

The words we use to describe suicide carry history, and with it, the power to heal or to harm. For centuries, suicide was framed in terms of *crime* and *sin*, and those echoes persist in phrases such as *committed suicide*. Many suicide prevention organizations and style guides now recommend the phrase *died by suicide*, which avoids criminal or moral judgment and instead acknowledges suicide as a cause of death (Samaritans, 2020; Centre for Addiction and Mental Health, 2020; International Association for Suicide Prevention, 2022).

This is more than a matter of politeness. Language shapes how people seek help, how communities respond, how the media reports, and how policy is written. Stigmatizing language may silence those in pain; compassionate and accurate language can open space for support, dignity, and prevention (Samaritans, 2020).

Edwin Shneidman (1985) cautioned against what he called "**semantic traps**"—terms such as *failed attempt*, *successful suicide*, or *suicidal gesture*. These phrases are misleading: they imply moral judgment, minimize suffering, or distort meaning. For Shneidman, precision in language was not an academic luxury but a clinical necessity, because words frame how we interpret and respond to human pain. To this day, avoiding semantic traps remains one of the most important tasks of suicidology.

A VERY SHORT HISTORY

The debate over suicide is as old as recorded history, and the meanings attached to it have shifted with philosophies, religions, laws, and local customs. In Rome, self-chosen death could be framed as honorable in specific circumstances, such as preserving dignity in the face of political disgrace or unavoidable defeat. Philosophers associated with Stoicism, including Seneca, defended it as a rational act when life's burdens outweighed its goods. Across antiquity, the vocabulary itself evolved. Early notions of *autothanasia* signaled a descriptive stance toward "self-death," which gradually gave way to the moralized term "suicide," a word that carried judgment and stigma as it entered medieval and early modern European discourse (Minois, 1999; van Hooff, 2002).

Cultural scripts around the world gave the act different meanings and social locations. In Japan, the ritual of *seppuku* developed within the samurai code as a codified form of atonement, protest, or restoration of honor, embedded in expectations of loyalty and courage rather than construed simply as transgression (Rankin, 2011). In parts of South Asia, religious and legal debates drew lines between self-sacrifice and self-destruction, with controversies over practices such as *sati* becoming flashpoints through which colonial and indigenous authorities negotiated power, gender, and morality (Mani, 1998). Jain traditions preserved a distinct discourse around *sallekhana*, a ritual fasting unto death framed as disciplined nonattachment and governed by stringent ethical conditions, which has continued to provoke debate about intention, coercion, and the boundary between ascetic practice and suicide in modern courts and scholarship (Dundas, 2002). In some Indigenous contexts, cosmologies that center kinship and obligations to ancestors and future generations have oriented conversations toward balance, reciprocity, and communal repair rather than purely individual moral judgment, reminding contemporary readers that risk and meaning are embedded in living worlds, not only in private minds (Gone et al., 2019).

Classical Greek thought pulled in different directions. Plato allowed tightly constrained exceptions in the face of unavoidable inevitabilities, while Aristotle condemned self-killing as an injustice against the polis. As Christianity spread in Europe, Augustine and later Aquinas consolidated a theological prohibition that shaped medieval law and custom. Penalties could include denial of Christian burial and the forfeiture of property, practices that extended moral condemnation into family life and memory (Minois, 1999; Adamiak & Dohnalik, 2023). Islamic jurisprudence, diverse across schools and eras, generally prohibited suicide while emphasizing compassion, the control of scandal, and duties of community care, reinforcing the communal responsibility to prevent harm and support the bereaved (Ghasemzadeh et al., 2018). Buddhist and Confucian traditions added further nuance, at times distinguishing between self-destructive acts and forms of self-sacrifice or protest interpreted through teachings on intention, duty, and relational harmony. The common lesson is variation within and between traditions, and the risk of reading any of them through a single lens.

European legal regimes intensified the moralization of suicide in the early modern period. English common law treated *felo de se* as a felony that could trigger posthumous punishments and property seizure, a stance that both reflected and reproduced stigma. Coroners' juries often returned verdicts of *non compos mentis* to spare families these penalties, a practice that quietly reframed many deaths as the result of impaired mind rather than criminal intent and foreshadowed later medicalization (Minois, 1999; Maris et al., 2000). By the Enlightenment, a new current emerged. David Hume's *Of Suicide* challenged blanket moral condemnation, arguing that choosing death need not be inherently immoral or irrational and reframing the question in terms of liberty, dignity, and the quality of life rather than its mere duration. Hume's position contested prevailing religious and legal doctrines and opened space for discourse on autonomy and the limits of state and ecclesial authority (Hume, 1757/1987).

The nineteenth century marked another turning point with Émile Durkheim's *Le Suicide*. Durkheim reframed suicide as a social fact, proposing that patterns of self-killing reflect degrees of social integration and regulation in collective life. His typology of egoistic, altruistic, anomic, and fatalistic suicides linked personal despair to social structure and cultural norms, providing a template for population-level inquiry that still informs public health approaches today, even as its categories are debated and revised (Durkheim, 1897/1951). At the same time, psychiatry and the emerging social sciences intensified efforts to classify and treat suicidal behavior, clarifying pathways to care while sometimes pathologizing difference or overlooking cultural meanings that matter for help-seeking and recovery (Maris et al., 2000).

Cultural history also shows how art and media shape behavior. The European reception of Goethe's *The Sorrows of Young Werther* in the late eighteenth century became a touchstone for discussions of imitation and contagion, later termed the "Werther effect." In the twentieth century, empirical work by Phillips linked certain forms of news coverage to subsequent increases in suicide, while more recent research has described a "Papageno effect," where stories of coping and mastery correspond to protective influences on audiences (Phillips, 1974; Niederkrotenthaler et al., 2010). These findings have fed into contemporary media guidelines that balance the public's right to know with practices that reduce harm.

Legal and policy landscapes shifted in the twentieth century. Many jurisdictions have decriminalized suicide, moving penalties away from individuals and toward support for prevention, crisis response, and postvention. In England and Wales, the Suicide Act 1961 removed criminal liability for the act itself while creating offenses related to assistance or encouragement, a model that influenced subsequent legal reforms elsewhere (Neeleman, 1996). The growth of crisis lines, community-based services, and national strategies reflected a public health view that suicide is preventable through coordinated action at individual, relational, community, and policy levels. Survivor and lived-experience movements widened the lens, insisting that what helps must be translated locally to be trustworthy and effective, and that dignity, autonomy, and cultural safety are not optional add-ons but core conditions for care.

A global view underscores plural histories rather than a single arc of progress. In East Asia, late imperial Chinese discourses sometimes valorized chaste widow suicide as emblematic of fidelity, a practice later criticized and legally discouraged as conceptions of virtue, gender, and the state changed in the nineteenth and twentieth centuries (Hinsch, 2012). In the Pacific, colonial encounters reframed local practices through imported moral and legal categories, often obscuring indigenous understandings of personhood and obligation. In Latin America, twentieth-century literary and public health conversations pulled between existential and social explanatory frames, with liberation theology, human rights discourses, and community mental health movements shaping prevention through attention to poverty, violence, and cultural identity. In parts of Africa, anthropological accounts document how accusations of witchcraft, land disputes, and gendered power dynamics inflect interpretations of suicidal death, and how communal reconciliation and customary law can guide responses distinct from biomedical models (Niehaus, 2001). These snapshots are not exhaustive. They are reminders that any claim about "what suicide means" must be situated in language, law, economy, kinship, gender, and faith as they are lived in place.

Contemporary research continues to braid these strands. Public health tracks rates and risk distributions. Clinical science studies warning signs, treatments, and care pathways. Sociology and anthropology map how social worlds regulate and make meaning. Religious studies and philosophy keep questions of value, dignity, and obligation salient. Media science refines guidelines that reduce harm and amplify hope. Lived-experience scholarship insists on humility, partnership, and the centrality of voice. When these threads are held together, they resist flattening and help practitioners adapt principles rather than export scripts.

Across eras and regions, one lesson persists. Suicide is never only an individual act removed from context. Its meanings have been moral, cultural, philosophical, medical, legal, and sociological, and they have not moved in a straight line. The act may look the same, yet interpretations, sanctions, and supports vary widely across time and place. A responsible history keeps difference in view, resists easy generalization, and treats culture not as a background variable but as a living world in which vulnerability, help-seeking, and recovery are made and remade (Hume, 1757/1987; Durkheim, 1897/1951; Phillips, 1974; Minois, 1999; Dundas, 2002; van Hooff, 2002; Niederkrotenthaler et al., 2010; Rankin, 2011).

DURABLE PATTERNS (WITHOUT HEAVY STATISTICS)

Even with wide historical and cultural variation, certain patterns in suicidal behavior recur across regions and eras. These are contours, not verdicts. They point to where risk concentrates and where protection often lives, while leaving room for substantial exceptions that depend on culture, context, and time.

GENDER PATTERNS AND METHODS

In many countries, men die by suicide more often than women, while women report more nonfatal attempts. This "gender paradox" is not universal, and it flexes with cultural norms and access to means. Where highly lethal methods are common and readily available, male mortality tends to be higher, partly because men more often use those methods. Where domestic pesticides are ubiquitous, for example, in parts of rural Asia, the gender gap has sometimes narrowed or even reversed, especially in earlier decades when young women's access to toxic agents intersected with acute interpersonal and household stressors (Turecki & Brent, 2016; World Health Organization, 2021, 2025). In the United States and several Latin American contexts, the availability of firearms corresponds to a higher proportion of deaths involving guns, and restricting access is associated with fewer fatalities without a full one-to-one substitution of other methods (Miller et al., 2002; Pirkis et al., 2015). In East Asia, the rise of charcoal-burning suicides in the late 1990s and 2000s illustrates how novel, highly lethal methods can diffuse culturally and reshape national patterns, and how targeted media guidance and environmental controls can curb that diffusion (Yip et al., 2004; Chen et al., 2015). These examples show that gender differences are mediated by method, opportunity, and meaning, not biology alone (Canetto & Sakinofsky, 1998; Canetto, 2008).

PLACE, MEANS, AND POLICY

Geography matters because it structures both culture and access. Rural regions often report higher suicide mortality than urban centers, a pattern linked to isolation, delayed emergency response, and greater access to lethal means, although this is not uniform across countries and can change over time with urbanization and shifting economies (Hirsch, 2006; Fontanella et al., 2015). Means safety stands out as a durable prevention lever. The detoxification of domestic gas in mid-twentieth-century Britain was followed by a marked drop in gas suicides and overall deaths, and the effect was not fully offset by substitutions to other methods. Pesticide bans and packaging reforms in Sri Lanka were associated with sustained reductions in national suicide rates. Barriers and safe design at bridges, railways, and high-risk locations repeatedly show local benefit. These are consistent lessons across countries with very different cultures and histories, and they require minimal assumptions about individual pathology to save lives (Kreitman, 1976; Pirkis et al., 2015; Knipe et al., 2017).

ECONOMY, POLITICS, AND COLLECTIVE SHOCKS

Suicide is sensitive to social weather. Economic downturns, austerity, and abrupt unemployment spikes have been linked to increases in suicide across Europe and the Americas, with stronger social protection blunting those effects. Conversely, classic observations describe temporary declines during periods of intense collective mobilization, such as major wars, followed by rebounds, although these patterns are uneven and do not erase within-group disparities (Durkheim, 1897/1951; Chang et al., 2013). Policy choices matter. National suicide prevention strategies that combine means safety, responsible media guidance, crisis care, and community interventions tend to show cumulative gains when implemented with fidelity and adapted to local culture (World Health Organization, 2021, 2025).

CULTURE, MIGRATION, AND MINORITY STRESS

Cultural worlds shape both vulnerability and protection. Religious participation and community obligations are often associated with lower risk, especially where congregations provide tangible support and moral discouragement of self-harm, although effects vary by doctrine, setting, and how inclusive those communities are for marginalized members (Stack, 2000; Kleiman & Liu, 2013). Among Indigenous peoples, risk can be exceptionally high in communities facing historical trauma and ongoing dispossession, while cultural continuity, self-governance, and language revitalization correspond to lower youth suicide in ecological studies, a reminder that culture can be a decisive buffer rather than a risk label (Chandler & Lalonde, 1998; Gone et al., 2019). Migrant and diaspora patterns are mixed. Some groups carry forward home country method profiles and timing, others converge toward host country patterns over generations. Acculturative stress, discrimination, loss of status, and barriers to care raise risk in some contexts, while expanded opportunities and social mobility lower it in others. The net effect depends on policy, reception, and intra-community support (Hjern & Allebeck, 2002; Nock et al., 2008; Spallek et al., 2015). For sexual and gender minority people, elevated risk is well documented and is linked to minority stress, family rejection, and violence, with affirming schools, families, and legal protections operating as protective conditions rather than mere niceties (Meyer, 2003; Marshal et al., 2011).

TIME, SEASONALITY, AND COMMUNICATION

Modest seasonal rhythms recur in many countries, with spring peaks more common than winter peaks, and weaker or different patterns in tropical regions and large cities. Day-of-week and holiday effects are small and inconsistent compared with other drivers, yet they reappear often enough to be noted in broad reviews. Media effects show more leverage. Sensational or detailed coverage can elevate risk through identification and modeling, while stories that highlight coping, treatment, and help-seeking correspond to protective influences, findings that have been replicated across languages and platforms and translated into practical reporting guidelines (Phillips, 1974; Ajdacic-Gross et al., 2007; Niederkrotenthaler et al., 2010; Christodoulou et al., 2012).

RISK AND PROTECTION THAT TRAVEL WELL

Across settings, a short list of signals consistently marks higher near-term risk. Prior suicide attempts, recent acute crises, social isolation, worsening mental health and substance use, and ready access to highly lethal means often cluster before death. Protective conditions also travel well. Stable belonging, trusted relationships, a sense of mattering, culturally safe and timely care, and confidence that help is available in a crisis are associated with lower risk and with recovery after attempts. These are simple statements, yet they are globally resilient in the literature and visible in practice when we listen for them carefully and document them well (Turecki & Brent, 2016; World Health Organization, 2021, 2025).

These patterns are guides, not guarantees. They are strongest when paired with local knowledge about culture, language, meaning, and law. They point us toward interventions that have saved lives in very different places without presuming that one script fits all. More than anything, they underscore a central theme of this book. Suicide is never reducible to one variable or one story. It unfolds at the intersection of personal vulnerability, relationships, and culture, and careful attention to language, context, and meaning is one way we keep the person, not the label, at the center.

CHAPTER SUMMARY

If this chapter has a single lesson, it is that the word "suicide" is deceptively small. In practice, it holds competing meanings: a wish to die and a wish to live pressed into the same breath, self-injury used to survive unbearable feelings rather than to die, and final writings that strain to translate what resists explanation. Definitions are never only academic. They change whether someone feels believed, whether their pain is recognized as real, and what we do next at the point of care.

History widens the lens. Cultures have read the act through dignity, honor, duty, sin, crime, illness, protest, and social fracture. Rome could frame self-chosen death as preserving status; Japan ritualized seppuku within codes of loyalty; Enlightenment debates raised autonomy; Durkheim linked despair to the weave of social life. None of these frames is universal, and within every tradition, there are countervoices. The lesson is not to pick one meaning but to ask which meanings are at work here, for this person, in this place.

Some durable contours still guide attention. Across many settings, men die more often, while women report more nonfatal attempts; risk often clusters at life's edges in youth and in later years; acute crises, isolation, and access to highly lethal means increase danger, while belonging, cultural continuity, and timely, culturally safe care protect. These are patterns, not verdicts. They help us anticipate and prevent, but they never replace listening.

Going forward, our stance is simple: keep people at the center. Attend to language, to relationships, to culture and identity, to power and place. Hold evidence close and use it with kindness. Prevention does not begin with a single theory or scale. It begins with humility in the face of complexity and with the practical, compassionate work of meeting someone where they are and helping them imagine a next step that feels possible.

RECOMMENDED READINGS

EDWIN S. SHNEIDMAN—*DEFINITION OF SUICIDE* (1985)

This foundational text articulates suicide as a conscious act driven by intolerable psychological pain (psychache), framing suicidology as a human science rather than a purely medical one. Shneidman's emphasis on meaning, ambivalence, and individuality directly informs this chapter's discussion of definition, intent, and ethical language. It is essential reading for understanding how modern suicidology emerged from clinical listening rather than moral judgment.

NORMAN L. FARBEROW—*THE MANY FACES OF SUICIDE* (1980)

Farberow expands early suicidological thinking beyond a single definition, illustrating suicide as a multifaceted human phenomenon shaped by culture, family, and communication. His work grounds the historical development of crisis intervention, suicide notes research, and prevention centers discussed in this chapter. This book complements Shneidman by emphasizing diversity of motive and meaning.

DAVID LESTER—*THEORIES OF SUICIDE: PAST, PRESENT, AND FUTURE* (1994)

Lester provides a clear historical overview of how suicide has been conceptualized across philosophical, sociological, and psychological traditions. This book helps readers situate contemporary definitions within a longer intellectual lineage. It is especially useful for understanding why definitional debates persist and why no single framework fully captures suicide.

KEY REFERENCES

Canetto S. S. (2008). Women and suicidal behavior: A cultural analysis. *The American Journal of Orthopsychiatry*, *78*(2), 259–266. https://doi.org/10.1037/a0013973

Canetto, S. S., & Sakinofsky, I. (1998). The gender paradox in suicide. *Suicide and Life-Threatening Behavior, 28*(1), 1–23.

Centre for Addiction and Mental Health. (2020). *Words matter: Language guidelines for talking about* suicide. https://www.camh.ca/-/media/files/words-matter-suicide-language-guide.pdf

Chandler, M. J., & Lalonde, C. E. (1998). Cultural continuity as a hedge against suicide. *Transcultural Psychiatry, 35*(2), 191–219.

Durkheim, É. (1951). *Suicide: A study in sociology* (J. A. Spaulding & G. Simpson, Trans.). Free Press. (Original work published 1897). https://doi.org/10.4324/9780203994320

Farberow, N. L., & Shneidman, E. S. (1961). *The cry for help.* McGraw-Hill.

Maris, R. W., Berman, A. L., & Silverman, M. M. (2000). *Comprehensive textbook of suicidology.* Guilford Press.

Niederkrotenthaler, T., Voracek, M., Herberth, A., Till, B., Strauss, M., Etzersdorfer, E., Eisenwort, B., & Sonneck, G. (2010). Role of media reports in completed and prevented suicide. *The British Journal of Psychiatry, 197*(3), 234–243.

Nock, M. K. (2009). Why do people hurt themselves? New insights into the nature and functions of self-injury. *Current Directions in Psychological Science, 18*(2), 78–83. https://doi.org/10.1111/j.1467-8721.2009.01613.x

Shneidman, E. S. (1985). *Definition of suicide.* Wiley.

Shneidman, E. S. (1993). Suicide as psychache. *Journal of Nervous and Mental Disease, 181*(3), 145–147. https://doi.org/10.1097/00005053-199303000-00001

2

THE ARCHITECTURE OF SUICIDE

Core Models Explained

WHY THEORIES MATTER

For much of history, suicide was framed as sin, crime, or social deviance. Those moral–legal lenses shaped community responses—punishment, concealment, stigma—far more than they shaped help. The modern era moved the conversation from blame to understanding. Today's theories give us practical levers for prevention:

DOI: 10.4324/9781003758792-2

how to listen, what to assess, which mechanisms to target, and which policies save lives. No single theory explains everything; each aims a flashlight at part of the terrain. Read together, they show where to step.

This chapter tours the major frameworks in clear, accessible language. For each, we answer four questions: What does it say? What does it help us see? Where does it fall short? What can we do tomorrow morning because of it? We also flag when the evidence is strongest at the population level (e.g., policy, media, means safety), the service level (e.g., care pathways, follow-up), or the bedside level (e.g., questions to ask, skills to teach, medications to consider).

It helps to think of suicide theory as three overlapping "waves," each adding tools rather than replacing what came before:

1. ***First generation (descriptive and sociological).*** Classic sociological work located suicide within social change, cohesion, and norms. Early psychological accounts emphasized meaning, ambivalence, and the wish to "escape the self." These ideas gave us empathy and a population lens, but they were light on short-term prediction and step-by-step clinical guidance.
2. ***Second generation (risk factors and diathesis).*** Biological and cognitive models introduced vulnerabilities—hopelessness schemas, impulsive aggression, serotonergic dysregulation, family loading, trauma histories—that interact with stressors. They taught us what to treat assertively and what to monitor over time, but could still miss why this person, now.
3. ***Third generation (states and transitions).*** Interpersonal, ideation-to-action, and volitional models explain how people move from thoughts to attempts: defeat → entrapment → intent; desire + capability; short-term crisis patterns marked by frantic hopelessness and cognitive flooding. These add stage-specific levers—safety planning, caring contacts, means safety, skills to widen options—and pair naturally with collaborative, suicide-focused treatments. Newer narrative identity and crisis models (including the Narrative Crisis Model [NCM] and the Existential Network of Suicidal Identity [ENSI]) show how stories, roles, time horizons, and cultural scripts can close—or reopen—the future.

THEORIES AT A GLANCE

- **Sociological:** how cohesion, change, and roles shape risk.
- **Psychodynamic and existential:** ambivalence, guilt, and escape from self.
- **Psychache:** intolerable psychological pain as a near-universal driver.
- **Cognitive/behavioral:** problem-solving deficits, attentional narrowing, hopelessness schemas, and the *suicide mode.*
- **Biological and stress–diathesis:** impulsive aggression, serotonin, sleep and substance effects; conditions and medications relevant to suicide risk.
- **Interpersonal:** thwarted belonging, perceived burdensomeness, and acquired capability.
- **Ideation to action (the Integrated Motivational–Volitional Model (IMV) of suicidal behavior/Three-Step Theory [3ST] of suicide):** defeat → entrapment → intent, plus volitional factors that govern the jump from thought to act.
- **Narrative identity and crisis (the ENSI/the NCM):** how character, setting, and script consolidate into a suicidal identity—and how to re-author a survivable plot.

DURKHEIM AND THE SOCIAL MATRIX

Durkheim's starting point is simple and unsettling: suicide bears the imprint of the society around it. He argued that its incidence rises and falls with two broad forces. The first is social integration, the degree to which people feel embedded in families, congregations, neighborhoods, and shared projects. The second is moral regulation, the clarity and stability of social rules, obligations, and expectations. When rapid change loosens norms and destabilizes expectations, a condition he called anomie, people can feel unmoored. Isolation and role loss then push toward what he termed "egoistic and anomic suicides." When ties are too tight or rules too rigid, people may die to meet collective demands or to escape oppression, patterns he labeled altruistic and fatalistic suicides (Durkheim, 1897/1951).

Durkheim's lens widens prevention beyond the clinic. If suicide reflects the social fabric, then improving the weave matters.

Practical levers include reducing access to highly lethal means, creating reliable income and housing supports, strengthening labor and education policy during shocks, promoting responsible media standards, and building connection in schools, workplaces, and civic life (Mann et al., 2005; Barber & Miller, 2014). The point is to install guardrails that make despair less likely and less lethal in the first place. The approach is compatible with contemporary public health. Population-level changes such as detoxifying domestic gas, restricting toxic pesticides, securing firearms, and adding barriers at hotspots repeatedly correspond with fewer deaths and do not result in full one-for-one substitution to other methods (Kreitman, 1976; Miller et al., 2002; Pirkis et al., 2015; Knipe et al., 2017).

There are strengths and limits. Durkheim's model explains why rates in a region climb after sudden unemployment or dislocation and why they sometimes fall during periods of intense collective mobilization, even when individual suffering remains (Durkheim, 1897/1951; Chang et al., 2013). It also helps interpret social gradients: groups with frayed ties, contested roles, or unclear futures often carry more risk. Yet the framework is a wide-angle shot rather than a close-up. It cannot tell you why this person is at the edge today. For that we need psychological mechanisms and clinical judgment that translate population signals into individualized care, such as models of interpersonal drivers and volitional processes that operate within crises (Joiner, 2005; O'Connor & Kirtley, 2010; Van Orden et al., 2010; Klonsky & May, 2015).

A social lens also benefits from cultural specificity. Integration is not the same in rural Sri Lanka as in suburban Canada, and regulation does not feel the same in a tightly knit Indigenous nation as in a rapidly urbanizing megacity. What counts as belonging and obligation is culture bound. A Durkheimian reading invites us to measure the local social world rather than treat "society" as an abstract average. It also cautions against ecological fallacy. Within a high-risk region, specific communities may be buffered by language continuity, land rights, or mutual aid, while others are exposed by discrimination or policy neglect. Bringing the social matrix to the bedside means asking what ties matter here, which rules have shifted, and who can help restore predictability and purpose.

Durkheim's thesis has been extended in modern systems work. Military and occupational prevention programs that combine leadership training, stigma reduction, policy change, and means safety have shown durable associations with fewer deaths and injuries, consistent with a social–ecological approach. The US Air Force program is a frequently cited example of multicomponent implementation with population impact, though replication and context matter for generalization (Knox et al., 2003; Mann et al., 2005). National strategies that braid together media guidance, school-based connection, crisis services, and lethal means reduction tend to accumulate benefit over time when implemented with fidelity and adapted to local culture (World Health Organization, 2021).

CLINICAL TRANSLATION

Clinically, a Durkheimian perspective reminds us that suicide risk does not arise only within the individual, but within the social matrix that shapes belonging, obligation, stability, and hope. This has important implications for assessment and intervention, as clinicians must look beyond symptoms to the patient's social world: recent role loss, unemployment, housing insecurity, family rupture, migration, cultural dislocation, discrimination, and weakened community ties may all intensify vulnerability by eroding integration and regulation. In practice, this means asking not only what the person feels but where they are situated, what social anchors have frayed, what expectations have collapsed, and which relationships, communities, or institutions might help restore predictability and meaning. This framework also supports collaboration between clinical care and public health by reinforcing the value of means safety, coordinated social supports, school and workplace connection, and culturally grounded community interventions that reduce the conditions under which despair becomes both more likely and more lethal.

LIMITATIONS

Despite its enduring value, Durkheim's framework has several limitations when applied to contemporary suicide theory and practice. Its strength lies in explaining population patterns, social gradients, and the effects of large-scale disruption, but it offers limited precision for understanding why a particular individual becomes suicidal at a specific moment. As an ecological model, it can understate the psychological, developmental, relational, and biological processes that mediate the link between social conditions and suicidal action. The framework also risks overgeneralization if concepts such as integration and regulation are applied without cultural and historical specificity, since belonging, obligation, and norm disruption are experienced differently across communities and contexts. For these reasons, Durkheim's model is best understood as a vital macro-level account of the social conditions of suicide, but one that requires integration with psychological and clinical theories to capture the lived immediacy and subjective meaning of suicidal crises.

PSYCHODYNAMIC AND EXISTENTIAL LINES

Early psychoanalytic writers treated suicide as a drama of the inner world. Freud proposed that when a loved or needed object is lost through death, betrayal, humiliation, or even threatened separation, the self identifies with the lost object. Anger initially directed outward turns against the self, producing self-reproach, punitive guilt, and, at the extreme, self-destruction (Freud, 1917/1957). Menninger described a triad of wishes, to kill, to be killed, and to die, arguing that suicidal behavior often condenses revenge, expiation, and escape into a single act (Menninger, 1938). Building on object relations, Klein emphasized internal good and bad objects. When envy, rage, and guilt toward internalized caregivers feel morally intolerable and unrepairable, annihilating the self can be experienced as the only way to silence persecutory states (Klein, 1940).

These accounts remain clinically useful because they give language to ambivalence and meaning. They explain why death can feel both punitive and relieving, why some patients speak in metaphors of cleansing or repair, and why shame can be the fuel that keeps the idea of death alive. They also give therapists handles for countertransference. Feelings of urgency or helplessness in the clinician can echo the patient's internal drama. Contemporary work has translated parts of these ideas into measurable constructs such as self-criticism, perfectionistic standards, and attachment insecurity, each linked to suicidality in diverse samples (Hewitt et al., 1992; Adam et al., 1996; Blatt, 2004).

Existential writers recast the territory in terms of meaning, freedom, isolation, and mortality. Binswanger and May, and later Frankl, emphasized crises of purpose and value. When the world no longer appears inhabitable, death can seem like the only coherent next chapter. Meaning-centered and dignity-conserving approaches operationalize these insights by rebuilding purpose, reconnecting people to chosen commitments, and restoring a future that feels livable, especially in palliative and chronic-illness contexts (Frankl, 1959/2006; Chochinov, 2007).

CLINICAL TRANSLATION

A psychodynamic–existential stance invites specific moves. Name and normalize ambivalence. Explore where guilt belongs and where it does not. Seek reparative pathways in relationships. Work directly with shame through compassion-focused strategies. When patients speak in moral languages of failure and unworthiness, ask what counts as repair to them, in their culture, for their people. Translate metaphors into actions that restore dignity.

LIMITATIONS

These traditions are rich interpretively and have seeded many therapeutic techniques, yet they require translation into operational markers for near-term risk and for stepped care. Without that translation, they struggle to guide moment-to-moment decisions in emergency settings. Combining them with cognitive, interpersonal, and volitional models improves predictive and practice utility (Rudd, 2006; Wenzel et al., 2009; O'Connor & Kirtley, 2010).

SUICIDE AS ESCAPE FROM SELF/PSYCHACHE

Baumeister's model reframes suicidal behavior as an attempt to shut down a punishing, hyper-self-aware state. The process unfolds in steps. A salient failure relative to high standards. Internal, global attributions such as "It is me, I am defective." Aversive self-awareness with ruminative focus. Intense negative affect. Cognitive deconstruction characterized by narrowed attention, present-tense thinking, and emotional numbing. Disinhibition toward extreme solutions when the self feels inescapable (Baumeister, 1990).

Attention narrows under threat, and people in crisis preferentially process suicide-related cues (Becker et al., 1999). Time and goal horizons collapse when entrapment is high, consistent with qualitative and experimental work on defeat and entrapment as key drivers of ideation (Williams, 1997; Williams & Pollock, 2000; Taylor et al., 2011). Cognitive therapy conceptualizes a suicide mode that, once activated, produces a recognizable pattern of perception, affect, and urges, which can be interrupted through targeted skills and meaning restoration (Wenzel et al., 2009).

For Shneidman, the common pathway is psychache, unbearable psychological pain arising from frustrated needs such as belonging, competence, love, and moral worth, coupled with the belief that no alternative will relieve it (Shneidman, 1997). Psychache is not a diagnosis. It is a felt state that many disorders and circumstances can produce. The lever is pragmatic. If pain is greater than available resources and the imagination of alternatives is near zero, suicide becomes thinkable. The clinician's task is to ask directly about the pain and its sources, locate the frustrated needs, and expand options for relief, from near-term soothing and social rescue to evidence-based treatments for co-occurring conditions and to system levers like means safety that create time for relief to work (Jobes, 2006; Stanley & Brown, 2012; Barber & Miller, 2014).

Psychache overlaps with other mechanisms. It co-travels with defeat and entrapment, hopelessness schemas, and interpersonal drivers of burdensomeness and thwarted belonging (Williams, 1997; Joiner, 2005; Wenzel et al., 2009; Van Orden et al., 2010). Measurement work suggests that indices of psychological pain often add explanatory value beyond depression severity. The Psychache Scale and the Orbach and Mikulincer Mental Pain constructs have each shown independent associations with suicidal thinking and behavior across samples, though findings are mixed and sensitive to method and comorbidity (Holden et al., 2001; Orbach et al., 2003).

CLINICAL TRANSLATION

Clinically, the escape from self and psychache frameworks direct attention to the unbearable inner state that makes suicide appear functional, not merely to the presence or absence of stated intent. These models suggest that assessment should explore experiences of humiliating failure, harsh self-appraisal, ruminative self-focus, cognitive narrowing, emotional numbing, and intolerable psychological pain linked to frustrated needs such as belonging, love, competence, and moral worth. In practice, this means helping patients name the pain, identify what is making the self feel unlivable, and locate where alternatives have collapsed in their imagination. These theories also support interventions aimed at interrupting the suicidal state by reducing arousal, restoring cognitive flexibility, strengthening near-term coping, addressing co-occurring disorders, re-establishing relational connection, and using safety planning and means restriction to create time for pain to recede. For clinicians, the task is to treat suicidality not only as risk to be contained but as a crisis of unbearable self-experience that requires relief, meaning restoration, and expansion of perceived options.

LIMITATIONS

Despite their considerable clinical and theoretical value, these models also have limitations. The escape from self and psychache perspectives offer powerful descriptions of the subjective pain and constricted consciousness associated with suicidal crises, but they may not fully explain why some individuals experiencing intense shame, failure, or psychological pain become suicidal, while others do not. Their emphasis on intrapsychic suffering can also underrepresent the broader relational, developmental, cultural, and structural contexts that shape how pain is interpreted and whether the self becomes experienced as intolerable. In addition, constructs such as psychache, cognitive deconstruction, and aversive self-awareness can overlap substantially with depression, hopelessness, defeat, and entrapment, making conceptual boundaries difficult to define with precision. These frameworks are therefore best understood as rich accounts of the phenomenology and internal logic of suicidal suffering, but not as complete explanatory models of suicidal behavior across all contexts.

CRY OF PAIN/ARRESTED FLIGHT

The Cry of Pain framework proposes that suicidal crises typically unfold as a sequence from defeat (e.g., humiliation, rejection, status loss) to entrapment (a felt absence of escape routes), intensified by no-rescue beliefs (expectations that help is unavailable or ineffective) (Williams, 1997; Williams & Pollock, 2000). Within this logic, suicide is construed as an "exit" when the person's appraisal system represents the situation as inescapable and unsupported. Temporal narrowing—an inability to envisage a future beyond the immediate impasse—often accompanies this configuration (Williams, 1997; Williams & Pollock, 2000).

Empirical cognitive work indicates that, compared to controls, suicidal individuals generate fewer solutions to stressors, evaluate potential solutions more negatively, and display attentional biases toward threat- or suicide-related cues, which narrows the perceived option space (Schotte & Clum, 1987; Becker et al., 1999). Conceptually, this line of research treats suicidal behavior as emerging from information-processing constraints—restricted fluency, pessimistic appraisal, and selective attention—that skew coping toward withdrawal or self-harm when stress is high.

CLINICAL TRANSLATION

Clinically, the Cry of Pain and problem-solving deficit frameworks suggest that suicide risk assessment should attend not only to expressed intent but also to the person's lived sense of defeat, entrapment, and perceived unavailability of rescue. In practice, this means exploring whether the individual feels trapped in an unbearable situation, whether they can imagine any realistic alternatives, and whether they believe help would matter if offered. These models also support interventions that directly target cognitive constriction by expanding the person's perceived option space, strengthening collaborative problem-solving, challenging hopeless appraisals, and increasing access to responsive interpersonal support. For clinicians, especially in crisis and acute care settings, the task is not simply to reduce symptoms but to help restore movement where the patient experiences only psychological dead ends, thereby interrupting the progression from humiliation or loss toward suicidal escape.

LIMITATIONS

Despite the clinical usefulness, the model has several limitations. The Cry of Pain framework and related cognitive theories provide a compelling account of proximal suicidal states, but they may underemphasize the broader developmental, relational, cultural, and identity-based contexts that shape how defeat and entrapment are experienced. Similarly, findings on problem-solving deficits and attentional bias help explain constricted coping under stress, yet they do not fully account for why some individuals with similar cognitive vulnerabilities become suicidal, while others do not. Much of this work also risks portraying suicidality in overly mechanistic cognitive terms, with less attention to narrative meaning, symbolic significance, and the personal logic through which suffering is interpreted. As a result, these frameworks are valuable for identifying acute pathways to suicidal crisis, but are best understood as partial explanations that require integration with broader psychosocial and existential models.

BECK'S COGNITIVE DIATHESIS AND THE "SUICIDE MODE," FLUID VULNERABILITY THEORY/MANN'S STRESS–DIATHESIS FORMULATION

Beck's cognitive account distinguishes enduring **diatheses** (e.g., hopelessness schemas, rigid standards) from **state-dependent distortions** that dominate attention during crises (e.g., selective attention to loss, dichotomous thinking) (Wenzel et al., 2009). In acute episodes, a coordinated **suicide mode** can activate: a temporarily organized pattern of thoughts, affect, physiological arousal, and action tendencies centered on self-destruction. The theory explains fluctuation by positing that stable schemas set the vulnerability landscape, while state processes determine when self-destructive patterns become dominant (Wenzel et al., 2009).

Fluid Vulnerability Theory (FVT) formalizes suicide risk as a time-varying system with two layers: (1) baseline vulnerabilities (cognitive, biological, behavioral) and (2) acute activation by triggers that transiently assemble a suicide-specific response pattern (Rudd, 2006). Repeated activations can produce sensitization, lowering the threshold for subsequent episodes. The theory thus explains recurrence and rapid shifts by modeling risk as a dynamic interaction between relatively stable diathesis and episodic stressor-linked activation (Rudd, 2006).

This model locates suicidal behavior at the intersection of stressors (loss, conflict, illness, intoxication) and a diathesis characterized by traits such as impulsive aggression, serotonergic dysfunction, family loading, early adversity, and psychiatric comorbidity (Mann et al., 2005). On this view, stress supplies proximal pressure, while diathesis determines the propensity to translate stress into suicidal behavior, accounting for heterogeneity across individuals exposed to similar life events (Mann et al., 2005; see also Apter et al., 1991).

CLINICAL TRANSLATION

Clinically, Beck's cognitive diathesis model, the suicide mode, FVT, and Mann's stress–diathesis formulation all underscore the importance of assessing suicide risk as both enduring and dynamic. These models suggest that clinicians must look beyond immediate suicidal thoughts and evaluate the broader vulnerability structure that shapes crisis emergence, including rigid hopeless schemas, prior sensitization to suicidal states, impulsive aggression, psychiatric comorbidity, early adversity, and stress-reactive patterns. In practice, this means combining longitudinal understanding with acute assessment: identifying baseline traits and historical vulnerabilities while also recognizing when a suicide-specific mode has become activated through cognitive constriction, physiological arousal, and action readiness. These theories support interventions that target both layers of risk, such as long-term work on maladaptive schemas and emotion regulation alongside immediate strategies for deactivation, safety planning, means restriction, trigger identification, and rapid support during episodes of acute escalation.

LIMITATIONS

Although these models are highly valuable for explaining fluctuation, recurrence, and individual differences in suicide risk, they also have important limitations. Their emphasis on cognitive, biological, and trait-based vulnerability can risk reducing suicidality to an intrapsychic or psychobiological process, with less attention to the relational, cultural, existential, and narrative meanings through which stressors are interpreted. While they explain why some individuals are more vulnerable than others under similar stress, they are less equipped to capture the symbolic and identity-based significance of suicidal crises, including how individuals come to understand self-destruction as a solution within the logic of their lives. In addition, constructs such as sensitization, suicide mode activation, and diathesis are clinically useful but can be difficult to operationalize with precision across settings. As a result, these theories are best viewed as strong explanatory models of vulnerability and acute activation, but not as complete accounts of the full psychological and contextual complexity of suicidal experience.

INTERPERSONAL THEORY OF SUICIDE/ IMV/3ST

The Interpersonal Theory of Suicide (IPTS) posits that lethal suicidal behavior requires the convergence of desire and capability. Desire is theorized to arise from thwarted belongingness (chronic social disconnection) and perceived burdensomeness (the belief that one is a liability to others), while capability accrues via habituation to fear and pain through painful and provocative experiences (e.g., injury, violence exposure, prior self-harm) (Joiner, 2005; Van Orden et al., 2010). The model treats desire as relatively common and fluctuating, whereas capability functions as a volitional gate that lowers natural inhibitions against lethal self-injury (Van Orden et al., 2010). Learning principles such as preparedness in fear acquisition and opponent process dynamics are invoked to explain how repeated exposure can blunt fear/pain responses over time, thereby augmenting capability (Solomon & Corbit, 1973; Öhman & Mineka, 2001).

The 3ST of suicide proposes that suicidal ideation develops first when a person experiences both intense psychological pain and hopelessness, meaning they are suffering and cannot see that things will improve. The second step suggests that this suicidal thinking becomes stronger when that pain outweighs a person's sense of connectedness to life, such as relationships, purpose, roles, or reasons for living. The third step explains that not everyone with strong suicidal ideation will attempt suicide, because an attempt usually requires the capacity to do so, including factors like reduced fear of death, greater tolerance for pain, and practical exposure to painful or provocative experiences (Klonsky & May, 2015). In this way, the theory separates the development of suicidal thoughts from the progression to suicidal behavior.

The IMV theory differentiates the **formation** of suicidal intent from the enactment of suicidal behavior.

- ***Premotivational phase*:** background factors (traits, adversity, biology) and current stressors establish susceptibility.
- ***Motivational phase*:** appraisals of defeat and entrapment generate ideation/intent, moderated by variables such as coping, problem-solving, social support, and beliefs about rescue.
- ***Volitional phase*:** the transition to behavior is governed by volitional moderators including capability, exposure to suicidal behavior, access to means, impulsivity, alcohol use, and planning (O'Connor et al., 2006; Dhingra et al., 2016).
- The model explains why many experience suicidal thoughts without acting (intent forms in the motivational phase) and why some progress to attempts (volitional moderators tip the system toward enactment).

CLINICAL TRANSLATION

Clinically, IPTS and the IMV/3ST family are especially useful because they help structure assessment around the distinction between wanting to die and being able or likely to act. These models direct clinicians to assess not only suicidal desire through experiences of isolation, burdensomeness, defeat, and entrapment but also the factors that increase the likelihood of transition to action, such as prior self-harm, exposure to violence or suicide, access to means, alcohol use, impulsivity, and planning. In practice, this supports a more layered formulation of risk in which social disconnection, hopeless appraisals, and failed rescue expectations are explored alongside volitional moderators that may increase enactment potential. These theories also have practical treatment implications: strengthening belonging, reducing burdensomeness, improving coping and problem-solving, limiting access to lethal means, and identifying when a patient has moved from motivational suffering into a more dangerous volitional phase marked by acquired capability or action readiness.

LIMITATIONS

Despite their strong clinical utility, IPTS and IMV/3ST also have limitations. Both models are highly valuable for distinguishing ideation from enactment, yet they can sometimes present suicidality in a stagelike or component-based manner that underrepresents the fluid, recursive, and meaning-laden nature of real suicidal crises. IPTS has been especially influential, but some of its core constructs, particularly acquired capability, have proven difficult to measure consistently and may not fully explain all suicidal behavior. Similarly, while IMV offers a more process-oriented account, its phases can still risk oversimplifying the complexity of how interpersonal pain, identity disruption, trauma, and existential collapse interact in lived experience. More broadly, both frameworks privilege motivational and volitional pathways but give less attention to narrative meaning, symbolic communication, and the developmental and cultural contexts through which belonging, burden, defeat, and escape are subjectively understood.

NCM/ENSI

The NCM is a diathesis–stress, multistage account in which trait vulnerabilities are activated by stressors to assemble a subacute suicidal narrative, which then escalates into an acute crisis phenotype—Suicide Crisis Syndrome (SCS)—that marks near-term risk and does not require self-reported ideation to be present (Galynker, 2017).

1. **Trait vulnerabilities:** enduring susceptibilities (e.g., temperament, identity, and cognitive tendencies) that increase the probability a stressful context will be interpreted through a suicidal lens (Rudd, 2006).

2. **Stressors:** proximal events or pressures that activate the diathesis (Mann et al., 2005).
3. **Suicidal narrative:** under activation, appraisal and meaning-making consolidate into a structured storyline characterized by seven recurrent schemas:

    - ***Perceived burdensomeness*** (belief that one is a liability to others) (Van Orden et al., 2010).
    - ***Thwarted belongingness*** (chronic disconnection from valued ties) (Van Orden et al., 2010).
    - ***Fear of humiliation*** (anticipation of shaming defeat) (Williams, 1997).
    - ***Social defeat*** (felt collapse of status/agency) (Williams & Pollock, 2000).
    - ***Entrapment*** (appraised impossibility of escape) (Williams, 1997; Williams & Pollock, 2000).
    - ***Goal process difficulty*** (e.g., failure to re-engage with attainable goals when old ones close) (Wenzel et al., 2009).
    - ***Perfectionism*** (often socially prescribed standards that rigidify self-evaluation) (Wenzel et al., 2009).

    These schemas cohere as a subacute cognitive storyline that renders suicide a "fitting" or "only" resolution once alternatives are appraised as closed.

4. **Acute crisis phenotype: the SCS:** when the narrative tightens, the person enters the SCS, defined by entrapment, affective turbulence, ruminative flooding, loss of cognitive control, hyperarousal, and acute social withdrawal (Galynker, 2017). Within NCM, SCS is the imminence state that bridges from narrative organization to near-term suicidal behavior.

The ENSI is an identity-narrative framework that maps how the self-structure reorganizes under strain until suicide becomes narratively coherent. Rather than staging symptoms, ENSI tracks an identity network built from three interlocking layers—character (who I am), setting (where/with whom I belong), and script (where I'm going)—and explains how progressive role narrowing, meaning erosion, and future-time constriction can consolidate a suicidal identity in which self-annihilation appears internally consistent with the person's lived story (Gay, 2026).

- ***Latent identity strain (chronic layer).*** Long-standing vulnerabilities in **existential**, **relational**, and **narrative identities create a brittle** self-structure (e.g., unstable self-definition, role discontinuities, fragile time horizon). These operate as background tensions within the identity network rather than symptoms in isolation (Gay, 2025).
- ***Stressor activation (network recruitment).*** Interpersonal or status-threatening stressors recruit the network: defensive positions and meaning-making intensify, and the self begins to organize around a **suicidal storyline** as a way to restore coherence to identity under pressure (Gay, 2025).
- ***Narrative deformation (form and time).*** The storyline deforms along two axes:
    - *Temporal constriction*—the felt future shrinks or collapses ("chronological collapse"), making only short-horizon endings appear credible (Gay, 2025).
    - *Discursive/narrative shifts*—voice fragmentation, metaphor hardening, and "performative" address (notes written as symbolic self-presentations), signaling tightening of the narrative frame (Gay, 2025).
- ***Crisis proximal configuration (accelerants inside identity).*** As deformation peaks, entrapment and defeat appraisals dominate the network's grammar; the plot converges on self-annihilation as a "fitting" resolution within the person's identity world (Gay, 2026).
- ***Bridge to imminence (compatibility with SCS).*** In the ENSI terms, this configuration readily co-occurs with the SCS phenotype—entrapment, affective disturbance, loss of cognitive control, hyperarousal, social withdrawal—which specifies the near-term, short-horizon state without requiring self-reported ideation (Galynker, 2017; Melzer et al., 2024).

CLINICAL TRANSLATION

Clinically, the NCM and ENSI frameworks are especially useful because they move assessment beyond checklist-style symptom detection and toward the evolving organization of suicidal risk across identity, narrative, and acute crisis states. Together, they suggest that clinicians should assess not only stressors and enduring vulnerabilities but also whether the person has begun to organize experience into a suicidal storyline marked by burdensomeness, disconnection, humiliation, defeat, entrapment, perfectionistic collapse, and difficulty imagining alternative goals or futures. In practice, this means listening closely for changes in how patients describe themselves, their relationships, and their future, including signs of temporal constriction, role loss, voice fragmentation, narrative rigidity, and withdrawal into a self-story in which death begins to feel fitting or inevitable. These models also support the importance of identifying SCS features as markers of near-term risk even when explicit ideation is absent, thereby encouraging clinicians to intervene at the level of narrative collapse, identity destabilization, and acute entrapment through relational engagement, safety planning, means restriction, restoration of future possibility, and efforts to reopen a livable storyline before self-annihilation becomes the dominant resolution.

LIMITATIONS

Despite their depth and clinical promise, the NCM and ENSI frameworks also have limitations. Both offer rich accounts of how suicidality emerges through meaning-making, vulnerability, and crisis escalation, but their complexity may make them harder to operationalize consistently in fast-paced clinical settings compared with briefer risk models. The NCM provides a strong structure for understanding the progression from trait vulnerability to suicidal narrative to acute crisis, yet some of its constructs may overlap with other cognitive and affective theories of entrapment, hopelessness, and stress activation. ENSI adds important explanatory depth by centering identity architecture, temporality, and narrative coherence, but as a broader interpretive framework it may be more difficult to standardize, measure, or validate across diverse populations and settings. In addition, both models risk requiring a high degree of clinician skill in narrative and phenomenological listening, which may not always be available in routine practice. For these reasons, they are best understood as powerful integrative frameworks that enrich suicide formulation and deepen clinical understanding, while still benefiting from continued empirical refinement and complementarity with more established assessment approaches.

Table 2.1 is designed to provide a comparative map of the major suicide theories presented in this chapter, highlighting what each framework uniquely reveals, the practical levers it supports, and its known limits. Its intent is not to rank theories or suggest that any single model is sufficient, but to help readers translate abstract concepts into *mechanism-informed action* at population, service, and bedside levels. The table should be read as a formulation aid: a way to select and combine theoretical lenses based on the question at hand—*what pattern am I seeing, what lever fits this moment, and where must this model be supplemented by others*—rather than as a menu from which to choose only one explanation.

Table 2.1 Summary of Suicide Theories

Theory Family	*Big Reveal*	*Practical Lever(s)*	*Limits*
Sociology (Durkheim)	Macro social forces (integration, regulation, anomie) shape population risk	Surveillance of rates; social policy; media guidance; postvention norms	Weak on "why this person, why now?"
Psychoanalytic/ existential	Suicidality expresses meaning, ambivalence, guilt, and escape from self	Explore ambivalence; name relief function; meaning-focused formulation	Variable empirical anchors; low short-term predictive utility
Psychache (Shneidman)	Intolerable psychological pain is the proximal driver	Ask about pain and frustrated needs; expand credible relief pathways	Mechanism-agnostic; broad construct
Cry of Pain/ Entrapment	Defeat → entrapment → "no rescue" appraisals	Detect defeat/ entrapment; restore credible escape/rescue pathways	Not all crises are framed as defeat

(*Continued*)

Table 2.1 (Continued)

Theory Family	*Big Reveal*	*Practical Lever(s)*	*Limits*
Beck (Cognitive Diathesis)/FVT	Diathesis vs. state; time-varying "suicide mode"	Mode detection/ deactivation; relapse-prevention focus	Requires longitudinal care and monitoring
Biological/ Stress–Diathesis	Impulsive aggression, serotonergic tone, and early adversity interact with stress	Treat agitation, insomnia, intoxication; optimize disorders; lithium/clozapine where indicated	Vulnerability ≠ destiny; doesn't explain micro-transitions
Interpersonal theory (desire + capability)	Thwarted belonging and burdensomeness fuel desire; capability gates action	Rebuild belonging/ contribution; reduce opportunity/ capability (means safety)	Capability hard to measure; drivers not universal
IMV/3ST	Distinguishes motivational (defeat → entrapment) from volitional (enactment) phase	Phase-specific targets: motivation (defeat/ entrapment), volition (means, alcohol, agitation)	Lives loop; phases can blur
The NCM	Traits + stressors → seven-schema suicidal narrative → SCS (ideation not required)	Monitor the narrative structure; track for SCS emergence	Requires structured assessment; stage map can feel linear
The ENSI	Identity network (character–setting–script) and time horizon organize risk	Map identity/ roles/time; restore anchors; reopen future horizon	Requires cultural fluency; adjunctive to stabilization

PUBLIC HEALTH AND CLINICAL "LEVERS"

By "levers," we mean the concrete actions that theories justify and guide. Examples include asking directly about unbearable psychological pain; spotting defeat and entrapment language; rebuilding belonging and reducing perceived burdensomeness; limiting access to highly lethal methods; using suicide-specific therapies and family repair; addressing agitation, insomnia, and substance use; and, where indicated, medications with anti-suicide effects. These are the actionable bridges between abstract concepts and real lives.

When time and capability are the gates between desire and death, making lethal action harder saves lives. Means safety reduces exposure to high-lethality methods (e.g., firearms, toxic medications) and increases the interval for help-seeking and de-escalation. Policy and clinical programs that restrict access or increase safe storage are associated with meaningful population-level reductions in suicide (Mann et al., 2005; Barber & Miller, 2014).

The Safety Planning Intervention organizes personalized warning signs, internal coping steps, social/professional contacts, and means safety on a single, portable plan. Coupled with proactive post-discharge contacts, it addresses the well-documented vulnerability window after emergency care and discharge (Horwitz et al., 2014; Currier et al., 2015). In practice, the pair functions as a continuity bridge between crisis stabilization and outpatient care (Currier et al., 2015).

COLLABORATIVE, FAMILY, AND SKILLS-BASED TREATMENTS

- Collaborative Assessment and Management of Suicidality (CAMS) centers a shared, suicide-specific case formulation using the Suicide Status Form, targeting the person's idiosyncratic drivers of suicidality (Jobes, 2006; Comtois et al., 2011).
- Dialectical Behavior Therapy (DBT) reduces suicidal and self-injurious behaviors among individuals at high risk with borderline personality disorder through skills in emotion regulation, distress tolerance, and interpersonal effectiveness (Linehan et al., 2015).

- Cognitive Behavioral Therapy for Suicide Prevention (CBT-SP) for suicidal patients targets hopelessness schemas, problem-solving, and cognitive processing of crisis cues; clinical applications are detailed in Beck-aligned manuals and reports (Wenzel et al., 2009).
- Attachment-Based Family Therapy (ABFT) repairs attachment ruptures and increases felt security for adolescents, with randomized evidence for benefits in youth with suicidal ideation (Diamond et al., 2010).

Systems takeaway: No single therapy fits all presentations. Effective programs align the treatment approach with the problem profile (mechanisms at play), developmental stage, and service context, integrating suicide-specific care with family engagement and structured follow-up (Jobes, 2006; Wenzel et al., 2009; Diamond et al., 2010; Linehan et al., 2015).

PREDICTION, ASSESSMENT, AND HUMILITY

Individual-level prediction remains limited: even sophisticated multivariate models have shown low positive predictive value in large clinical samples (Goldstein et al., 1991), and classic debates over "equivocal" suicides illustrate the fallibility of expert judgment (Litman et al., 1963). The implication is design, not nihilism: build care pathways that assume uncertainty—routine safety planning when indicated, rapid caring contacts after transitions, and "no-wrong-door" return access—while using theory to guide iterative formulations rather than static risk labels (Mann et al., 2005; Horwitz et al., 2014).

CHAPTER SUMMARY

This chapter traced how understandings of suicide moved from moral judgment to plural, mechanism-based models that actually help us see—and do—more. Sociological work reminded us that suicide is patterned by integration, regulation, and change. Psychoanalytic and existential accounts returned us to meaning, ambivalence, and the wish to escape a punishing self. Cognitive and stress–diathesis models clarified how enduring vulnerabilities interact with acute appraisals, attention, and problem-solving limits to produce crises that wax and wane over time. Interpersonal and ideation-to-action frameworks explained why desire for death is common, but action is rare without capability, access, and volitional accelerants. Clinical imminence work specified a short-horizon phenotype (SCS). Narrative approaches—the ENSI and the NCM—showed how identity, story form, and time horizons can narrow until a suicidal ending feels coherent within the person's world.

Across traditions, several themes converge:

- ***No single theory suffices.*** Each framework is a flashlight; together they illuminate population patterns, individual mechanisms, and near-term danger.
- ***Risk is dynamic and layered.*** Separate baseline diathesis from state activation; expect recurrence; plan for change.
- ***From ideation to action requires gates.*** Capability, access, intoxication, agitation, and planning shape the leap from thoughts to behavior.
- ***Entrapment is pivotal.*** Whether described as "cry of pain," motivational defeat, SCS, or narrative foreclosure, the felt absence of exits is the hinge of many crises.
- ***Identity and time matter.*** Narrative form (genre, role, plot) and temporal constriction help explain why suicide can feel "fitting"—and therefore where coherence might be rebuilt.
- ***Prediction is limited; design is decisive.*** Because individual forecasting is imprecise, systems must assume uncertainty and prioritize continuity, safety planning, caring contacts, and easy return pathways.
- ***Mechanisms point to levers.*** Theories earn their keep when they clarify what to monitor (e.g., defeat/entrapment, burdensomeness/belonging, volitional accelerants), what to map (identity, roles, time horizon), and how to organize care at population, service, and bedside levels.

RECOMMENDED READINGS

THOMAS JOINER—*WHY PEOPLE DIE BY SUICIDE* (2005)

Joiner's IPTS reshaped the field by distinguishing suicidal desire from suicidal capability. This book is central to understanding perceived burdensomeness, thwarted belonging, and acquired capability as interacting mechanisms. It is recommended here because it provides one of the clearest bridges from theory to clinical assessment.

MATIAS GAY—*INTEGRATING NARRATIVE IDENTITY IN SUICIDOLOGY: A CLINICAL EXPLORATION OF STORY, IDENTITY, AND SUICIDE*

This book explores how suicide can be better understood through the stories people construct about who they are, where they belong, and where their lives are going. It shows how disruptions in identity, meaning, relationships, and future orientation can shape suicidal suffering beyond symptoms alone. It brings together narrative theory, suicidology, and clinical practice to help readers understand suicide as a crisis of self, story, and existential coherence. Written for clinicians and helping professionals, it offers a deeper framework for assessment, formulation, and compassionate intervention.

RONALD W. MARIS, ALAN L. BERMAN, MORTON M. SILVERMAN, AND DAVID A. JOBES—*COMPREHENSIVE TEXTBOOK OF SUICIDOLOGY* (2000)

This authoritative textbook offers the most complete synthesis of suicide theory, research, clinical practice, and prevention available in a single volume. It systematically compares sociological, psychological, biological, and developmental models, making it an ideal companion for a chapter devoted to architectural frameworks. We recommend it here because it teaches readers how theories fit together across levels of analysis rather than competing for dominance.

KEY REFERENCES

Adam, K. S., Sheldon-Keller, A. E., & West, M. (1996). Attachment organization and history of suicidal behavior in clinical adolescents. *Journal of Consulting and Clinical Psychology, 64*(2), 264–272.

Baumeister, R. F. (1990). Suicide as escape from self. *Psychological Review, 97*(1), 90–113. https://doi.org/10.1037/0033-295X.97.1.90

Jobes, D. A. (2006). *Managing suicidal risk: A collaborative approach*. Guilford Press.

Litman, R. E., Curphey, T. J., Shneidman, E. S., Farberow, N. L., & Tabachnick, N. D. (1963). Investigations of equivocal suicides. JAMA, 184(12), 924–929. https://doi.org/10.1001/jama.1963.03700250060008

Mann, J. J., Apter, A., Bertolote, J., Beautrais, A., Currier, D., Haas, A., Hegerl, U., Lönnqvist, J., Malone, K., Marusic, A., Mehlum, L., Patton, G., Phillips, M., Rutz, W., Rihmer, Z., Schmidtke, A., Shaffer, D., Silverman, M., Takahashi, Y., Värnik, A., … Hendin, H. (2005). Suicide prevention strategies: A systematic review. *JAMA, 294*(16), 2064–2074. https://doi.org/10.1001/jama.294.16.2064

Menninger, K. (1938). *Man against himself.* Harcourt, Brace.

Orbach, I., Mikulincer, M., Sirota, P., & Gilboa-Schechtman, E. (2003). Mental pain and suicide. *Suicide and Life-Threatening Behavior, 33*(3), 231–241.

Rudd, M. D. (2006). Fluid vulnerability theory: A cognitive approach to understanding the process of acute and chronic suicide risk. In T. E. Ellis (Ed.), *Cognition and suicide: Theory, research, and therapy* (pp. 355–368). American Psychological Association. https://doi.org/10.1037/11377-016

3

CLUES AND MEASURES

Risk Factors, Warning Signs, and Tools

DISTINGUISHING VULNERABILITY FROM DANGER

This chapter draws a bright line between what raises a person's *long-term* likelihood of suicidal behavior and what signals *short-term* danger. In practice, that distinction prevents category errors—using a static checklist to "predict" an imminent act. Distal factors mark

DOI: 10.4324/9781003758792-3

background vulnerability that accumulates across years; proximal factors are fast-moving states and situations that change over hours or days; and protective factors buffer both horizons. Read this way, risk formulation becomes layered rather than linear: distal risk tells us who is more combustible, proximal signs tell us how close the flame is to the fuse, and protective elements tell us how readily a spark will catch (Jobes, 2006; Neimeyer et al., 2013).

Distal factors are the developmental and contextual conditions that make suicidal behavior more likely over the lifespan. Recurrent examples include prior attempts and self-harm; mood, psychotic, and substance use disorders; childhood maltreatment and attachment disruption; and trait-level impulsive–aggressive tendencies that increase the probability of acting under stress (Neimeyer et al., 2013; Stillion & McDowell, 1996). Distal risk also reflects *where* a person lives in the social world. Minority stress and discrimination raise baseline vulnerability among sexual and gender minority youth, in part by eroding belonging and safe disclosure, while community-level adversity—poverty, isolation, and weak service access—adds friction to help-seeking (Borenstein, 2020; Kingsbury et al., 2022). Population surveillance makes these patterns visible: national and provincial reports document differences by sex/gender, shifts by age cohort, and the role of method availability in shaping mortality trends. In Canada, method profiles have changed over time, with hanging/asphyxiation remaining prominent and method shares evolving across decades; these patterns track with changes in access and prevention policy (Public Health Agency of Canada, 2019; Liu et al., 2021; Province of Nova Scotia, 2022; Public Health Agency of Canada, 2022). Distal factors do not announce *when* danger will peak, but they explain why two people exposed to the same stressor can diverge in outcome.

Proximal factors are the short-horizon signals that a crisis is intensifying. Across cognitive and imminence models, a characteristic profile emerges: acute defeat and entrapment appraisals ("no way out"), ruminative flooding and narrowed time horizons, psychophysiological arousal marked by agitation or insomnia, and disinhibiting conditions such as intoxication (Williams, 2014; Galynker, 2017). Proximal context matters as well. Transitions of care—recent discharge from inpatient or emergency settings—are repeatedly implicated in near-term events, as are disciplinary or legal crises that combine humiliation, loss, and perceived lack of rescue (Sakinofsky, 2014; Chammas et al., 2022). Finally, access to highly lethal means shortens the window between impulse and fatal outcome; method-specific literatures (e.g., hanging) illustrate why seemingly small environmental differences can translate into large differences in survival (Gunnell et al., 2005). Proximal factors, by definition, move quickly; watching their *direction of travel*—worsening, stabilizing, or resolving—often tells us more about immediate danger than any static risk ledger (Jobes, 2006; Galynker, 2017).

Protective factors operate both across timescales and at multiple levels—individual, relational, and structural. On the individual side, reasons for living, future commitments, and problem-solving efficacy can widen perceived options when stress spikes. Relationally, belonging and supportive, non-punitive family climates reduce isolation and facilitate early help-seeking. Structurally, timely access to care, culturally and spiritually grounded prohibitions against self-harm, and practical home safety measures lower the probability that vulnerability becomes action (Neimeyer et al., 2013; Beattie & Devitt, 2015; Public Health Agency of Canada, 2019). Equity overlays all of this. Because sexual and gender minority youth face elevated baseline risk from stigma and structural barriers, protective design must be adapted to their realities—privacy-sensitive screening, affirming environments, and service pathways that do not presume supportive households (Borenstein, 2020; Kingsbury et al., 2022). Protective factors are not mere opposites of risk; they are independent forces that can interrupt the translation from distress to behavior even when distal vulnerabilities are substantial.

Taken together, these layers give clinicians and systems a common map. Distal factors outline the background landscape, proximal factors signal the weather moving in, and protective factors describe the shelter on hand. The map does not eliminate uncertainty—individual prediction remains limited—but it replaces one-size-fits-all risk lists with a time-sensitive formulation that better matches how crises actually unfold (Jobes, 2006; Neimeyer et al., 2013; Galynker, 2017).

What separates what raises a person's long-term likelihood of suicidal behavior (distal risk) from what signals short-term danger (proximal state)? The distinction is practical: distal factors describe background vulnerability that accumulates over years, whereas proximal factors describe states and situations that can shift over hours or days. A third strand—protective factors—buffers both horizons. Keeping these layers straight prevents a common error: treating a long list of static risks as if it could forecast an immediate act (Jobes, 2006; Neimeyer et al., 2013; Large et al., 2017). The clinical task is to formulate how vulnerabilities, stressors, and acute states interact *now*, and to target changeable elements.

Key claim: Distal ≠ predictive of *when*; proximal ≈ informative about *now*; protective = leverage for *change*.

DISTAL FACTORS: BACKGROUND LIABILITIES THAT ACCUMULATE

Distal factors are enduring conditions and life patterns that elevate *baseline* likelihood of suicidal thoughts and behavior. They rarely indicate *immediacy* on their own. Common classes include:

1. **History and development**
    - Prior suicide attempts or self-harm, exposure to suicide or violent loss
    - Early relational trauma, attachment disruption, neglect, maltreatment
    - Adverse childhood experiences and chronic invalidation across development (Stillion & McDowell, 1996; Kingsbury et al., 2022)
2. **Psychiatric and medical comorbidity**
    - Mood, anxiety, and psychotic disorders; substance use disorders
    - Chronic pain and disabling medical conditions (Jobes, 2006; Stillion & McDowell, 1996)

3. **Temperament and personality features**
   - Impulsive–aggressive traits, perfectionism, cognitive rigidity, hopelessness
   - Interpersonal sensitivities (e.g., burdensomeness, thwarted belonging) (Joiner, 2005; O'Connor & Kirtley, 2010)
4. **Sociocultural and structural context**
   - Minority stress and discrimination, economic precarity, isolation
   - Community-level adversity and access to highly lethal means (O'Connor & Pirkis, 2016; Borenstein, 2020)

Reading tip: Distal factors are *necessary context* but *insufficient* for timing. Use them to map vulnerability and to anticipate *what kinds of stressors* and *which acute states* are likely to precipitate crisis.

PROXIMAL FACTORS: STATES THAT TIGHTEN THE WINDOW

Proximal factors are dynamic conditions, stressors, and symptoms that correlate with *near-term* risk. They often evolve over hours to days and are sensitive to intervention.

1. **Escalating suicidal cognition**
   - Worsening frequency, intensity, rehearsal (planning, preparing)
   - Narrowing to specific method or time, acquisition of means (Jobes, 2006)
2. **Entrapment and temporal constriction**
   - Feeling no way out, foreshortened future, "time is closing in"
   - Narrative foreclosure and loss of authorship (O'Connor & Kirtley, 2010; Gay, 2025)
3. **Arousal and dysregulation syndromes**
   - Agitation, severe anxiety, insomnia, acute anhedonia, or panic

- Intoxication or withdrawal, abrupt mood lability (Galynker, 2023)

4. **Suicide Crisis Syndrome**
   - Frantic hopelessness, affective disturbance, ruminative flooding, panic-dissociation, hyperarousal; often without a fixed plan early on (Galynker, 2023)
5. **Psychotic and mixed affective states**
   - Command hallucinations, nihilistic delusions, mixed/manic features (Stillion & McDowell, 1996)
6. **Acute interpersonal or role threats**
   - Shaming events, legal or financial shock, relationship rupture, forced identity transitions (O'Connor & Kirtley, 2010)

Reading tip: Proximal factors demand time-sensitive decisions (means safety, observation level, crisis-oriented interventions) and rapid follow-up.

PROTECTIVE FACTORS: BUFFERS AND LEVERS

Protective factors are conditions that *reduce* the likelihood of transition from ideation to attempt and support recovery. They function as both *buffers* and *targets* for care.

- **Relational supports**: reliable attachment, social connectedness, caring contacts
- **Meaning and commitments**: reasons for living, valued roles, future projects
- **Skills and access**: problem-solving, emotion regulation, cultural/spiritual resources, timely access to evidence-based care
- **Environmental safety**: secure storage or removal of lethal means, supportive settings (Jobes, 2006; O'Connor & Pirkis, 2016)

Reading tip: Name the *specific* buffer (who/what/where), then convert it into an *actionable plan* (how to mobilize, when, and by whom).

Putting the layers together in formulation: A practical way to synthesize is to write a single sentence (or diagram) that captures **Trait × Stressor × State → Near-term risk**, then add **Buffers/Levers**:

> A history of childhood maltreatment and perfectionistic self-standards (distal) combined with a public professional setback (stressor) has precipitated entrapment, insomnia, and method rehearsal (proximal); risk is elevated in the next 24–72 hours. Protective anchors include a committed partner and a pending project deadline, both of which can be activated today (protective).

CLINICAL LEVERS BY LAYER

- *Distal*: long-term psychotherapy targets (schema work, identity repair, substance treatment); social determinants (income, housing, discrimination)
- *Proximal*: crisis-focused measures (safety planning, collaborative means safety, brief cognitive behavioral therapy/dialectical behavior therapy skills, medication for agitation/insomnia, observation when indicated)
- *Protective*: concrete activation (warm handoffs, scheduled caring contacts, family meetings, spiritual/cultural resources, return-to-purpose tasks).

COMMON INTERPRETIVE ERRORS—AND HOW TO AVOID THEM

1. **Risk stratification fallacy**
   Assigning patients to static "low/moderate/high" bins is weakly informative and may be unsafe; prioritize individualized formulation and modifiable drivers over labels (Large et al., 2017).
   Fix: Document the *mechanism* of risk, the *time window*, and the *intervention plan*.
2. **List inflation**
   Presenting long lists of distal risks as if they forecast imminence.
   Fix: Separate sections in notes: **Distal** vs. **Proximal** vs. **Protective**.

3. **Tool absolutism**

   Treating screeners as outcome measures or as substitutes for clinical judgment.

   Fix: Use tools to structure inquiry and track change; retain synthesis and narrative context.

4. **Under-specifying protection**

   Naming "supportive family" without operationalizing *how* support will be used.

   Fix: Convert each protective factor into a task with a person, place, and time.

PRACTICE BOXES

Box 1 Quick Prompts for Proximal Risk

- "What has changed in the last 48–72 hours?"
- "What are you rehearsing in your head?"
- "When does the urge feel strongest, and what predicts it?"

Box 2 Turning Buffers into Plans

- From *"my sister helps"* → *"Sister will stay tonight; remove medications to locked storage; check-in calls at 10am/7pm; calendar invite sent before discharge."*

Box 3 Documentation Scaffold

- **Distal** (baseline vulnerability)
- **Stressors** (recent triggers)
- **Proximal** (current states/signs)
- **Protective** (buffers to mobilize)
- **Plan** (interventions mapped to each layer)

Table 3.1 is designed to operationalize the chapter's central distinction between distal vulnerability, proximal warning signs, and protective buffers by placing them side by side in a single, time-sensitive framework. Its intent is to help clinicians avoid a common category error—treating long-standing risk factors as indicators of imminent danger—by clarifying which factors inform *baseline vulnerability*, which signal *near-term escalation*, and which offer *leverage for immediate intervention*. The table should be read as a formulation aid rather than a predictive tool: it supports layered clinical reasoning by linking *what has accumulated over years*, *what is changing right now*, and *what can be strengthened today* to reduce risk and widen the person's future.

Table 3.1 Summary of Proximal, Distal, and Protective Suicide Factors

Layer	*Typical content*	*Illustrative sources*
Distal (chronic vulnerability)	Prior attempts/self-harm; mood, psychotic, and substance disorders; impulsive–aggressive traits; childhood maltreatment/attachment problems; minority stress; community disadvantage	Stillion & McDowell, 1996; Neimeyer et al., 2013; Kingsbury et al., 2022; Borenstein, 2020
Proximal (short-term warning signs)	Defeat/entrapment; frantic hopelessness; ruminative flooding; agitation/insomnia; intoxication; recent discharge or disciplinary stress; access to lethal means	Williams, 2014; Galynker, 2017; Sakinofsky, 2014; Chammas et al., 2022; Gunnell et al., 2005
Protective (buffers)	Connectedness; supportive family climate; culturally grounded prohibitions/purposes; timely access to care; practical home safety	Public Health Agency of Canada, 2019; Neimeyer et al., 2013; Beattie & Devitt, 2015

SCREENS AND SCALES—WHAT THEY MEASURE AND WHAT THEY DON'T

Brief screeners are quick checks that tell us who needs a full, person-to-person assessment. They do not diagnose suicide risk on their own. Here's a plain-language guide to the most common tools and what the evidence says.

ASK SUICIDE-SCREENING QUESTIONS

What it is: Four yes/no questions (with one quick follow-up if any answer is "yes"). Designed to be done in under a minute.

Where it fits: Emergency departments (EDs), primary care, and medical units—especially with children, teens, and young adults.

What studies show: In pediatric EDs, Ask Suicide-Screening Questions (ASQ) caught **most youth who were at risk** (sensitivity about **97%**) while missing few (specificity about **88%**) (Horowitz et al., 2012). In adult inpatients, it also performed well (sensitivity **100%**, specificity **89%**) (Horowitz et al., 2020). Outpatient studies support use beyond the ED (Aguinaldo et al., 2021).

Strengths: Very fast, easy to teach, and ties into a ready workflow (ASQ → Brief Suicide Safety Assessment, or BSSA) (NIMH, 2017).

Considerations: Like any quick screen, it can produce false positives; scores must be read in context of the person and setting.

COLUMBIA-SUICIDE SEVERITY RATING SCALE

What it is: A short, structured interview that organizes what someone is thinking (from "wish to die" to "intent and plan") and what they've done (attempts, aborted or interrupted attempts, preparatory acts).

Where it fits: EDs, mental health clinics, inpatient units—anywhere teams need a shared language to document the level of ideation and behaviors linked to near-term risk.

What studies show: Strong initial validation across adolescents and adults (Posner et al., 2011). Some youth ED studies show certain Columbia-Suicide Severity Rating Scale (C-SSRS) scores predict short-term attempts (Gipson et al., 2015). In general ED cohorts, prediction is modest, so results must be paired with clinical judgment (Salvi, 2019; Brown et al., 2020).

Strengths: Clear, common terminology; ensures behavior history is captured.
Considerations: Categorical cutoffs can overidentify some youth; the tool cannot forecast who will act on its own.

PATIENT HEALTH QUESTIONNAIRE-9

What it is: A single question inside the depression screen asking about thoughts of death or self-harm.

Where it fits: Primary care and mental health settings where the Patient Health Questionnaire-9 (PHQ-9) is already used.

What studies show: Marking item 9 as positive is linked to higher short-term risk of attempts and deaths in large health system samples (Simon et al., 2013; Louzon et al., 2016; Rossom et al., 2017). But many people who later attempt or die had answered "not at all" on their last PHQ-9 (Louzon et al., 2016), and a meta-analysis concludes item 9 isn't enough as a stand-alone suicide screener (Na et al., 2018).

Strengths: Ubiquitous and quick—helps flag who needs follow-up.
Considerations: Not suicide-specific; a "yes" includes passive death wishes—it should **trigger a conversation**, not a label.

CRISIS-STATE MEASURES (SCS)

What they are: Short measures of acute states linked to imminent risk—e.g., frantic hopelessness, entrapment, ruminative flooding, affective turmoil, loss of cognitive control—the cluster known as SCS (Galynker, 2023).

Where they fit: As add-ons when teams suspect imminent risk even if someone denies ideation.

What studies show: The Suicide Crisis Inventory-2 (SCI-2) shows good validity and short-term predictive utility across inpatient and outpatient samples (Bloch-Elkouby et al., 2021; Menon et al., 2024).

How to use: Read alongside routine assessment and observation—not instead of them.

Strengths: ability to detect imminent suicide risk beyond stated ideation.

Considerations: though they are most effective when used to supplement, they do not replace comprehensive clinical assessment.

TWO CROSS-CUTTING CAUTIONS

- **Screen ≠ diagnosis.** A positive screen means **"talk more and plan for safety,"** not **"this person is suicidal."**
- **No tool is an Oracle.** Individual-level prediction is modest even with structured tools; simple risk bins(low/moderate/high) have poor positive predictive value (PPV) (Franklin et al., 2017; Large et al., 2017). Pair screening with observation of proximal signs, a clear story of the current episode, and attention to environment and means.

EQUITY, METHOD, AND CONTEXT

Risk is not distributed evenly. National and provincial data show differences by sex/gender and by method, with shifts over time in the means used and in the lethality of first attempts—patterns that matter for prevention and aftercare design (McKean et al., 2018; Liu et al., 2021). Youth who identify as sexual or gender minorities face higher rates of ideation and attempts, reflecting minority stress and barriers to supportive environments, while stigma and discrimination continue to impede disclosure and help-seeking across groups (Borenstein, 2020; Kingsbury et al., 2022). These realities require that screening and assessment be culturally attuned, trauma-informed, and sensitive to confidentiality and safety in families and schools (Neimeyer et al., 2013; Beattie & Devitt, 2015).

BOX: BRIEF SCREENING VERSUS COMPREHENSIVE ASSESSMENT (WHY BOTH MATTER)

Brief screening answers a narrow question—*is there a credible signal that this person could be at risk right now?*—and does so quickly, using a few standardized questions and a clear follow-up pathway. Comprehensive assessment is slower and integrative. It clarifies history and diathesis (distal risks and protective anchors), reconstructs the current episode (defeat, entrapment, substance use, sleep, access), and documents the living context (family climate, school or workplace pressures, cultural and legal considerations). The former triages; the latter explains. Good services treat them as sequential steps recorded in standard clinical notes or structured templates rather than as competing philosophies (Jobes, 2006; Neimeyer et al., 2013; Galynker, 2017).

CHAPTER SUMMARY

This chapter shows how to read suicide risk in layers. Distal factors (development, diagnoses, traits, and social context) raise *baseline* vulnerability over years; they tell us who may be at risk but not when. Proximal factors (acute thoughts, method rehearsal, entrapment/temporal constriction, agitation, intoxication, psychotic or mixed states, and fresh interpersonal or role shocks) shift over hours to days; they tell us when danger is rising and guide time-sensitive actions. Protective factors (people, purposes, skills, access to care, and safer environments) buffer both horizons and give us levers for change.

Brief screeners (ASQ, C-SSRS, PHQ-9 item 9) help busy teams find who needs a deeper, person-to-person assessment; positive screens should trigger brief safety assessment, means safety, and follow-up, not a label. Because some imminent crises unfold without declared ideation, measures of SCS can add value by capturing the phenomenology of imminence when it matters most. Across all tools, we avoid the risk stratification fallacy and document instead the mechanism × time window × plan for this person, today (Jobes, 2006; Large et al., 2017).

WHY PREDICTION STAYS HARD—AND WHAT TO DO INSTEAD

Even strong, multivariate models cannot forecast individual suicide with high accuracy; many who die were never labeled "high risk," and many labeled "high risk" do not die (Neimeyer et al., 2013). The practical response is design, not fatalism: use screens to open conversations; watch for proximal change even when the distal profile is familiar; document clearly using standardized templates; and pair measurement with relationship, follow-up, and environmental safety (Jobes, 2006; Galynker, 2017; Public Health Agency of Canada, 2019).

KEY TAKEAWAYS

- **Distal ≠ timing. Proximal ≈ timing. Protective = leverage.** Keep the layers separate in notes and in team talk.
- **Screen, then assess.** Use ASQ/C-SSRS/PHQ-9 item 9 to triage; a positive screen prompts brief safety assessment, means safety, and follow-up (Posner et al., 2011; Horowitz et al., 2012; NIMH, 2017).
- **Don't over-trust labels.** Static low/moderate/high bins have poor PPV; write the mechanism, time window (e.g., 24–72 h), and plan instead (Large et al., 2017).
- **Watch the near-term state.** Escalating ideation/rehearsal, entrapment, agitation/insomnia, substance effects, psychosis/mixed states, and fresh relational shocks drive next-few-days risk (Jobes, 2006; O'Connor & Kirtley, 2010).
- **Imminence can be quiet.** Consider SCS/SCI-2 when ideation is denied but frantic hopelessness/rumination/loss of control is evident (Galynker, 2023).
- **Convert buffers to actions.** Name *who/what/when* and schedule caring contacts, family roles, and access changes today (O'Connor & Pirkis, 2016; PHAC, 2019).
- **Care is relational.** Pair tools with collaborative conversation, warm handoffs, and timely follow-up (Jobes, 2006).

RECOMMENDED READINGS

ALAN L. BERMAN, RONALD W. MARIS, JOHN T. MALTSBERGER, AND ROBERT I. YUFIT (EDS.)—*ASSESSMENT AND PREDICTION OF SUICIDE* (1992)

This edited volume is a classic, clinically oriented deep dive into how suicidology has tried (and often struggled) to translate risk knowledge into assessment and prediction. It's most valuable for Chapter 3 because it highlights the limits of static risk lists while still teaching structured clinical reasoning, documentation logic, and decision-making under uncertainty. We recommend it here as a "measurement-and-judgment" backbone that matches this chapter's central distinction between distal vulnerability and proximal danger.

DAVID A. JOBES—*MANAGING SUICIDAL RISK: A COLLABORATIVE APPROACH* (2016)

Jobes' Collaborative Assessment and Management of Suicidality framework reframes assessment as a collaborative, patient-centered process focused on drivers of suicidal suffering. This book aligns directly with this chapter's emphasis on formulation over prediction and proximal over distal risk. It is essential for translating risk theory into everyday clinical practice.

MICHAEL D. ANESTIS—*GUNS AND SUICIDE: AN AMERICAN EPIDEMIC* (2018)

This book explains, in clear public health terms, how access to a highly lethal method changes outcomes even when suicidal desire is constant—making it directly relevant to this chapter's emphasis on what drives near-term risk. Anestis is especially useful here because he focuses on the mechanism of lethality and practical capability rather than vague general risk. We recommend it for this chapter because it strengthens the reader's ability to integrate "access + time + lethality" into real-world risk formulation and safety planning.

KEY REFERENCES

Brown, G. K., Currier, G. W., Jager-Hyman, S., & Stanley, B. (2020). Detection and classification of suicidal behavior and nonsuicidal self-injury behavior in emergency departments. *Journal of Clinical Psychiatry, 81*(2), 19m12964. https://doi.org/10.4088/JCP.19m12964

Franklin, J. C., Ribeiro, J. D., Fox, K. R., Bentley, K. H., Kleiman, E. M., Huang, X., Musacchio, K. M., Jaroszewski, A. C., Chang, B. P., & Nock, M. K. (2017). Risk factors for suicidal thoughts and behaviors: A meta-analysis of 50 years of studies. *Psychological Bulletin, 143*(2), 187–232. https://doi.org/10.1037/bul0000084

Gunnell, D., Bennewith, O., Hawton, K., Simkin, S., & Kapur, N. (2005). The epidemiology and prevention of suicide by hanging: A systematic review. *International Journal of Epidemiology, 34*(2), 433–442.

Large, M. M., Ryan, C. J., Carter, G., & Kapur, N. (2017). Can we usefully stratify patients according to suicide risk? *BMJ, 359*, j4627. https://doi.org/10.1136/bmj.j4627

Neimeyer, R. A., et al. (2013). *Treatment of Suicidal People*. Taylor & Francis.

O'Connor, R. C., & Kirtley, O. J. (2010). The integrated motivational–volitional model of suicidal behaviour. *Philosophical Transactions of the Royal Society B: Biological Sciences, 373*(1754), 20170268. https://doi.org/10.1098/rstb.2017.0268

O'Connor, R. C., & Pirkis, J. (2016). The international handbook of suicide prevention (2nd ed.). Wiley Blackwell.

Salvi, V. (2019). The role of risk assessment in suicide prevention. *BJPsych Advances, 25*(1), 25–32. https://doi.org/10.1192/bja.2018.31

4

ROOTS OF VULNERABILITY

HOW RISK TAKES ROOT OVER TIME

Suicidal risk rarely begins with a single event. It develops over time as life experiences, health conditions, and social circumstances shape how a person understands themselves and copes with stress. Some influences sit in the background for years—early adversity, chronic illness, personality and coping styles, stigma

DOI: 10.4324/9781003758792-4

and discrimination, poverty or rural isolation. These are **distal** factors: they set the stage but do not, on their own, cause a suicidal act. Other influences are **proximal**—they arise in the hours, days, or weeks before a crisis, such as a relationship breakup, a shame-laden setback, a spike in agitation or insomnia, or sudden access to a lethal method. Suicidal behavior becomes more likely when proximal stress lands on top of long-standing vulnerabilities, especially if protective supports are thin (O'Connor & Kirtley, 2010; Liu & Miller, 2014).

Across the lifespan, three elements reliably shape risk:(1) **vulnerability**—the background load a person carries; (2) **stress**—what is happening now; and (3) **buffers**—what helps the person hold steady. Buffers include a sense of belonging, reasons for living, identity affirmation, and timely, respectful access to care. When these buffers erode, ordinary stress can feel unbearable and the future can appear closed off (Jobes, 2006; Lawrence et al., 2015).

Developmental experiences matter. Adverse childhood experiences (ACEs)—especially sexual, physical, and chronic emotional abuse—can distort how safety, shame, and self-worth are encoded, increasing the odds of suicidal ideation and later attempts (Mina & Gallop, 1998; Martin et al., 2004; Afifi et al., 2008). Bullying and social exclusion add further strain, particularly in children and adolescents, where peer status and belonging are central (Cook et al., 2010). In adolescence and emerging adulthood, rapid biological and social changes heighten self-consciousness and amplify interpersonal stress; clusters and contagion effects also appear more often in these age groups (Gould et al., 1990; O'Connor et al., 2014).

Identity and culture shape risk and protection. Sexual- and gender-minority youth face higher rates of ideation and attempts in the context of stigma, rejection, and violence, whereas affirming families, schools, and communities are protective (King & Merchant, 2008; Kingsbury et al., 2022). Religious or spiritual communities can protect through belonging and moral commitments—so long as they do not introduce shame or exclusion (Lawrence et al., 2015). In some cultural settings, "honor," face, or perfectionistic ideals can intensify shame after setbacks and suppress help-seeking, which clinicians must name and gently counter (Lester, 1997; Chambers, 2010).

Health conditions and substances also load the system. Mood, anxiety, bipolar, psychotic, and substance use disorders often co-occur with suicidal thoughts or behavior; alcohol and drugs can lower inhibition, increase agitation, and make a lethal attempt more likely during a surge of distress (Cash & Bridge, 2009; O'Connor & Kirtley, 2010). Chronic pain and medical illness can narrow horizons and tax coping. For some groups—such as military personnel—repeated exposure to pain, injury, or death may increase **capability for suicide**, meaning greater fearlessness and tolerance for pain; capability can also be **acquired** through prior attempts, self-injury, or practice with methods (Joiner et al., 2009; Bryan et al., 2013).

Social determinants shape both risk and access to help. Poverty, food or housing insecurity, rurality, racism, and barriers to transportation or childcare can make it hard to reach care and harder still to stay connected. Patterns in Canada reflect these influences: hanging is the most common method nationally, with trends varying by region; timely access to primary care, crisis supports, and coordinated follow-up remain key levers for prevention (Public Health Agency of Canada, 2019; Liu et al., 2021; Province of Nova Scotia, 2022).

This chapter translates these roots into practice. We differentiate distal from proximal factors to avoid a common error: using long lists of static risks to predict an immediate act. Instead, we focus on **how** vulnerabilities and current stress combine in the presence—or absence—of buffers. We describe typical developmental patterns from childhood through older adulthood, examine identity-based and relational influences; outline health and substance factors, and summarize social determinants clinicians can act on. Throughout, we return to a practical question: *What can we strengthen right now to widen the person's future and reduce near-term risk?* (Jobes, 2006; O'Connor & Kirtley, 2010).

Clinically, the stance is simple: be curious about the person's story; map their background loads; listen for today's pressures; probe capability (fearlessness, pain tolerance, prior self-harm, method familiarity); and grow buffers—belonging, reasons for living, tangible supports, and access pathways that do not drop them after the crisis visit. Risk rises when stress tips a thinly buffered system; it falls when relationships, skills, and environments are shored up (Owens et al., 2002; Hawton et al., 2003; Jobes, 2006).

Finally, we provide a visual "balance" figure to keep the clinical logic in view: vulnerabilities on one side, buffers on the other, and current stress as the slider that tips the beam. The goal is not to label people as "high risk" but to understand *what is heavy right now* and *what we can strengthen next* (Joiner et al., 2009; Liu & Miller, 2014; Lawrence et al., 2015).

DEVELOPMENTAL FOUNDATIONS

CHILDHOOD

Early life lays much of the groundwork for later vulnerability. Research on ACEs shows that repeated exposure to abuse, neglect, or family dysfunction increases the odds of suicidal thoughts and attempts across the lifespan. Emotional and sexual abuse, in particular, appear to carry stronger and more enduring effects than neglect alone (Afifi et al., 2008; Miller et al., 2013). Children exposed to these environments often internalize patterns of shame, fear, and helplessness that can become part of their identity and coping style.

When suicide occurs in childhood, it often reflects a tragic collision of immaturity and stress. Psychiatric diagnoses are less common than in adolescents and adults; instead, acute relational triggers—particularly conflict with parents or caregivers—are prominent (McIntire & Angle, 1980; Freuchen et al., 2012). Children's limited grasp of permanence and death may mean their actions are more about escape from an unbearable moment than a clear intention to die, which complicates prevention and highlights the importance of supportive communication and early intervention.

Bullying adds another layer of risk. Both victims and perpetrators show higher rates of suicidal ideation and behavior, though the burden is often heavier for girls. Repeated humiliation or exclusion erodes belonging, a critical buffer at this age (Cook et al., 2010; Losey, 2011). Clinicians should remember that children may not disclose bullying directly; instead, they may show withdrawal, school refusal, or sudden irritability.

ADOLESCENCE AND EMERGING ADULTHOOD

Adolescence brings rapid physical, social, and psychological changes. Pubertal development heightens self-consciousness, peer comparison becomes central, and expectations about the future grow weighty. Failures or rejections during this period—whether a breakup, falling grades, or family conflict—can feel overwhelming and identity-defining (O'Connor et al., 2014).

Suicidal clusters—multiple deaths in a community within a short period—occur more often in adolescent populations, reflecting both contagion effects and the heightened sensitivity to peer influence at this stage (Gould et al., 1990). Exposure to suicide in family or peers triples the risk for adolescents, underscoring the importance of safe messaging, supportive debriefing, and careful monitoring after a suicide in schools or communities (Schaffer et al., 2016).

Identity-based stressors are particularly salient. LGBTQIA+ and transgender youth report markedly elevated rates of suicidal ideation and attempts, largely due to stigma, rejection, and minority stress (King & Merchant, 2008). Protective factors are clear: supportive families, affirming school climates, and inclusive community spaces dramatically reduce risk (Kingsbury et al., 2022). For clinicians, this means that asking directly about acceptance and affirmation is not optional—it is central to understanding vulnerability and designing effective care.

ADULTHOOD AND MILITARY CONTEXT

In adulthood, vulnerabilities often stem from the cumulative impact of life events. Traumas that were survivable when isolated can pile up—unemployment, divorce, caregiving stress, medical illness, and chronic pain—creating a load that overwhelms coping resources. Mood, anxiety, and substance use disorders often intersect with these stressors, magnifying risk.

For military personnel and veterans, exposure to combat, injury, and death can change the way pain and fear are processed. Repeated exposure may foster a kind of fearlessness or desensitization—what some theories call "acquired capability for suicide." This can increase the likelihood that thoughts are acted upon, especially during transitions out of service, when isolation and burdensomeness often rise (Bryan et al., 2013). The military context underscores how social role shifts and identity disruption can interact with capability, creating unique vulnerabilities that demand culturally informed and trauma-aware care.

RELATIONAL, CULTURAL, AND CONTEXTUAL VULNERABILITIES

RELATIONAL AND FAMILY CONTEXT

Families are the first and most enduring relational environment. Patterns of warmth, control, and communication in childhood and adolescence strongly shape suicide risk later in life. Research shows that when parental care is low and control is high—a dynamic sometimes described as "affectionless control"—youth face higher rates of suicidal thoughts and behaviors (Goschin et al., 2013). Separation from caregivers, high conflict, or persistent misunderstandings can further amplify risk, particularly when young people lack other sources of belonging and stability.

Family history adds another layer. Parental suicidal behavior independently predicts suicidality in offspring, with stronger effects when the mother has attempted or died by suicide. Sensitivity can peak as children approach the age at which their parent died, suggesting that developmental milestones can activate vulnerability (Geulayov et al., 2012). For many children and adolescents, open conflict with parents is the most common immediate trigger before an attempt, underscoring the need for family-focused prevention and repair (Freuchen et al., 2012).

IDENTITY, CULTURE, AND MINORITY STRESS

Identity shapes both the burdens people carry and the protections available to them. Minority stress—including discrimination, victimization, and invalidation—adds weight to the diathesis, contributing to earlier onset and more frequent suicidal thoughts and behaviors. Sexual- and gender-minority youth, for example, report significantly higher rates of suicidal ideation and attempts compared to their peers (King & Merchant, 2008). However, supportive families, affirming schools, and safe community spaces can dramatically reduce these risks (Kingsbury et al., 2022).

Cultural frameworks also matter. In some contexts, suicide is framed through honor, shame, or collective obligation. These beliefs can intensify pressure to conceal distress and may inhibit help-seeking, as disclosure could be seen as weakness or dishonor (Chambers, 2010). Conversely, strong religious affiliation often protects against suicide by offering belonging, moral proscriptions against self-harm, and supportive community structures. Importantly, this protection depends on whether faith communities foster inclusion rather than shame (Lawrence et al., 2015).

TRAUMA, GRIEF, AND CHRONIC STRESSORS

Trauma and grief accumulate across the lifespan, leaving deep marks on vulnerability. Sexual violence and chronic emotional abuse are especially powerful predictors of later suicide attempts and self-harm, often re-emerging in adult life as triggers for crisis (Mina & Gallop, 1998; Martin et al., 2004). Grief can operate similarly, particularly after sudden or stigmatized loss, narrowing a person's capacity to imagine a viable future.

Acute stressors often cluster in the days and weeks before a death. Relationship breakups, legal or financial problems, and health crises are common precipitants. Yet these stressors rarely act in isolation; their impact depends on the vulnerabilities already present and the buffers still intact (Liu & Miller, 2014). Many people who die by suicide have recently seen a healthcare professional, highlighting that opportunities for recognition, continuity, and timely intervention are often missed (Schaffer et al., 2016).

HEALTH CONDITIONS AND SUBSTANCE USE

Psychiatric and medical conditions contribute substantially to risk. Mood disorders, psychotic illnesses, anxiety, and bipolar spectrum conditions are consistently associated with suicidal behavior across adolescence and adulthood (Cash & Bridge, 2009). Substance use further compounds vulnerability: alcohol and drugs can increase impulsivity, intensify mood swings, lower inhibition, and provide access to lethal means. This combination makes the transition from suicidal thoughts to suicidal action more likely (O'Connor & Kirtley, 2010).

SOCIAL DETERMINANTS: POVERTY, RURALITY, AND ACCESS TO CARE

Social and structural conditions shape both exposure to stress and the ability to access help. Poverty and unstable housing create daily strain, erode coping resources, and restrict options for timely support. Rural residence can add further challenges—greater isolation, reduced availability of mental health professionals, and, in some regions, easier access to highly lethal methods such as firearms or hanging (Public Health Agency of Canada, 2019; Liu et al., 2021). Transportation barriers, long wait times, and fragmented services mean that many people experiencing suicidal distress encounter obstacles at precisely the moment they most need care.

Across North America, these systemic factors are closely linked with suicide patterns. Hanging has become the most common method in Canada and remains a leading cause of death in the United States, reflecting broader shifts in means over time (Liu et al., 2021). Public health strategies consistently stress the importance of upstream prevention: ensuring access to primary care, expanding crisis services, improving coordination after emergency visits, and addressing the broader inequities that make help harder to reach (Public Health Agency of Canada, 2019).

CAPABILITY FOR SUICIDE: TRAIT AND ACQUIRED

Not everyone who thinks about suicide is able to act on those thoughts. The concept of "capability" helps explain why some people cross from ideation to attempt while others do not. Borrowing from ideation-to-action frameworks, capability includes both trait factors and acquired factors (Joiner et al., 2009).

Trait capability refers to relatively stable characteristics that reduce fear of death or increase tolerance for pain. Some people are temperamentally more fearless or less reactive to pain. Personality features such as high impulsivity, aggression, or sensation-seeking can add to this baseline capability, though they do not predict suicide in isolation.

Acquired capability develops through life experiences. Repeated exposure to painful or provocative events—self-injury, prior attempts, medical procedures, combat, abuse, or witnessing violence—can lower a person's natural resistance to death. With time, this exposure breeds familiarity with pain and reduces the body's instinctive fear response. Familiarity with lethal means (e.g., firearms, hanging methods, medication stockpiles) further increases risk because it bridges thought and action.

Prior attempts are one of the most reliable predictors of later death. The methods people choose often track intent: more lethal methods signal higher risk, and many who die use the same or a more lethal method than in past attempts (Nishimura et al., 1999; Runeson et al., 2010). This is especially important when working with adolescents, where "impulsivity" is often overstated. While some youth make sudden decisions, many attempts involve planning—even when the outward trigger seems small or ordinary (Witte et al., 2008; Horwitz et al., 2014). Clinicians should therefore avoid dismissing a prior attempt as "just impulsive" and instead explore planning, rehearsal, and capability in detail.

PROTECTIVE ASSETS AND BUFFERS

If capability lowers barriers to action, protective assets help keep the balance from tipping. These are the relational, psychological, and practical forces that sustain life even in the midst of pain.

- **Belonging and connection:** Feeling valued by family, peers, or community reduces risk. Family acceptance, affirming schools, and supportive workplaces are powerful buffers, especially for LGBTQIA+ youth (Kingsbury et al., 2022).
- **Purpose and reasons for living:** Goals, identities, and commitments that matter to the person—parenting, caregiving, creative projects, spirituality—counteract suicidal pull (Lawrence et al., 2015).
- **Access to care:** Ready access to responsive, collaborative, and respectful care makes it more likely that distress will be contained rather than acted upon.

- **Community and faith ties:** Religious or community groups can provide belonging and moral guidance, but only if they foster inclusion rather than shame (Lawrence et al., 2015).

At the clinical level, practical tools strengthen buffers: collaborative safety planning gives structure and hope; lethal means counseling buys time and reduces immediate danger; warm handoffs after emergency visits ensure people do not leave care unsupported (Owens et al., 2002; Hawton et al., 2003; Jobes, 2006). These interventions reduce short-term risk while longer-term skills and relationships are rebuilt.

TRANSLATING THE ROOTS INTO PRACTICE: LIFESPAN QUICK GUIDE

- **Children:** Watch for shame, withdrawal, or sudden silence after bullying or discipline. Involve caregivers early and teach concrete coping and repair routines (Cook et al., 2010; Freuchen et al., 2012).
- **Adolescents:** Ask about relationship losses, family conflict, minority stress, and social media exposure. Assess capability directly: history of self-harm, rehearsals, or access to lethal means. Avoid assuming attempts are purely "impulsive" (Gould et al., 1990; Witte et al., 2008; Kingsbury et al., 2022).
- **Adults:** Screen for cumulative trauma, substance use, chronic pain, financial/legal stress, and role loss. Strengthen belonging and problem-solving while restricting means (Jobes, 2006; Liu & Miller, 2014).
- **Older adults:** Explore grief, medical illness, caregiver burden, and isolation. Attend to method access and prioritize primary care and home-based supports (Liu & Miller, 2014; Public Health Agency of Canada, 2019).

Clinical Sidebar: Reading the Balance

A practical approach is to visualize suicidal risk as a balance with vulnerabilities on one side, buffers on the other, and current stressors acting as the tipping weight. Clinicians can:

1. **Map vulnerabilities.** Early adversity, chronic illness, identity stress, family conflict.
2. **Identify current stressors**. Acute loss, agitation, entrapment, shame events.
3. **Probe capability**. Fearlessness, pain tolerance, prior attempts, rehearsals, means access.
4. **Strengthen buffers**. Belonging, reasons for living, access to responsive care, cultural or religious supports.
5. **Co-author a safety plan.** Pair relationship and monitoring with environmental safety—restricting means, arranging follow-up, and engaging family or community supports (Jobes, 2006; Joiner et al., 2009; Galynker, 2017).

The central task is not to predict who will act but to understand what is heavy right now and what can be reinforced immediately.

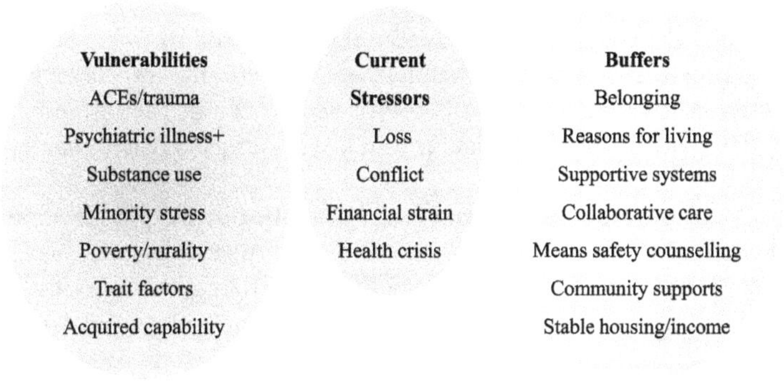

Figure 4.1 Vulnerability–buffer balance

Figure 4.1 illustrates a two-pan balance. **Left pan (Vulnerabilities)** lists ACEs/trauma; psychiatric and substance conditions; minority stress; family conflict; poverty/rurality; trait factors (impulsivity, perfectionism, fearlessness/pain insensitivity); acquired capability (prior self-harm, rehearsals, lethal means familiarity). **Right pan (Buffers)** lists belonging/identity affirmation; reasons for living; supportive family/school/work; timely access to collaborative care; means safety; spiritual/community supports; stable housing/income. A central slider labeled **Current Stressors** (loss, conflict, legal/financial strain, health crisis) tips the beam. *Risk emerges when stress adds weight to vulnerabilities and buffers are thin* (Jobes, 2006; Joiner et al., 2009; Liu & Miller, 2014; Lawrence et al., 2015).

CHAPTER SUMMARY

This chapter has explored the deep foundations of suicidal risk—the developmental, relational, cultural, health, and social contexts that shape how a person becomes vulnerable and the protective forces that can buffer against crisis. The central message is that suicide does not arise from a single cause. Instead, it grows out of a complex interplay between long-standing vulnerabilities, current stressors, and the availability (or absence) of buffers.

KEY POINTS ACROSS THE LIFESPAN

- **Childhood:** ACEs such as abuse, neglect, and bullying can set patterns of shame and helplessness that endure into later life. Even at young ages, conflict with parents can be the immediate trigger for suicidal behavior, often without psychiatric diagnoses in the background.
- **Adolescence and emerging adulthood:** Rapid developmental changes amplify stress and make peer rejection, breakups, and family conflict especially destabilizing. Suicide clusters are more common, and exposure to suicide in peers or family significantly increases risk. LGBTQIA+ and trans youth carry higher risk due to minority stress, but affirming environments act as strong protective factors.
- **Adulthood and military contexts:** Cumulative trauma, substance use, mood disorders, and role or economic losses can weigh heavily. In military and veteran populations, combat exposure can increase "acquired capability" through habituation to pain and fear, raising risk particularly during transitions back to civilian life.
- **Older adults:** Risk often centers around grief, declining health, chronic pain, caregiver burden, and social isolation. These

factors highlight the need for home- and community-based supports that reduce loneliness and maintain dignity.

RELATIONAL AND CULTURAL INFLUENCES

Families can either buffer or amplify vulnerability. Low warmth, high conflict, or parental suicidal behavior increases risk, while support and open communication protect. Cultural values and beliefs shape whether distress is spoken about or hidden. While some frameworks of shame and honor may discourage help-seeking, faith and community groups often provide belonging and purpose that safeguard against suicide.

TRAUMA, HEALTH, AND SOCIAL DETERMINANTS

Trauma and grief, especially sexual violence and chronic emotional abuse, have long-lasting effects. Many crises arise when acute stressors—such as relationship breakups, legal or financial strain, or health crises—collide with these deeper vulnerabilities. Psychiatric and substance use disorders are frequent companions to suicidal risk, with alcohol and drugs in particular increasing the likelihood that suicidal thoughts are acted upon. Structural forces—poverty, housing insecurity, rural isolation, and lack of timely care—further magnify these risks, shaping both who becomes vulnerable and who can access help.

CAPABILITY FOR SUICIDE AND PROTECTIVE BUFFERS

Not everyone who thinks about suicide acts on those thoughts. Capability—a mix of trait factors (fearlessness, pain tolerance) and acquired factors (habituation through trauma, prior attempts, means familiarity)—lowers the barrier between thought and action. Prior attempts are among the strongest predictors of later suicide, often by the same or more lethal method.

On the other side of the balance are protective buffers: belonging, reasons for living, supportive environments, access to collaborative care, community and spiritual connections, and stable housing and income. At the clinical level, practical tools like safety planning, means restriction, and warm handoffs after emergency visits strengthen these buffers and buy time for recovery.

CONCLUSION: WHAT CLINICIANS AND HELPERS CAN DO

The roots of vulnerability remind us that suicide prevention is not only about responding to immediate crises but about **understanding the person's full context**—their history, relationships, identity, health, and living conditions. Clinicians should:

1. **Map vulnerabilities.** Look beyond the surface to early trauma, chronic illness, minority stress, and family dynamics.
2. **Identify stressors.** Name the specific losses, conflicts, or crises weighing on the person right now.
3. **Assess capability.** Ask directly about prior attempts, rehearsals, fearlessness, and means access.
4. **Strengthen buffers.** Support belonging, highlight reasons for living, engage family and community, and secure timely, coordinated care.
5. **Pair relationship with environment.** Build trust while ensuring safety through practical steps like restricting means and arranging follow-up.

KEY TAKEAWAYS (EASY TO REMEMBER)

- **Suicidal risk grows over time.** Distal vulnerabilities interact with proximal stressors.
- **Capability matters.** Fearlessness, pain tolerance, and prior exposure lower the barrier to action.
- **Buffers protect.** Belonging, reasons for living, and access to care reduce risk and create hope.
- **Context is crucial.** Families, culture, health conditions, and social determinants shape both risk and protection.
- **The goal is balance.** Risk rises when vulnerabilities outweigh buffers; prevention strengthens the protective side of the scale.

RECOMMENDED READINGS

ANTOON A. LEENAARS—*PSYCHOTHERAPY WITH SUICIDAL PEOPLE: A PERSON-CENTRED APPROACH* (2004)

Leenaars focuses on how suicidal vulnerability develops through lived psychological pain, self-concept, and relational history rather than isolated symptoms. This book fits a chapter on roots because it treats suicidality as a multidimensional malaise shaped over time by meaning, attachment, and internalized suffering. It is recommended here to ground vulnerability in personhood rather than pathology.

DANUTA WASSERMAN (ED.)—*OXFORD TEXTBOOK OF SUICIDOLOGY AND SUICIDE PREVENTION* (2009)

This authoritative textbook synthesizes biological, psychological, social, and cultural contributors to suicide risk across the lifespan. It is especially useful in this chapter for mapping long-term vulnerabilities without collapsing them into prediction. We recommend it as a stabilizing reference that prevents oversimplified accounts of "risk factors."

DIEGO DE LEO AND VITA POŠTUVAN (EDS.)—*REDUCING THE TOLL OF SUICIDE: RESOURCES FOR COMMUNITIES, GROUPS, AND INDIVIDUALS* (2019)

This edited volume pulls suicide prevention out of theory-only space and into practical, community-facing resources across groups, settings, and levels of risk. It belongs in this chapter because "vulnerability" is not only individual or developmental; it is also shaped by social design, access, and the scaffolding (or absence) of supports around a person. We recommend it here because it gives readers concrete prevention architecture that fits this chapter's roots-and-context emphasis.

KEY REFERENCES

Afifi, T. O., Enns, M. W., Cox, B. J., Asmundson, G. J., Stein, M. B., & Sareen, J. (2008). Population attributable fractions of psychiatric disorders and suicide ideation and attempts associated with adverse childhood experiences. *American Journal of Public Health, 98*(5), 946–952. https://doi.org/10.2105/AJPH.2007.120253

Kingsbury, M., Hammond, N., Colman, I., & Bulloch, A. (2022). Suicidality among sexual minority and transgender adolescents: A nationally representative population-based study of youth in Canada. *CMAJ, 194*(22), E767–E774. https://doi.org/10.1503/cmaj.212054

Lawrence, R. E., Oquendo, M. A., & Stanley, B. (2015). Religion and suicide risk: A systematic review. *Archives of Suicide Research, 20*(1), 1–21. https://doi.org/10.1080/13811118.2015.1004494

Lester D. (1997). The role of shame in suicide. *Suicide & life-threatening behavior, 27*(4), 352–361.

Liu, L., Capaldi, C. A., Orpana, H. M., Kaplan, M. S., & Tonmyr, L. (2021). Changes over time in means of suicide in Canada: An analysis of mortality data from 1981 to 2018. *CMAJ, 193*(10), E331–E338. https://doi.org/10.1503/cmaj.202378

Liu, R. T., & Miller, I. (2014). Life events and suicidal ideation and behavior: A systematic review. *Clinical Psychology Review, 34*(3), 181–192. https://doi.org/10.1016/j.cpr.2014.01.006

Losey, B. (2011). *Bullying, suicide, and homicide: Understanding, assessment, and prevention.* Routledge.

McIntire, M. S., & Angle, C. R. (1980). *Suicide attempts in children and youth.* HarperCollins.

5

TURNING POINTS

Triggers Across a Life

WHEN STRESS BECOMES CRISIS

This chapter clarifies how specific catalysts—for example, a breakup, humiliation at school or work, sudden legal or financial trouble, an adverse diagnosis or injury, or an abrupt role change (e.g., job loss, retirement, custody shift)—can flip background vulnerability into acute risk. We track how these triggers show up across

DOI: 10.4324/9781003758792-5

development (childhood through late life), noting that the *same* category of event carries *different* meanings at different ages and in different identities and cultures (Värnik, 2012; Turecki & Brent, 2016; Hawton et al., 2024).

Our focus is the *mechanism* that makes triggers dangerous. A rapid tightening of attention, options, and time—often called temporal constriction and entrapment—in which escape by suicide begins to feel like the *only* way to stop overwhelming defeat, shame, pain, or exposure (Turecki & Brent, 2016). We pair this with gendered and contextual patterns (e.g., performance and provider norms for men; relational rupture and caregiving overload for women; rurality, minority stress, and method access for many groups) that shape when and how people act (Denning et al., 2000; Rutz & Rihmer, 2007; Schrijvers et al., 2012).

The aim is practical. Help clinicians notice *what just changed*, link that change to a person's developmental stage, roles, and identity meanings, and respond *quickly* with targeted supports—especially means safety, follow-up, and problem-solving around the precipitant (Beautrais, 2000; World Health Organization [WHO], 2014).

WHY TRIGGERS MATTER: FROM VULNERABILITY TO ACUTE DANGER

Many patients carry distal vulnerabilities for years—prior self-harm, trauma histories, psychiatric comorbidity, chronic pain, substance use, social disconnection—but acts are more often preceded by proximal shifts: a breakup, arrest, diagnosis, public humiliation, or sudden debt (Beautrais, 2000; Nock et al., 2010; Turecki & Brent, 2016; Hawton et al., 2024). After such blows, risk escalates through a short cascade:

1. **Defeat or status loss:** Something important is lost or publicly threatened (relationship, role, reputation, freedom, solvency). Shame and exposure loom large in youth and working-age adults, while dependency and dignity threats weigh heavily later in life (Agerbo, 2005; King & Merchant, 2008; Kjølseth et al., 2010).

2. **Entrapment (the "felt trap"):** Cognition and attention narrow—time collapses into "right now," alternatives seem to vanish, and escape becomes the central goal. Patients begin to use "stuck," "cornered," "no way out," or "only one option" language (Hawton et al., 2013; WHO, 2014; Turecki & Brent, 2016).
3. **Volitional drivers:** The shift from desire to action depends on *how* a person might act (e.g., access to lethal means, negative urgency/impulsivity, exposure to others' suicide, increasing pain tolerance/fearlessness). These factors shorten the window between thought and attempt and raise case fatality (Nock et al., 2010; Turecki & Brent, 2016).

Classic clinical descriptions capture the same pattern. A narrowing of attention and options (often labeled *constriction*or *entrapment*) that follows defeat, with suicidal ideation emerging as a compelling escape (Turecki & Brent, 2016; Hawton et al., 2024). Similar dynamics are reflected in "pre-suicidal syndrome" accounts and contemporary models that link defeat and humiliation to entrapment and then to action via volitional moderators (Qin & Nordentoft, 2005; WHO, 2014).

Train yourself to listen for the pairing of:

- A fresh trigger (what changed this week?)
- Trap language ("I'm boxed in," "they're better off," "only one way").

When that pairing appears—especially with method research/rehearsal, organizing affairs, sudden calm after crisis, or increased substance use—treat it as a near-term danger signal and move immediately to means restriction, collaborative safety planning, and active follow-up (Qin & Nordentoft, 2005; Hawton et al., 2013; WHO, 2014).

Quick clinical tell. Escalating talk about being "trapped," "a burden," or "out of options" in the days after a discrete setback—especially alongside method rehearsal (e.g., searching, scouting locations) or sorting affairs—signals imminent risk that warrants rapid, concrete intervention (Hawton et al., 2013; WHO, 2014).

ACROSS THE LIFE COURSE: HOW TRIGGERS DIFFER BY STAGE

CHILDHOOD (≤12)

Typical triggers: In children, the events that tip risk are often *everyday* disruptions that feel outsized to a developing mind: being scolded or losing privileges, changing schools or teachers, ongoing family conflict, or an early bereavement. Adverse childhood experiences (ACEs)—such as abuse, neglect, and household dysfunction—raise baseline vulnerability and sensitize children to later stressors (Dube et al., 2001). Population data also show that even at younger ages, elevated distress and suicidal behaviors can emerge when belonging and safety feel threatened (Wasserman et al., 2005). Because executive functions and abstract problem-solving are still maturing, children are more likely to react impulsively to acute interpersonal stress without imagining alternatives or time-delaying choices (WHO, 2014).

How the mechanism operates in this stage: Following a setback (e.g., harsh criticism, peer exclusion), children can rapidly enter a narrowed state—time feels immediate, options seem "all or nothing," and escape-seeking rises. Entrapment here is less about complex rumination and more about a sudden, overwhelming affect storm in a child who lacks skills to regulate it (WHO, 2014; Hawton et al., 2024).

Clinical pivot: Secure the relationship field first: restore caregiver attunement, clarify expectations, and reduce harsh or inconsistent discipline. Teach concrete coping in child-friendly terms (name feelings; take space; ask an adult for help). Complete a means safety audit at home (lock medications, secure cords/knives/tools) and build a brief, visual safety plan the child and caregivers can remember (Borowsky et al., 2001; WHO, 2014).

Look-fors in practice: Sudden withdrawal after reprimand; statements like "no one cares" or "I should disappear"; giving away favorite items; impulsive risk after an argument—all warrant same-day intervention and caregiver coaching (Wasserman et al., 2005; WHO, 2014).

ADOLESCENCE AND EMERGING ADULTHOOD (13–25)

Typical triggers: Romantic breakups, peer humiliation (including online), academic failure or disciplinary action, identity-based victimization (e.g., homophobic or racist bullying), family separation, and exposure to a peer's suicide are frequent precipitants (Beautrais, 2000; Borowsky et al., 2001; Gould & Kramer, 2001; Wasserman et al., 2005; King & Merchant, 2008).

How the mechanism operates in this stage: A pattern of defeat or humiliation → entrapment is common: social status losses or shame moments collapse a young person's sense of future, especially in those who ruminate, recall negative memories readily, and interpret setbacks globally ("I'll *never* recover") (Kessler et al., 1999; Turecki & Brent, 2016; Hawton et al., 2024). Concurrency with depression, anxiety, substance use, and trauma histories increases the chance that trigger-driven entrapment converts to suicidal ideation and behavior (Nock et al., 2010).

Clinical pivot: After a precipitating event (e.g., breakup), tighten follow-up in the first one to two weeks. Co-create a collaborative safety plan that names personal warning signs, reasons for living, and specific help-seeking steps; involve family or trusted adults with consent; coordinate with school or campus services; and restrict access to high-lethality means (Shaffer & Craft, 1999; WHO, 2014). When identity-based victimization is present, address safety and belonging directly (King & Merchant, 2008).

Look-fors in practice: "Stuck" or "no way out" talk after public embarrassment; late-night method searches; sudden calm after a crisis; increased substance use to blunt distress—all mark near-term danger (Gould & Kramer, 2001; WHO, 2014).

YOUNG TO MID-ADULTHOOD (26–55)

Typical triggers: Legal problems, job loss or demotion, public professional failure, escalating debt, relationship dissolution or custody conflict, and untreated substance spirals are common catalysts (Stack, 2000; Agerbo, 2005; McLaughlin et al., 2012). For many, these events signal role collapse (provider, partner, parent) and perceived public exposure.

How the mechanism operates in this stage: Defeat and threatened identity lead to entrapment, then to action when volitional factors line up: ready access to lethal means, negative urgency (acting rashly under intense affect), and rehearsals or exposure to others' suicide shorten the path from thought to attempt (Nock et al., 2010; Turecki & Brent, 2016).

Clinical pivot—move on two tracks: (1) practical problem-solving around the precipitant (e.g., legal/financial navigation, workplace liaison, expedited counseling) and (2) means restriction with explicit storage or removal plans. Add alcohol and substance use interventions where relevant and schedule active follow-up contacts, as small, repeated touches reduce short-term risk (Turecki & Brent, 2016; Hawton et al., 2024).

Look-fors in practice: Expressions of burdensomeness after job loss ("they're better off without me"), making wills or sorting finances, scouting locations or methods, or a sudden brightening after days of crisis may signal decision and preparation—treat as urgent (Agerbo, 2005; McLaughlin et al., 2012).

LATE LIFE (≥56)

Typical triggers: Accumulated medical illness, chronic pain, loss of function, bereavement, caregiver burden, social isolation, transitions to assisted living, and fears about dependency or dignity are prominent precipitants (Conwell & Brent, 1995; Kjølseth et al., 2010; Shah et al., 2016).

How the mechanism operates in this stage: Triggers often activate hopelessness and perceived burdensomeness; when autonomy feels threatened and supports thin, entrapment consolidates. Older men may disclose less, even as risk increases (Oliffe et al., 2011).

Clinical pivot: Treat pain and depression aggressively; address loneliness with structured social prescriptions (e.g., community groups, befriending programs); support autonomy and dignity via occupational therapy, assistive devices, and collaborative care planning; and perform thorough means safety reviews with family involvement (Nordentoft, 2011; WHO, 2014).

Look-fors in practice: Statements about "not wanting to be a burden," giving away possessions, detailed end-of-life planning without medical indication, or abrupt disengagement from activities merit immediate, concrete countermeasures (Kjølseth et al., 2010; Shah et al., 2016).

PSYCHOLOGICAL ENGINES THAT "LOCK IN" TRIGGERS

1. **Temporal constriction and entrapment:** After acute defeat, attention narrows, the future collapses into the present, and options feel binary. Poor problem-solving and ruminative style intensify this felt trap, converting pain into escape motivation (Hawton et al., 2013; Turecki & Brent, 2016).
2. **From desire to attempt:** Capability and volitional factors. Whether ideation becomes an attempt depends on *how* a person can act: access to lethal means, negative urgency/impulsivity, exposure to suicide, rising pain tolerance/fearlessness, and vivid suicidal imagery hasten enactment and raise fatality (Nock et al., 2010; Turecki & Brent, 2016). Repetition and rehearsal strengthen capability over time (Nock et al., 2010).
3. **Future thinking collisions:** Many people oscillate between an implicit plan to escape via suicide and competing hopes; close to an attempt, future-tense language may drop and planning narrows to immediate steps—a linguistic sign of constriction consolidating (Turecki & Brent, 2016; Hawton et al., 2024).

GENDERED PATTERNS THAT SHAPE TRIGGERS AND ACTION

- **Men:** Performance, status, and provider role scripts heighten the impact of work, legal, and financial crises; masculine norms can suppress help-seeking and emotional disclosure (Rutz & Rihmer, 2007; Cleary, 2012; Schrijvers et al., 2012). Lethal methods are used more often, and marital disruption increases risk (Denning et al., 2000; Kposowa, 2000; Qin et al., 2003).
- **Women:** Higher rates of nonfatal attempts; triggers often cluster around relational rupture, victimization, and caregiving strain, with patterns moderated by culture and method availability (Beautrais, 2002; Yip et al., 2004; Vijayakumar, 2005; Bridge et al., 2006).

- **Older men:** Depression with low openness to discussing distress can mask acute risk despite high lethality when attempts occur (Oliffe et al., 2011).
- **Clinical note:** In both sexes, interpersonal conflict and failed relationships are frequent precipitants; ambivalence is common, with expressions of love, apology, and instruction even during high risk—leverage these remaining bonds and obligations as anchors in care (Bridge et al., 2006; King & Merchant, 2008).

METHOD ACCESS AS A TRIGGER AMPLIFIER

When acute triggers occur in contexts with ready access to high-lethality means, deaths increase—even if underlying distress is similar (Hawton et al., 2013; Turecki & Brent, 2016). Interventions that change the environment—such as installing barriers at hotspots, limiting large-quantity medication access (e.g., blister packs), or improving firearm storage—reduce suicide deaths without clear substitution (WHO, 2014). Timing also matters: seasonal rhythms (e.g., spring peaks) and calendar effects (e.g., shifts around major holidays or school transitions) interact with exposure and social connectedness, suggesting periods when surveillance and support should be intensified (Värnik, 2012; WHO, 2014).

CLINICAL SYNTHESIS ACROSS STAGES

- Always pair the precipitant you can name (e.g., "disciplinary hearing," "breakup," "new diagnosis") with the trap language you can hear ("no options," "only one way," "everyone's better off") to gauge *immediacy*.
- Act on volitional risks immediately (means access, impulsivity under distress, exposure/rehearsal).
- Tailor responses to developmental needs (child skills coaching, youth school–family linkages, adult practical problem-solving, late-life autonomy and pain control).
- Expect ambivalence; mobilize bonds, values, and reasons for living as *real-time* buffers (WHO, 2014; Turecki & Brent, 2016).

Table 5.1 is designed to translate the chapter's core mechanism—how a discrete trigger becomes acute risk—into a lifespan-sensitive

Table 5.1 Common Triggers, Psychological Meanings, and Practice Responses Across Life Stages

Life stage	*Common triggers*	*Likely psychological meanings*	*Near-term red flags*	*Practice responses*
Childhood	Acute discipline or loss; school transitions; family conflict/ bereavement	Threats to belonging/ safety; concrete, all-or-none appraisals	Sudden withdrawal; impulsive acts after scolding	Caregiver coaching; emotion labeling; routine + means safety (locking meds/cords) (Stillion, 1996; Dube et al., 2001). Suicide, History and Culture
Adolescence	Breakup; bullying/humiliation (including online); academic failure; identity-based victimization; exposure to suicide	Defeat → **entrapment**; shame; thwarted belonging	"Stuck/nowhere to go," method research, giving away items	Collaborative safety planning; school–family team; means restriction; warm follow-up (Beautrais, 2000; Gould & Kramer, 2001). Suicide Theory
Young adults	Legal trouble; job loss; debt; custody conflict; substance spiral; public failure	Role collapse; threatened status/identity; escape motive	Sudden calm after crisis; will changes; high-risk method access	Practical problem-solving + means safety; alcohol use care; brief contact interventions (Agerbo, 2005; McLaughlin et al., 2012). Suicide Theory

(*Continued*)

Table 5.1 (Continued)

Life stage	*Common triggers*	*Likely psychological meanings*	*Near-term red flags*	*Practice responses*
Midlife	Divorce/separation; chronic pain/illness; caring for ill relatives; unemployment	Burdensomeness; trapped caregiver; erosion of agency	"They're better off without me"; rehearsals	Pain/depression treatment; respite; legal/financial supports; firearm/storage counseling (Hawton et al., 2013; Qin & Nordentoft, 2005)
Late life	Multimorbidity; bereavement; functional loss; institutional moves; isolation	Hopelessness; dignity/autonomy fears	Stated desire to avoid dependency; tidy-up behavior	Social prescribing; grief care; occupational therapy; lethal means audit (Conwell & Brent, 1995; Kjølseth et al., 2010; Shah et al., 2016)

clinical reference. Its intent is to help clinicians rapidly link a specific precipitating event to its likely psychological meaning, recognize near-term red flags, and select stage-appropriate practice responses in real time. Rather than treating triggers as generic "stressors," the table emphasizes that the *same* event carries different meanings and risks at different developmental stages, and that effective intervention depends on matching the response to those meanings, not merely naming the event itself.

PRACTICE: TURNING RECOGNITION INTO ACTION

Goal: move from noticing a precipitant to executing a brief, structured response that reduces near-term danger and restores options.

1. **Name the trigger and the trap**
   What to do (2–3 minutes)

- **Elicit the precipitant.** "What changed in the last few days?" (e.g., *custody hearing, breakup, job loss, public humiliation*).
- **Reflect the felt trap** in the person's own words. "You've said 'there's no way out' and 'everyone's better off'—that sounds like you're feeling boxed in."
- **Link event → meaning → state**. "The breakup (event) feels like proof you're unlovable (meaning), and now everything seems all-or-nothing (state)."
- **Name time compression.** "When the future shrinks to only tonight, suicide can look like the *only* exit. Let's widen the time window together."

Why it matters. Pairing a **discrete trigger** with **entrapment language** surfaces the mechanism that drives acute risk—temporal constriction and escape motivation—so you can target it directly (WHO, 2014; Turecki & Brent, 2016; Hawton et al., 2024)

Document. Record the precipitant, the patient's exact "trap" quotes, and any change from baseline. Note protective counter-statements (e.g., responsibilities, values) (WHO, 2014).

2. **Act on volitional risks (the "how" of an attempt)**
   Rapid audit (ask, don't assume)

- **Means access:** "What methods have crossed your mind? What do you *have* access to right now—medications, belts/cords, firearms, high places?" (Hawton et al., 2013; Turecki & Brent, 2016).
- **Exposure and rehearsal:** "Have you searched locations or doses, driven by any sites, or practiced how it might go?" (Turecki & Brent, 2016).
- **Imagery:** "Do you *see* it in your mind—like a movie?" (Turecki & Brent, 2016).
- **Negative urgency/substances:** "When the feeling spikes, do you act fast or use alcohol/drugs to numb it?" (Nock et al., 2010).

Immediate actions (concrete, collaborative)

- **Restrict/transfer means** *today*. Lock or remove medications (consider blister packs); secure cords/ligatures;, remove or externally store firearms; block access to known hotspots; confirm who will do what by *when* (Hawton et al., 2013; WHO, 2014).
- **Interrupt rehearsal and imagery.** Block web searches; avoid scouting; replace intrusive images with a brief competing task (call, walk, cold-water splash) (Turecki & Brent, 2016).
- **Treat negative urgency.** Teach one distress tolerance skill the person will actually use (paced breathing, countdown, brief cold stimulus), and add a **24-hour rule** ("no irreversible actions for 24 hours; we recheck together") (Zylstra, 2002; WHO, 2014).
- **Reduce intoxication risk.** Set a no-use plan for the next 72 hours; add a supporter check-in at typical drinking hours (WHO, 2014).

Document. Specify exact storage locations, key holders, and verification plan; note rehearsals you interrupted and skills chosen (WHO, 2014).

3. **Use collaborative, measurement-guided care**
   Structure the visit around the suicidal problem, not only diagnosis

- **Collaborative Assessment and Management of Suicidality (CAMS)-style stance:** Validate the *suicidal driver* (pain, shame, entrapment), map reasons for living, and co-author a *single-session stabilization plan* with concrete next steps and follow-ups (Jobes, 2006; WHO, 2014).
- **Brief, repeatable measures:** Track ideation severity, entrapment/defeat language, and access to means at each contact; use the same questions so change is visible over days/weeks (WHO, 2014).
- **Safety planning (collaborative):** List personal warning signs, internal coping, people/places for distraction, supporters to call, professionals and urgent options, and the **means safety** plan you just made. Rehearse it once in the room (Zylstra, 2002; WHO, 2014).
- **Active follow-up:** Schedule phone/text/visit touches in 24–72 hours and again within 7 days; brief "caring contacts" reduce near-term risk (WHO, 2014).

Document. Record patient-generated wording for reasons to live and the top one to two drivers you're targeting this week; list exact follow-up dates and modalities (Jobes, 2006; WHO, 2014).

4. **Expect ambivalence—and use it**

Even at the edge, suicide notes and diaries often show mixed motives: love, apology, instruction, and care persist alongside despair (Leenaars, 1988; Meyer, 2017). These threads can anchor safety work.

How to leverage ambivalence (in session)

- **Name both sides.** "Part of you wants the pain to stop *now*; another part worries about your kids and the mess this would leave." (Leenaars, 1988).
- **Amplify obligations and attachments.** Identify *specific* people, pets, roles, or commitments that still matter; translate them into near-term tasks ("read to Maya Friday," "walk the dog at 7 pm") (Meyer, 2017).
- **Time-bridging tasks.** Write a short note to tomorrow's self; schedule one valued action within 24 hours; enlist a supporter to co-complete it (WHO, 2014).

- **Language shift.** Replace "no way out" with "no good options I can see *yet*"; small qualifiers reopen agency (Turecki & Brent, 2016).

Document. Quote the person's own "reasons to live," the task you scheduled, and who will confirm completion (WHO, 2014).

AT-A-GLANCE CHECKLIST

- **Trigger named?** (what changed) **Trap quoted?** ("no way out," "burden") (WHO, 2014)
- **Volitional audit done?** means/exposure/imagery/urgency/substances (Hawton et al., 2013; Turecki & Brent, 2016)
- **Means plan finalized?** items secured/removed; who holds keys; verification time (WHO, 2014)
- **Stabilization plan written and rehearsed?** (Zylstra, 2002; Jobes, 2006)
- **Follow-ups scheduled?** 24–72 hours and 7 days caring contacts (WHO, 2014)
- **Ambivalence anchored?** named attachments; one valued task in next 24 hours (Leenaars, 1988; Meyer, 2017)

CHAPTER SUMMARY

We showed how specific life events—like a breakup, public humiliation, job loss, debt, illness/injury, legal trouble, or a sudden role change—can flip background vulnerability into acute suicidal risk. The same kind of event means different things at different ages and in different identities and cultures, so we track **childhood through late** life and highlight what to watch for in each stage (Värnik, 2012; Turecki & Brent, 2016; Hawton et al., 2024).

The engine underneath: After a sharp setback, many people move through a short sequence: defeat or loss → entrapment (time narrows, options feel closed) → **action**, especially if there is access to lethal means, high distress-driven impulsivity, prior exposure/rehearsal, or vivid suicidal imagery (Nock et al., 2010; Turecki & Brent, 2016). **Listening for trap language**—"stuck," "no way out," "they're better off without me"—is crucial because it marks near-term danger (Qin & Nordentoft, 2005; WHO, 2014).

LIFESPAN PATTERNS

- In **children**, everyday disruptions (scolding, school changes, family conflict, bereavement) can feel enormous; acts tend to be impulsive and tied to belonging/safety (Dube et al., 2001; Wasserman et al., 2005).
- In **adolescents/young adults**, triggers cluster around social status and identity (breakups, humiliation, bullying, exposure to suicide); defeat → entrapment is common, especially with rumination and comorbidity (Beautrais, 2000; King & Merchant, 2008; Nock et al., 2010).
- In **young to mid-adulthood**, role collapse (job, legal, financial, custody) and substances loom large; means access and negative urgency often shorten the time from thought to act (Agerbo, 2005; McLaughlin et al., 2012).
- In **late life**, medical illness, pain, functional loss, bereavement, isolation, and fears about dependency drive risk; disclosure may be muted, especially in older men (Conwell & Brent, 1995; Kjølseth et al., 2010; Shah et al., 2016).

Gendered and contextual shape: Men are disproportionately affected by triggers that threaten performance, status, and provider roles, and are more likely to use lethal methods; marital disruption adds risk (Denning et al., 2000; Kposowa, 2000; Schrijvers et al., 2012). **Women** show higher nonfatal attempts, with triggers centered on relational rupture, victimization, and caregiving strain, moderated by culture and method availability (Beautrais, 2002; Vijayakumar, 2005). **Access to means** amplifies any trigger, and population-level changes (e.g., blister-pack limits, barriers at hotspots) reduce deaths without clear substitution (Hawton et al., 2013).

What to do in practice: Move fast on four steps: (1) name the trigger and the trap out loud; (2) act on volitional risks (audit and restrict means, interrupt rehearsal, manage negative urgency); (3) use collaborative, measurement-guided care (CAMS stance, safety planning, caring contacts); and (4) expect **and leverage ambivalence**—love, obligation, and values that still matter—to anchor safety (Leenaars, 1988; Jobes, 2006; WHO, 2014; Meyer, 2017).

CONCLUSION

Triggers are not just "events"—they are meaningful shocks to identity, role, and future time. The lethal turn happens when defeat meets entrapment and opportunity. Clinicians can change that trajectory by naming the mechanism, closing off the path to action (means, rehearsal, intoxication), and opening time and options through rapid, collaborative planning and follow-up. Tailoring this approach to developmental stage, gendered scripts, and context (rurality, minority stress, method availability) turns general knowledge into actionable care (WHO, 2014; Turecki & Brent, 2016; Hawton et al., 2024).

KEY TAKEAWAYS

- **Triggers are developmental and contextual.** The same category (e.g., loss) plays out differently at 12, 22, 45, and 80—read each event through the person's roles, culture, and identity meanings (Värnik, 2012; Turecki & Brent, 2016; Hawton et al., 2024).
- **Defeat → entrapment is the pivot.** When fresh setbacks combine with rumination, poor problem-solving, and all-or-none thinking, the **felt trap** closes; language like "trapped," "burden," or "only way" is a red flag for **near-term risk** (Qin & Nordentoft, 2005; WHO, 2014).
- **Means, timing, and gender norms matter.** Lethal access and social calendars shape outcomes; performance/provider scripts heighten risk for men, while relational and caregiving burdens weigh heavily for women (Denning et al., 2000; Rutz & Rihmer, 2007; Schrijvers et al., 2012).
- **Act fast on the "how."** Audit and restrict methods, interrupt rehearsal and imagery, and manage intoxication and negative urgency; small environmental changes prevent deaths (Hawton et al., 2013; Turecki & Brent, 2016).
- **Collaborate and follow up.** Use a CAMS-style stance, write a safety plan together, and schedule caring contacts within 24–72 hours; repetition saves lives (Jobes, 2006; WHO, 2014).
- **Use ambivalence as a lifeline.** Even at the edge, bonds, duties, and values persist—name them, schedule one valued

task within 24 hours, and enlist supporters (Leenaars, 1988; Meyer, 2017).

Figure 5.1 visually summarizes the chapter's central pathway from **Trigger → Trap → Turn**, showing how a precipitating event can collapse time and options (entrapment) and then convert into action through volitional drivers such as means access, impulsivity, exposure, and rehearsal. Its intent is to provide a shared mental model that helps clinicians move beyond static risk factors and focus on *process*: what just happened, how the person is now thinking and feeling, and what conditions make action more likely *right now*. Used alongside the text, the figure is meant to guide rapid formulation, sharpen listening for "trap language," and support timely, mechanism-targeted intervention.

Figure 5.1 shows a three-step flow from Trigger (defeat, humiliation, loss, or role shock) to Trap (temporal constriction, "no way out" language, rumination, threat-to-self) to Turn (volitional drivers such as access to lethal means, distress-driven impulsivity, exposure/rehearsal, and vivid suicidal imagery).

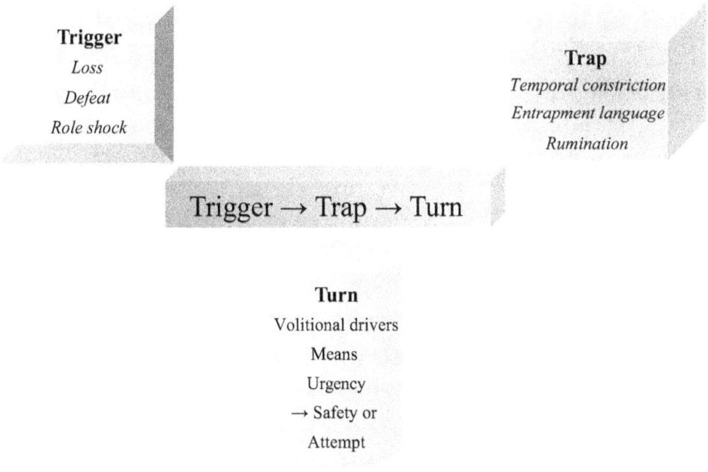

Figure 5.1 Trigger → Trap → Turn: From precipitating event to felt entrapment to volitional drivers across the lifespan

RECOMMENDED READINGS

ANTOON A. LEENAARS—*PSYCHOTHERAPY WITH SUICIDAL PEOPLE: A PERSON-CENTRED APPROACH* (2004)

Leenaars focuses on how suicidal vulnerability develops through lived psychological pain, self-concept, and relational history rather than isolated symptoms. This book fits a chapter on roots because it treats suicidality as a multidimensional malaise shaped over time by meaning, attachment, and internalized suffering. It is recommended here to ground vulnerability in personhood rather than pathology.

DANUTA WASSERMAN (ED.)—*OXFORD TEXTBOOK OF SUICIDOLOGY AND SUICIDE PREVENTION* (2009)

This authoritative textbook synthesizes biological, psychological, social, and cultural contributors to suicide risk across the lifespan. It is especially useful in this chapter for mapping long-term vulnerabilities without collapsing them into prediction. We recommend it as a stabilizing reference that prevents oversimplified accounts of "risk factors."

IGOR GALYNKER—*THE SUICIDAL CRISIS: CLINICAL GUIDE TO THE ASSESSMENT OF IMMINENT SUICIDE RISK* (2ND ED., 2023)

This belongs in the acute states chapter because it centers imminent risk as a recognizable syndrome-like process rather than a vague escalation of ideation. It helps clinicians detect danger through entrapment, affective turmoil, dyscontrol, and hyperarousal even when intent is minimized or denied. We recommend it here because it gives a precise clinical language for the "last mile" of suicidal crisis.

KEY REFERENCES

Agerbo, E. (2005). Midlife suicide risk, mental health, illness and social adversity in a longitudinal study: A cohort analysis of 223,372 suicides in Denmark. *BMJ, 330*(7489), 347–354.

Beautrais, A. L. (2000). Risk factors for suicide and attempted suicide among young people. *Australian & New Zealand Journal of Psychiatry, 34*(3), 420–436.

Borowsky, I. W., Ireland, M., & Resnick, M. D. (2001). Adolescent suicide attempts: Risks and protectors. *Pediatrics, 107*(3), 485–493.

Bridge, J. A., Goldstein, T. R., & Brent, D. A. (2006). Adolescent suicide and suicidal behavior. *Journal of Child Psychology and Psychiatry, 47*(3–4), 372–394.

Kjølseth, I., Ekeberg, Ø., & Steihaug, S. (2010). Why suicide? Elderly people who committed suicide and their experience of life in the period before their death. *International Psychogeriatrics, 22*(2), 209–218.

Schrijvers, D. L., Bollen, J., & Sabbe, B. G. (2012). The gender paradox in suicidal behavior and its impact on the suicidal process. *Journal of Affective Disorders, 138*(1–2), 19–26.

Shaffer, D., & Craft, L. (1999). Methods of adolescent suicide prevention. *Journal of Clinical Psychiatry, 60*(Suppl 2), 70–74.

Stillion, J. M. (1996). *Suicide across the lifespan.* Taylor & Francis.

6

SUICIDAL SCHEMAS

Narrative Pathways of Risk

HOW THE SUICIDAL STORY ORGANIZES THE SELF

Suicidal suffering seldom arrives as a single thought; it arrives as a story that keeps rewriting the self. Inside that story, several strands braid together: a core belief about who one is, a moral logic about what one owes others, a felt sense of where one stands with one's

DOI: 10.4324/9781003758792-6

group, and a lived horizon of time. When pressure mounts, these strands tighten one another. A person who thinks "I've failed" does not merely feel sad; they begin to view themselves through a moral lens—"I am costing them"—and to experience time as shorter and options as fewer. That is why we treat suicidal schemas as small but powerful storylines rather than stray cognitions (McAdams, 2001; Wenzel et al., 2009).

Narratives interact first by selecting what gets noticed. A burdensomeness plot, for example, acts like a filter: it highlights evidence of being a weight and edits out signs of mattering. Rumination then rehearses this plot, strengthening its plausibility while crowding out alternatives (Morrison & O'Connor, 2008). In parallel, goal processes shift. When perfectionistic standards meet blocked progress, the capacity to disengage and re-engage goals falters; flexibility gives way to rigid "must/should" rules, which makes the story less negotiable (Wrosch et al., 2003; Heckhausen et al., 2010). The storyline and the self-regulatory system, in other words, begin to lock each other in place.

The social world is not a backdrop to this process; it is the stage on which the plot advances. After public setback or humiliation, people often read the event through rank and audience: who saw me fall, what status was lost, and what roles are now closed (Price et al., 1994; Williams, 1997). That social reading then recruits the interpersonal engine described by the Interpersonal Theory: perceived burdensomeness ("I harm those I love") and thwarted belonging ("I am outside the membrane") combine to amplify suicidal desire (Joiner, 2005; Van Orden et al., 2010). The narrative is no longer only about the self; it is about the self-in-relation, with suicide cast as relief for others or as an exit from social shame.

Time is the third strand that binds the plot. As defeat and isolation accumulate, the future stops behaving like a wide, branching path and starts to feel like a wall. People say "tomorrow is blank," and that language is not poetic exaggeration—it reflects a real, embodied narrowing of temporal imagination. At its extreme, this becomes entrapment, a locked-in state strongly associated with short-term risk and a key bridge from story to action (O'Connor & Kirtley, 2010; Taylor et al., 2011). In the Suicide Crisis Syndrome (SCS), the body joins the story: arousal spikes, attention tunnels, and the urge is to flee an unbearable state, not to pursue death as an abstract ideal (Galynker, 2017). Once the body is racing inside a no-exits plot, argument is futile; the work shifts to down-shifting arousal and reopening even a sliver of tomorrow.

Culture and genre supply the script grammar. People borrow forms—tragedy, defeated quest, honorable exit—and those forms carry moral rules about what "counts" as a coherent ending. In the Suicide Semiotics Model, we describe this as genre grammar: metaphors, plot arcs, and moral axioms that make certain moves feel inevitable (e.g., "only a clean break is honorable") and others feel forbidden (e.g., "asking for help means deeper shame"). When a genre hardens into narrative foreclosure, the future is not merely bleak; it is narratively impossible. Baumeister's account of escape from a failed, morally judged self fits here: suicide appears as a way to exit a story that can no longer be borne (Baumeister, 1990).

These strands also feed one another in loops. A burden plot prompts withdrawal to protect others; withdrawal deepens not-belonging; isolation removes corrective feedback and everyday roles that prove contribution; the absence of roles shrinks the future still further. The loop is not only cognitive but attentional and behavioral: suicidal attempters show selective attention to suicide-relevant cues, which pulls the mind back toward the same storyline (Becker et al., 1999). Meanwhile, the nervous system learns that escape behaviors briefly reduce intolerable arousal, negatively reinforcing the urge to flee the self (Baumeister, 1990). The narrative, the body, and the environment thus collaborate in tightening the plot.

Because these are interaction effects, small, ordinary buffers carry outsized power. Tangible social integration—roles at work or school, faith or cultural rituals, reliable check-ins—supplies counter-scenes in which the person is visibly of use and expected tomorrow. That is not superficial "activity scheduling"; it is narrative repair, reintroducing characters, settings, and scenes that contradict burden and restore belonging, which population evidence links with lower suicide risk (Tsai et al., 2015). At the same time, structured clinical practices—collaborative safety planning with scheduled follow-up—convert an abstract "future" into near-term scenes held by other people (Comtois et al., 2011).

Integrating theories clarifies why our chapter's practices work. Social rank and cry-of-pain models explain why witnessed defeat and blocked escape push stories toward entrapment (Price et al., 1994; Williams, 1997). The Interpersonal Theory explains why burden and not-belonging are the interpersonal "fuel" of desire (Joiner, 2005; Van Orden et al., 2010). Lifespan motivation and goal adjustment research explain why flexibility around unattainable goals is protective (Wrosch et al., 2003; Heckhausen et al., 2010). Cognitive models explain how attention, memory, and reasoning narrow under schema pressure (Morrison & O'Connor, 2008; Wenzel et al., 2009). The SCS explains the embodied, time-compressed endgame where escape, not argument, governs behavior (Galynker, 2017). Brought together in the Existential Network of Suicidal Identity (ENSI)/Narrative Crisis Model framing we use throughout, these theories describe one process with multiple lenses rather than a pile of disconnected ideas.

The clinical significance follows directly. We are not simply listing risks; we are reading a living plot. That is why we ask for a headline, listen for moral logic, test the time horizon, and identify the governing schema. It is why we prioritize arousal reduction and means safety when entrapment is active, and why we stage small, socially anchored scenes that place the person back inside a story with other people and a near-term tomorrow (Jobes, 2006; Comtois et al., 2011; Barber & Miller, 2014). And it is why documentation names the active schemas and the person's place on the arc: so the next clinician can pick up the thread and continue co-authoring a survivable story with the patient.

Finally, the interactional view keeps hope honest. We do not have to dismantle an entire life story in one encounter. If we can soften one strand—reduce arousal, widen belonging, loosen a perfectionistic rule, or restore one hour of future—the braid begins to slacken. That slack is not just relief; it is clinical leverage. It creates room for medications, therapies, family meetings, and community supports to take hold, and it makes survival feel narratively possible again (Jobes, 2006; Rudd, 2006; Tsai et al., 2015).

WHAT A SCHEMA IS

When pressure becomes unbearable, most people don't speak in diagnoses; they speak in stories. Suicidal schemas are the short, powerful storylines that organize those stories: "I am a burden," "there is no future," "I've been publicly ruined," "if I can't be who I promised, nothing else counts." These are not fleeting thoughts; they are organizing beliefs that filter attention, bias memory, and narrow problem-solving so that self-preservation can feel logically impossible (Baumeister, 1990; McAdams, 2001; Wenzel et al., 2009). Rumination and cognitive rigidity keep the story closed, rehearsing the same plot while excluding disconfirming details (Morrison & O'Connor, 2008). As these schemas strengthen, people commonly move along a predictable arc—goal failure → humiliation/defeat → burdensomeness and thwarted belonging → entrapment and "no future" (Williams, 1997; Joiner, 2005; Van Orden et al., 2010; Galynker, 2017). This arc is explicitly mapped in the Suicidal Narrative phases used throughout this book.

Clinically, three quick checks help surface schemas: (1) ask for the person's headline ("If today were a newspaper, what's the title of your story?"); (2) listen for moral logic ("Who gets protected or harmed in this story?"); and (3) test time ("How far into the future can you imagine right now—hours, days, weeks?"). Short answers often reveal the governing plot and how closed the future has become (Baumeister, 1990; Williams, 1997).

SUICIDAL NARRATIVES ACROSS FIVE MODELS

Read as stories, the major theories of suicide are best understood as complementary camera angles on how a life plot tightens and, under certain conditions, turns into action. The Integrated Motivational–Volitional (IMV) model asks how pain becomes intent and how intent becomes an act. In its motivational phase, experiences of defeat and humiliation (often socially witnessed) funnel into entrapment via "threat-to-self" processes such as rumination, problem-solving deficits, and memory biases; these processes consolidate suicidal ideation and intent. In its volitional phase, the model shows how the closed plot is enacted through volitional moderators: access to and knowledge of means, exposure and modeling, past self-injury, fearlessness and pain tolerance, and facets of impulsivity that accelerate transition from urge to behavior (O'Connor & Kirtley, 2010; Dhingra et al., 2016). In narrative terms, IMV tracks a shift from "there are no exits" to "a door is present and I can use it," linking meaning to enactment with specific, testable levers.

Baumeister's escape theory is a deep interior account of the same closure. It traces a descent from aversive self-awareness and self-blame into "cognitive deconstruction"—a constricted, concrete, present-tense mental state in which the future feels unreal, nuance collapses, and inhibitory controls weaken (Baumeister, 1990). The suicidal act is thus framed not as a pursuit of death per se but as an attempt to escape a persecutory, failed self when re-authoring one's standards seems impossible. Narratively, this is the "no-future" chapter written from the inside out: language flattens, time collapses, and the next act is chosen for its immediate, felt relief.

J. Mark G. Williams's cry of pain theory adds the social architecture of collapse. Suicidal behavior is most likely where three conditions converge: defeat, no escape, and no rescue (Williams, 1997; Williams & Pollock, 2000). Because social rank and audience shape the meaning of defeat, humiliation in front of others—who saw me fall, what status or role was lost—often matters more than the objective magnitude of the setback. When escape routes are not perceived and potential rescuers are absent or disbelieved, the story freezes into entrapment. Put narratively, this is the classic external "no-exits" scene: "I am ruined, there is nowhere to go, and no one is coming."

Galynker's SCS brings the lens right up to the acute, measurable bridge between story and attempt. SCS identifies a proximal state—frantic hopelessness, felt entrapment, affective turmoil, cognitive rigidity, and acute social withdrawal—that predicts near-term suicidal behavior beyond static risk factors (Galynker, 2017). Related prospective work shows how panic-laden "fear of dying" and crisis-specific arousal can accompany this locked-in state (Yaseen et al., 2010, 2012). Read narratively, SCS operationalizes the locked room chapter of the plot: the motive is escape from unbearable arousal rather than an abstract wish to die, and the clinical task is to down-shift arousal, widen perceived exits, and restore even a sliver of tomorrow.

The ENSI used throughout this book widens the frame to the story's long arc and symbolic grammar. Drawing from narrative identity research and clinical suicidology, ENSI follows how perfectionistic or inherited identities and misaligned goals erode flexibility; how socially witnessed defeat ruptures dignity; how perceived burdensomeness and thwarted belonging recast the moral logic of the self-in-relation; and how the lived future narrows toward foreclosure. It treats suicidal schemas—"I am a burden," "I don't belong," "there is no future," "I am ruined"—as compact storylines that select evidence, shape memory, and dictate what feels permissible next (Morrison & O'Connor, 2008; Wenzel et al., 2009; Van Orden et al., 2010). It also incorporates lifespan motivation and goal adjustment science to explain why difficulty disengaging from unattainable goals (and failure to re-engage elsewhere) stiffens the plot (Wrosch et al., 2003; Heckhausen et al., 2010). In ENSI, culture supplies genre grammar—tragedy, defeated quest, perceived honorable exit—that can harden into narrative foreclosure unless deliberately reopened.

Compared head-to-head, the correspondences become clear. IMV's motivational path from defeat to entrapment to ideation dovetails with Williams's triad of defeat/no escape/no rescue, and both align with ENSI's mid-arc phases where humiliation, burdensomeness, and not-belonging dominate the plot (Williams, 1997; Williams & Pollock, 2000; O'Connor & Kirtley, 2010; Van Orden et al., 2010). IMV's volitional phase maps onto the moment SCS is most clinically salient: when arousal spikes and attention tunnels, moderators like access to means, prior exposure, and fearlessness determine whether the closed story gains the tools to enact itself (O'Connor & Kirtley, 2010; Galynker, 2017). Baumeister and Williams can be read as interior and exterior versions of the same tightening: the former describes how time and language collapse inside the self; the latter explains how social rank, audience, and absence of perceived rescue collapse options outside the self (Baumeister, 1990; Williams, 1997). ENSI supplies the developmental and symbolic glue, showing how distal identity work, cultural scripts, and goal processes set the stage on which IMV's mechanisms, Williams's social physics, and SCS's acute physiology play out (Wrosch et al., 2003; Heckhausen et al., 2010; Van Orden et al., 2010; Galynker, 2017).

These convergences have practical consequences. If a person's story is organized by burdensomeness and not-belonging, the Interpersonal Theory points to rebuilding mattering and belonging as direct antidotes; population evidence supports the protective role of social integration (Van Orden et al., 2010; Tsai et al., 2015). If the plot shows public defeat with no perceived rescue, Williams suggests making exits and rescuers visible now; IMV clarifies that we must also neutralize volitional moderators—especially access to lethal means—so the story cannot easily be enacted (Williams, 1997; O'Connor & Kirtley, 2010; Barber & Miller, 2014). If the interior feels compressed to the present moment with flattened language and urgency to flee, Baumeister and SCS justify prioritizing arousal reduction and time-reopening before any cognitive debate (Baumeister, 1990; Galynker, 2017). And if perfectionistic identity and blocked goals are stiffening the narrative, lifespan motivation research supports intentional goal disengagement and re-engagement to restore flexibility (Wrosch et al., 2003; Heckhausen et al., 2010). Taken together, the models describe one narrative architecture—from long-arc identity and culture, through social defeat and interpersonal meanings, into acute no-exits physiology—with multiple entry points for care.

FROM NARRATIVES TO SCRIPT: HOW MEANINGS TIGHTEN OVER TIME

Across settings we see the same tightening. Perfectionistic identity and the promise of future relief ("If I do it right, I'll be okay") meet misalignment and blocked goals; if disengagement and re-engagement fail, the self hardens around "must/should" rules and loss of flexibility (Wrosch et al., 2003; Heckhausen et al., 2010). Social defeat or humiliation then ruptures standing and face—especially when the loss is witnessed—amplifying shame and isolation (Price et al., 1994; Williams, 1997). The next turn is interpersonal: the self is recast as harmful to others (perceived burdensomeness) while feeling cut off from any stable "we" (thwarted belongingness), conditions that potentiate suicidal desire (Joiner et al., 2002; Van Orden et al., 2010).

Buffers matter throughout: ordinary, tangible integration—roles at school or work, reliable check-ins, faith or cultural communities—slows or reverses tightening by restoring mattering and routine (Tsai et al., 2015).

Mini-vignette for practice: a high-achieving student misses several deadlines (blocked goals), receives public criticism (defeat), starts saying "I'm dragging everyone down" (burden), withdraws from group chats (belonging), and begins to report that "tomorrow feels blank" (no future). Each step is a cue for intervention—especially the **time collapse**.

CORE SUICIDAL NARRATIVES (WITH CLINICAL CUES)

- **I am a burden:** heard as "I cost them too much," "they'd be relieved." Often appears after failure relative to one's standards; shame is framed as care for others. This belief mediates the link between perfectionism/failed self-determination and suicidal ideation (Van Orden et al., 2010; Rasmussen et al., 2012).

  What to ask: "Do you ever think others would be better off without you?" "How much of this is about protecting them?"

  Near-term moves: validate intent ("You're trying not to hurt them"); add *mattering micro-evidence* (who still invests in you, what would be lost); schedule prosocial tasks that create visible contribution (Van Orden et al., 2010).
- **I don't belong:** "Even with people, I'm alone," "not one of us." Belonging is a basic need; when it collapses, loneliness becomes existential, not just social (Williams, 1997; Joiner, 2005). Sense of belonging via everyday community roles is powerfully protective (Tsai et al., 2015).

  What to ask: "Where, if anywhere, do you feel even 10% 'with' others?" "Who notices if you disappear?"

  Near-term moves: re-establish **thin ties** (one teammate, one colleague), text-based check-ins, and brief, predictable contact that the person doesn't have to initiate.
- **There is no future:** a felt collapse of narrative time. In acute states, this pairs with entrapment—the "locked-in" experience most closely linked to imminent risk (O'Connor & Kirtley, 2010; Taylor et al., 2011).

  What to ask: "How far ahead can you picture right now?" "If tomorrow at 10 a.m. had to happen, what exactly would you be doing?"

Near-term moves: externalize time (write tomorrow's micro-schedule), reduce arousal first (breathing, grounding), then generate **one actionable next step** that is socially anchored (Comtois et al., 2011).

- **I am ruined (defeat/shame):** the meaning of public loss—disgrace, ostracism—often matters more than its objective magnitude. Clinically, ask "Who witnessed it?" and "What was lost in reputation or role?" (Price et al., 1994; Williams, 1997).

  Near-term moves: separate event from identity ("something bad happened" vs. "I am bad"), identify repairable roles (apology, restitution, alternative paths), and widen the audience—who still sees you as redeemable?
- **Escape at any cost:** in the **SCS**, arousal spikes, attention narrows, and time compresses; people may deny explicit suicidal intent even hours before an attempt because the experience is an escape imperative, not a straightforward wish to die (Yaseen et al., 2010, 2012; Galynker, 2017).

  Markers to track: frantic hopelessness, ruminative flooding, agitation, social withdrawal, and somatic fear (including "fear of dying" during panic) (Yaseen et al., 2010, 2012).

  Near-term moves: treat it as imminent risk—down-shift arousal (skills, medication when indicated), remove or lock lethal means (Barber & Miller, 2014), complete a collaborative safety plan with scheduled follow-up (Jobes, 2006; Comtois et al., 2011), and mobilize supportive others (Mann et al., 2005).

BRINGING THE PIECES TOGETHER FOR PRACTICE

1. **Surface the headline.** Invite a one-line story and listen for moral logic and time horizons (Baumeister, 1990; McAdams, 2001).
2. **Locate the tightening.** Blocked goals/perfectionism (Wrosch et al., 2003; Heckhausen et al., 2010) → defeat/shame (Price et al., 1994) → burden/belonging (Joiner, 2005; Van Orden et al., 2010) → entrapment/no future (Williams, 1997; Galynker, 2017).

3. **Screen for SCS.** If present, prioritize arousal reduction, means safety, and rapid follow-up (Jobes, 2006; Comtois et al., 2011; Barber & Miller, 2014; Galynker, 2017).
4. **Reopen time and agency.** Use micro-commitments anchored to people and places (e.g., "At 10 a.m. I meet my uncle at the clinic"), then widen belonging via small, reliable roles (Tsai et al., 2015).
5. **Document clearly.** State the dominant schema(s), current phase on the narrative arc, SCS markers (present/absent), means access, and the specific protective steps initiated today (Jobes, 2006; Wenzel et al., 2009).

FROM SCHEMAS TO CRISIS: THE SCS BRIDGE

As suicidal schemas consolidate, the story of the self stops moving forward and begins to circle. What was once a painful appraisal—"I failed," "I'm a burden"—fuses with a bodily sense of being cornered. People describe it as a narrowing hallway, a locked room, a tunnel with no exits. This is the phenomenology of entrapment, and when it combines with frantic hopelessness, affective turbulence, cognitive rigidity, and abrupt social withdrawal, we are in the territory of the SCS (Galynker, 2017). Empirical work shows that entrapment sits on the pathway from defeat to suicidal ideation and is among the most powerful short-term predictors of attempts (O'Connor & Kirtley, 2010; Taylor et al., 2011). In this phase, arguing about logic rarely helps. The task is to stabilize arousal so the nervous system can downshift, to validate how trapped it feels without endorsing the conclusions, and to reopen time by identifying the next concrete hour and the next supportive contact. Once even a sliver of tomorrow is back in view, other forms of care can do their work.

"SCHEMA-TO-SCRIPT" INTERVIEWING IN PLAIN LANGUAGE

A practical way to keep assessment inside the person's story is to ask for the headline and then follow the plot. Begin with an opener like "If today were a newspaper, what's the title of your story?" Then listen for the governing schema—burden, not-belonging, no-future, or ruin—and invite the person to elaborate its moral logic: "In this story, who gets protected and who gets hurt?" When burdensomeness is present, you might wonder aloud, "Do you ever worry others would be better off without you? When that thought shows up, how heavy does it feel and what does it push you to do?" If loneliness sits at the center, stay with the experience rather than the headcount: "Even when you are with people, does it still feel like you're on the outside looking in?" Where entrapment is active, shift gently toward agency and time: "Right now it feels like there are no doors. If any small window could exist, what would it look like later today or tomorrow morning?" This interviewing stance mirrors the Suicidal Narrative algorithm used throughout the book: map the arc, reflect the meaning, test time, and co-author a next scene that is specific, observable, and socially anchored.

TWO BEGINNER-FRIENDLY REPAIR MOVES

Symbolic anchoring is a simple counterweight to the pull of closed stories. Together, you name one balanced truth that can actually be held in the present—"I have cost, and I am wanted"; "I cannot see beyond tonight, and tomorrow at 10 a.m. I will sit with my aunt in the clinic waiting room"—and you attach it to a physical cue such as a note on the phone lock screen, a photo in a wallet, or an object with relational meaning. During spikes, the person rehearses the sentence aloud while holding the cue. The goal is not to win an argument with the schema but to steady the body and reopen the next hour (Jobes, 2006; Rudd, 2006). A companion practice is dialogue between stories. Invite the persecutory voice to write a few lines—"I am a burden"—and then invite a compassionate witness to answer—"You are terrified and trying to protect them." A third voice, often drawn from values, culture, community, or faith, offers perspective and alternatives—"Protection can also look like asking for help and letting others carry part of this." These brief exchanges loosen the dominance of a single plot, create room for safety planning, and pair naturally with structured follow-up (Comtois et al., 2011).

MYTHS AND FACTS ABOUT "TALKING SOMEONE OUT OF IT"

A common myth is that if a person can articulate plans for the future, they are not suicidal. In practice, future talk and suicidal intent often coexist; ambivalence is a basic feature of suicidal minds, and many people move rapidly between "I have reasons to live" and "there is no way out" within the same day. Plans do not negate acute risk, nor does hope guarantee safety. The clinical response is to put the ambivalence to work—acknowledging the part that wants escape while recruiting the part that still reaches for attachment and tomorrow (Shneidman, 1996; Joiner, 2005).

Myth: Conversations plant the idea.
Fact: Open, compassionate conversation increases connection and reduces isolation—protective factors in their own right (Durkheim/Joiner line; community integration).
Myth: Holidays are the "danger time."
Fact: Rates tend to dip around major holidays—connection matters; risk often rebounds after (Phillips & Wills, 1987; Gabennesch, 1988).

PUTTING IT TOGETHER: A SCHEMA-INFORMED MINI-FORMULATION

1. **Map the dominant schema(s)** (burden; no future; defeat/shame).
2. **Locate the person on the Suicidal Narrative arc** (goals → defeat → burden/belonging → entrapment).
3. **Probe for SCS** markers (frantic hopelessness; time collapse; hyperarousal).
4. **Act on volitional factors** (means, negative urgency, exposure) while building buffers (practical belonging, safe adults, structured follow-up, community roles).

CHAPTER SUMMARY

This chapter argued that suicidality is best understood as a story the mind tells under unbearable pressure, not as a scattered set of symptoms. We called these compact storylines suicidal schemas—organizing beliefs like "I am a burden," "I don't belong," "there is no future," and "I am ruined"—because they filter attention, bias memory, and narrow what feels possible next (McAdams, 2001; Wenzel et al., 2009). We showed how these schemas rarely operate alone; instead, they braid together with blocked goals, public defeat, and interpersonal meanings to create a tightening plot that can culminate in an acute, locked-in state (Baumeister, 1990; Price et al., 1994; Williams, 1997; Van Orden et al., 2010). We then placed that plot inside a practical arc—from identity and goal dynamics, through defeat and interpersonal meanings, to temporal collapse and the SCS—and we identified the "volitional bridge" factors that turn a closed story into an act (Dhingra et al., 2016; Galynker, 2017). Throughout, the emphasis remained clinical and accessible: ask for the headline, listen for moral logic, test the time horizon, stabilize arousal, and co-author near-term scenes that are socially anchored and auditable in documentation (Jobes, 2006; Comtois et al., 2011).

HOW INTERNAL NARRATIVES INTERACT WITH RISK PROCESSES

Narratives select evidence. In a burdensomeness plot, the mind overweights signs that one is a cost and underweights everyday "mattering," while rumination rehearses that plot and keeps alternatives off stage (Morrison & O'Connor, 2008; Van Orden et al., 2010). Goal processes strengthen the clamp: when perfectionistic standards collide with blocked progress, difficulty disengaging and re-engaging goals stiffens the story's rules from "I prefer" to "I must," making revision feel morally forbidden (Wrosch et al., 2003; Heckhausen et al., 2010). Social context then gives the script its public stakes. After a witnessed setback, people read the event through rank and audience—who saw me fall and what role did I lose—so the same objective loss can feel catastrophic if it threatens face and standing (Price et al., 1994; Williams, 1997). Over time, these strands compress the future; people begin to report that "tomorrow is blank," a felt temporal collapse that empirical work links to entrapment and short-term risk (O'Connor & Kirtley, 2010). In the acute SCS state, the body joins the story: arousal spikes, attention tunnels, and the motive is escape from an unbearable state rather than a considered wish to die (Yaseen et al., 2010, 2012; Galynker, 2017).

Read narratively, the IMV shows how defeat and humiliation funnel into entrapment and ideation (motivational phase), and how moderators such as means access, exposure, capability, and negative urgency convert ideation into action (volitional phase) (O'Connor & Kirtley, 2010; Dhingra et al., 2016). Baumeister's escape theory describes the interior of that funnel: aversive self-awareness and self-blame collapse into "cognitive deconstruction," a narrow present tense in which the future feels unreal and inhibitions weaken (Baumeister, 1990). Williams's cry of pain account provides the social physics—defeat, no escape, no rescue—explaining why public loss with absent rescuers accelerates entrapment (Williams, 1997; Williams & Pollock, 2000). SCS then operationalizes the endgame with five measurable features—frantic hopelessness, entrapment, affective turmoil, cognitive rigidity, and acute withdrawal—that predict near-term attempts beyond static risk (Galynker, 2017). Within this chapter's ENSI framing, these models are complementary camera angles on one process: identity and culture set a fragile arc, social defeat and interpersonal meanings narrow it, time collapses, the body locks in, and volitional levers determine enactment. The clinical payoff is specificity: if social defeat dominates, make exits and rescuers visible now; if the interior is deconstructed and time has collapsed, down-shift arousal and rematerialize the next hour before any cognitive debate; if desire is riding on burdensomeness and not-belonging, rebuild mattering and belonging in ordinary, visible scenes (Baumeister, 1990; Williams, 1997; O'Connor & Kirtley, 2010; Van Orden et al., 2010; Galynker, 2017).

WHAT BUFFERS DO—AND WHY ORDINARY ROLES ARE NOT "SOFT" INTERVENTIONS

Tangible social integration—work or school roles, reliable check-ins, cultural or faith rhythms—adds counter-scenes to the plot, where contribution is visible and tomorrow is expected (Tsai et al., 2015). This is not cosmetic activity scheduling; it is narrative repair. It contradicts burdensomeness, restores thin-tie belonging, and provides temporal punctuation that competes with entrapment. Means safety and structured follow-up function similarly: they weaken the volitional bridge and convert an abstract "future" into near-term appointments held by other people (Comtois et al., 2011; Barber & Miller, 2014).

PRACTICE SYNTHESIS—WHAT TO DO AT THE BEDSIDE

Begin by surfacing the headline: "If today were a newspaper, what's the title of your story?" Listen for the governing schema and its moral logic—who is protected, who is harmed—and test the time horizon directly: "How far ahead can you picture right now?" When the language points to defeat and social audience, ask who witnessed the loss and what role felt forfeited; when burdensomeness or not-belonging dominates, recruit micro-evidence of mattering and re-establish thin ties that the person does not have to initiate (Joiner, 2005; Van Orden et al., 2010). If features of SCS are present, treat imminence as the priority: down-shift arousal, lock or remove lethal means, complete a collaborative safety plan, and schedule follow-up before the person leaves (Comtois et al., 2011; Barber & Miller, 2014; Galynker, 2017). Document in auditable language: active schemas, position on the narrative arc, SCS markers present/absent, means access, and specific protective steps initiated today (Jobes, 2006; Wenzel et al., 2009).

RECOMMENDED READINGS

EDWIN S. SHNEIDMAN—*THE SUICIDAL MIND* (1996)

Shneidman's exploration of psychache, ambivalence, and meaning makes this a foundational text for understanding suicidal schemas. This book treats suicidal thinking as a coherent inner logic rather than a collection of distorted cognitions. We recommend it here because it directly supports a narrative understanding of suicidal identity.

THOMAS JOINER—*MYTHS ABOUT SUICIDE* (2010)

Joiner examines culturally embedded beliefs that quietly structure suicidal thinking and clinical misunderstanding. This book fits a chapter on schemas because myths function as inherited narrative rules about burden, strength, and inevitability. We recommend it here to help readers identify socially reinforced cognitive traps.

DAN P. MCADAMS—*THE STORIES WE LIVE BY: PERSONAL MYTHS AND THE MAKING OF THE SELF* (1993)

McAdams provides the foundational narrative identity framework for understanding how people construct selfhood through story, memory, and future imagining. This belongs in this chapter because suicidal schemas often function as narrative foreclosure: the person cannot imagine a credible next chapter. We recommend it here because it gives the theoretical backbone for your "storyline" approach to suicidal risk.

KEY REFERENCES

Baumeister, R. F. (1990). Suicide as escape from self. *Psychological Review, 97*(1), 90–113. https://doi.org/10.1037/0033-295X.97.1.90

Becker, E. S., Strohbach, D., & Rinck, M. (1999). A specific attentional bias in suicide attempters. *The Journal of Nervous and Mental Disease, 187*(12), 730–735. https://doi.org/10.1097/00005053-199912000-00004

Gabennesch, H. (1988). When promises fail: A theory of temporal fluctuations in suicide. *Social Forces, 67*(1), 129–145.

Galynker, I. (2017). *The suicidal crisis: Clinical guide to the assessment of imminent risk*. Oxford University Press.

Heckhausen, J., Wrosch, C., & Schulz, R. (2010). A motivational theory of life-span development. *Psychological Review, 117*(1), 32–60. https://doi.org/10.1037/a0017668

McAdams, D. P. (2001). The psychology of life stories. *Review of General Psychology, 5*(2), 100–122. https://doi.org/10.1037/1089-2680.5.2.100

Williams, J. M. G., & Pollock, L. R. (2000). The psychology of suicidal behaviour. In K. Hawton & K. van Heeringen (Eds.), *The international handbook of suicide and attempted suicide* (pp. 79–93). John Wiley & Sons. https://doi.org/10.1002/9780470698976.ch5

Wrosch, C., Scheier, M. F., Miller, G. E., Schulz, R., & Carver, C. S. (2003). Adaptive self-regulation of unattainable goals: Goal disengagement, goal reengagement, and subjective well-being. *Personality and Social Psychology Bulletin, 29*(12), 1494–1508. https://doi.org/10.1177/0146167203256921

7

CRISIS AT THE CORE

Acute Suicidal States

RECOGNIZING SUICIDAL STATES IN REAL TIME

Acute suicidal states are not a personality type and they are not permanent. They are short-lived, high-arousal mental states that emerge when a person feels both trapped and out of time. In this window—often hours to a few days—traditional risk inventories

DOI: 10.4324/9781003758792-7

and even direct questions about "intent" can fail to detect what drives immediate danger: a rapidly intensifying cluster of entrapment, affective turmoil, loss of cognitive control, physiological hyperarousal (especially insomnia and agitation), and abrupt social withdrawal (Galynker, 2017, 2023; Melzer et al., 2024). The construct of Suicide Crisis Syndrome (SCS) names this cluster and has growing prospective support, including validation of the Suicide Crisis Inventory (SCI-2) for predicting near-term outcomes independent of self-reported suicidal ideation (Galynker, 2017, 2023; Bloch-Elkouby et al., 2021). This chapter centers these fast-moving processes to help readers recognize imminent risk in plain language and respond with concrete actions. The emphasis is practical and evidence-informed: what changes quickly predicts danger more reliably than long lists of static vulnerabilities (Fawcett et al., 1990; Ballard et al., 2016; Large et al., 2016).

WHAT AN ACUTE SUICIDAL STATE IS

In straightforward terms, an acute suicidal state is a panic-like storm organized around the appraisal, "there is no livable way out." People describe feeling cornered, desperate to escape, and unable to imagine a tomorrow in which the pain eases. Several features tend to co-occur. First, entrapment—the sense of being stuck in an intolerable situation with no acceptable exit—accelerates the search for escape (Galynker, 2017, 2023). Second, there is affective disturbance, experienced as surging emotional pain, frantic anxiety, and a form of hopelessness that feels urgent rather than merely sad (Ballard et al., 2016; Galynker, 2017). Third, many experience loss of cognitive control: racing or looping thoughts that will not shut off, intrusive images, and decision paralysis; this "ruminative flooding" is frequently reported and may be physically felt as head pressure or "bursting" (Halari et al., 2009; Galynker, 2017). Fourth, hyperarousal—notably near-global insomnia and psychomotor agitation—supplies the energy that makes action more likely (Fawcett et al., 1990; Wong et al., 2011). Fifth, there is acute social withdrawal, a pulling away from people and places that could interrupt the crisis (Galynker, 2017). In some presentations, fear of dying during panic paradoxically coexists with suicidal danger and prospectively predicts attempts in depressed samples (Katz et al.,

2011; Yaseen et al., 2013). These features can intensify over minutes to hours; without interruption, the combination of entrapment, hyperarousal, and cognitive dyscontrol can culminate in an attempt—even when a person denies suicidal intent (Hubers et al., 2016; Bloch-Elkouby et al., 2021; Melzer et al., 2024).

Most people in crisis begin in ambivalence: one part wants to live, and another wants the pain to stop. As stressors accumulate and coping fails, time narrows. The future appears closed, options feel binary, and the next few hours become the only imaginable horizon. Classic time-related predictors in mood disorders and contemporary SCS findings converge on this point: rapid shifts in affect, arousal (especially sleep loss), cognition (rumination and rigidity), and connection (withdrawal) mark the transition from chronic vulnerability to imminent risk (Fawcett et al., 1990; Ballard et al., 2016; Galynker, 2017, 2023). Recognizing this shift—naming entrapment, asking about ruminative flooding and near-global insomnia, noticing sudden isolation—allows helpers to act on the state itself rather than relying only on ideation checklists or distant background risks (Large et al., 2016; Bloch-Elkouby et al., 2021; Melzer et al., 2024).

Near-term risk often declares itself through a recognizable pattern of feelings, body states, and behaviors rather than through an admitted plan. One common presentation is frantic anxiety with fear of dying. People say things like "I feel doomed" and "my heart is going to stop," or describe panic dissociation—feeling unreal, sped up, or "about to go over an edge." In depressed samples, *fear of dying during panic* prospectively predicts suicide attempts and helps explain how people move from thoughts to action (Katz et al., 2011; Yaseen et al., 2013).

A second marker is ruminative flooding—relentless, looping thoughts that will not shut off. Individuals describe "my head is bursting," crushing indecision, and head pressure or headache that tracks with cognitive overload. Ruminative styles are linked to impaired decision-making and worse symptoms in serious mental illness and are frequently observed in the hours to days preceding attempts (Halari et al., 2009; Galynker, 2017).

Third, global insomnia and agitation are common accelerants. People report difficulty falling asleep, repeated awakenings, and rising exhausted; daytime psychomotor agitation ("I can't sit still") often overlaps with the frantic anxiety above and has been associated with near-term attempts in multiple samples, including adolescents (Fawcett et al., 1990; Wong et al., 2011; Hochard et al., 2017).

Fourth, acute social withdrawal—dodging calls, disappearing from routines, avoiding people who would notice danger—removes natural interrupters of crisis and narrows options for rescue (Galynker, 2017).

Finally, many experience anhedonia under pressure: activities that once brought relief no longer register, and motivation collapses. In severe depression and schizophrenia, anhedonia reflects disruptions in reward processing and goal-directed behavior that can intensify entrapment when stress mounts (Van Os & Kapur, 2009; Treadway & Zald, 2011).

These red flags commonly co-occur. When they cluster—especially *fear of dying* plus *ruminative flooding* plus *global insomnia/agitation*—risk can escalate over minutes to hours even without stated intent (Yaseen et al., 2014; Melzer et al., 2024).

WHY CAPABILITY, PLANNING, AND ACCESS MATTER IN THE "LAST MILE"

As the acute state peaks, three practical factors shape whether crisis becomes an attempt: capability, planning, and access. Capability refers to the acquired capacity to enact lethal self-harm—habituation to pain and fear through prior self-injury, trauma exposure, or repeated rehearsal (Smith & Cukrowicz, 2010). Planning includes concrete steps such as choosing a location or time, writing notes, or rehearsing methods. Access means proximity to methods and their lethality (e.g., loaded firearms, large medication supplies). In short windows, these "last mile" variables often determine outcomes more than distal traits; reducing access to high-lethality means and interrupting rehearsals lowers the probability that an acute state becomes fatal (Smith & Cukrowicz, 2010; Cai et al., 2022).

ASSESSMENT THAT SEES THE STATE (NOT JUST THE STORY OF RISK)

Look beyond "Do you want to die?" Many people who die by suicide never disclose intent, and ideation alone is an unreliable marker of near-term outcomes. Meta-analytic and cohort work shows that ideation predicts death only modestly; widely used ideation-anchored tools such as the Columbia-Suicide Severity Rating Scale (C-SSRS) have limited sensitivity and specificity in routine care (Hubers et al., 2016; Large et al., 2016; Steeg et al., 2018; Salvi, 2019).

BRIEF, SCS-INFORMED QUESTIONING TARGETS THE SYNDROME DIRECTLY

- *Entrapment:* "Right now, does it feel like there's no livable way out?"
- *Frantic anxiety/fear of dying:* "Do you feel a sense of doom or fear your body is about to give out?"
- *Ruminative flooding:* "Are your thoughts looping or bursting so you can't decide or rest?"
- *Global insomnia/agitation:* "Have you slept at all? Are you too keyed up to sit still?"
- *Acute withdrawal:* "Have you been avoiding people who usually steady you?"

Saving explicit suicide questions for last can reduce defensive underreporting while still identifying imminent risk. Structured measures such as the SCI-2 and the Suicide Trigger Scale (STS-3) operationalize these features and have shown prospective validity for near-term outcomes—often *independent* of ideation (Yaseen et al., 2014; Bloch-Elkouby et al., 2021; Galynker, 2017, 2023). Pair state-focused assessment with concrete checks on capability, planning, and access, since these determine what happens next (Smith & Cukrowicz, 2010; Cai et al., 2022).

IMMEDIATE RESPONSE PLAYBOOK (CLINICALLY AGNOSTIC, HUMAN FIRST)—EXPANDED

(1) Stabilize the Moment

Goal: lower arousal enough to think together.

How: invite one slow thing at a time—"Let's do six slow breaths together," "Put your feet flat; press them into the floor," "Hold this cold cloth to your face," "Let's dim the lights and move to the quieter chair." Sit at eye level, keep your voice low and steady, and narrate safety ("We can slow this down; we'll make a next step together"). These co-regulation moves counter the physiologic activation that fuels near-term attempts—agitation, panic sensations, and insomnia—creating a brief window for problem-solving (Fawcett et al., 1990; Wong et al., 2011; Galynker, 2017, 2023).

Watch for: rapid pacing, hand wringing, "I can't breathe," "I'm going to die," inability to stay seated.

Do not: debate logic while arousal is high; postpone grounding because "we need to finish the form."

(2) Build a Safety Plan Now

Goal: produce a usable, written plan before the encounter ends.

Components (co-authored, in the person's words):

a. Personal warning signs ("What tells you you're sliding into the bad state?").
b. Internal coping (brief activities the person can do alone—shower, music, prayer, pet, walk around the block).
c. People/places for distraction and support (names + numbers + where to go).
d. Live contact options (family/friends/clinicians/warmlines/crisis lines) and how to reach them tonight.
e. Clear thresholds for emergency care ("If X happens, I will go to the ED/call 911").
f. One concrete next action to do immediately after the visit ("I will text my sister and ask to stay tonight").

Close by rehearsing the plan out loud and photographing or printing it. Frame the plan as *active and revisable* ("Use this tonight; we'll update tomorrow"). Collaborative, skills-focused planning with prompt follow-up is central to modern suicide-specific care (Jobes, 2023).

Do not: rely on "no-suicide contracts"; they do not prevent attempts and can undermine collaboration (Jobes, 2023).

(3) Secure the Means (Means Safety)

Goal: reduce access to high-lethality methods during the risk window.

How: ask permission to talk practically: "Because this feels dangerous tonight, can we make the environment safer?" Then: remove or lock firearms; store ammunition separately; lock or dispense medications (small, blister-packed quantities); restrict access to ligatures, sharps, and toxic chemicals; change digital access (codes, passwords) when relevant; ask a trusted person to temporarily hold keys/codes/medications. Document who will do what and by when.

Why: lethality and proximity vary widely by method; changing access changes outcomes even when desire is unchanged (Cai et al., 2022).

Do not: assume "they'll be fine because they promised"; verify the concrete step (who holds which item, where it is stored).

(4) Caring Contacts and Fast Follow-Up

Goal: keep connection alive in the hours–days when risk is highest.

How: before the visit ends, schedule the next contact (call, text, visit). Send a brief supportive message within 24–72 hours: "I'm glad we talked. I'll call tomorrow at 10. Your plan is attached; we'll make coffee the next step." Arrange transportation/reminders if needed; involve one supporter (with consent) who agrees to check in and help with means safety. Rapid continuity converts advice into action and counters isolation (Jobes, 2023).

Tip: put follow-up on your calendar while the person is present.

(5) Treat the *State*, Not Just the Story

Goal: directly target SCS features that carry near-term danger.

- **Sleep:** create a same-day sleep plan (wind-down routine; screens off; hot shower; cool/dark room; get out of bed if awake >20 minutes; short-term pharmacologic support per local guidance). Even one improved night can reduce arousal and catastrophic thinking (Wong et al., 2011).

- **Anxiety/agitation**: teach a 60-second reset (paced breathing four to six, cold splash, wall push, name five things); brief medication per scope and guidelines when indicated.
- **Ruminative flooding**: externalize loops—write the looped thought once, set a ten-minute timer, then shift to a one-step task (dishwasher, short walk, call a friend). Use "one-decision only" framing to shrink overwhelm.
- **Connection**: restore *one safe human* and *one routine* today (text a friend; attend a faith/community meeting; go to work/school for one hour).

These moves align with evidence that imminent danger tracks arousal, cognitive dyscontrol, and sudden withdrawal more than distal traits (Ballard et al., 2016; Galynker, 2017, 2023; Melzer et al., 2024).

Do not: wait for "motivation" before acting; give the person a small, scheduled first step.

(6) If Imminent Danger Is Present

Indicators: inability to commit to safety for the next hours; escalating agitation with plan/access; psychotic command content; intoxication; no reliable supervision.

Actions: do not leave the person alone; activate on-site supports; call emergency services or accompany to the emergency department (ED). Use a structured handoff (e.g., Situation, Background, Assessment, Recommendation): state the SCS features you observed (entrapment, fear of dying, ruminative flooding, insomnia/agitation, acute withdrawal); brief history and recent stressors; actions already taken (means safety steps, safety plan, contacts engaged); request (medical/psychiatric evaluation, observation). Abbreviated SCS checklists can support ED decision-making (Karsen et al., 2023; Galynker, 2017, 2023).

Do not: discharge alone at night without a specific plan, contact, and means safety check.

Documentation essentials (one to two minutes):

- Presenting SCS features and quotes ("feels doomed," "head is bursting," "slept 0–2 h").
- Safety plan elements (who, what, when); means safety steps (what was removed/locked; who holds it).
- Follow-up arrangements (date/time; who will call whom).
- Involvement and consent of supporters.
- Rationale for disposition (link to observed state rather than only distal risk lists).

CLINICIAN EMOTIONS ARE DATA

Strong clinician emotions often *track* near-term risk. Feelings such as dread, urgency to rescue, irritation, or unusual relief can signal sharp shifts in the patient's state and—if unspoken—can erode alliance. Brief, real-time consultation or supervision, explicit co-regulation strategies, and shared safety planning protect both patient and clinician. Empirical work links therapist emotional responses and alliance to short-term suicidal outcomes, and prospective pilot data show that conflicting clinician emotions are associated with near-term suicidal behaviors (Yaseen et al., 2017; Soulié et al., 2018; Barzilay et al., 2018, 2019). Figure 7.1 illustrates the SCS-informed pathway from early signals to acute crisis and bifurcation.

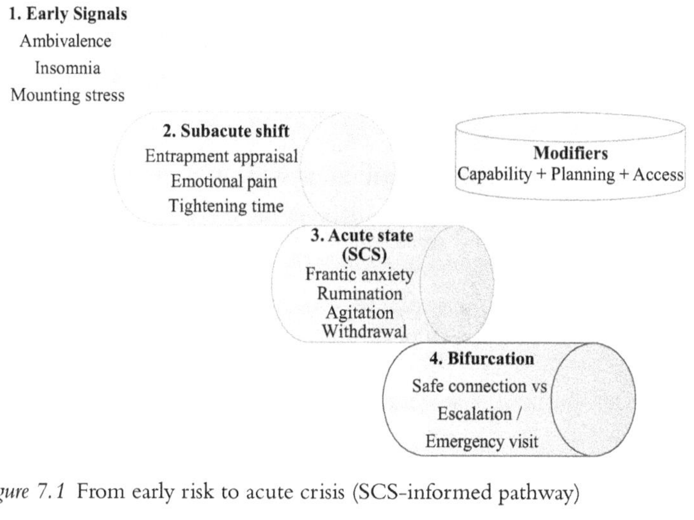

Figure 7.1 From early risk to acute crisis (SCS-informed pathway)

CHAPTER SUMMARY

This chapter reframed imminent suicide risk as a short-lived syndrome rather than a stable trait. When people feel entrapped and out of time, a recognizable cluster of fast-moving changes—affect, cognition, arousal, and connection—can emerge over hours to days. This pattern is captured by SCS and is prospectively associated with very near-term suicidal behavior, often independent of whether a person discloses intent (Galynker, 2017, 2023; Bloch-Elkouby et al., 2021; Melzer et al., 2024). In other words, what changes quickly is more informative for immediate danger than long lists of static or historical risk factors (Fawcett et al., 1990; Ballard et al., 2016).

We translated SCS into plain language. Acute states often sound like a panic-organized storm around the appraisal, "There is no livable way out." Common near-term red flags include frantic anxiety and fear of dying, ruminative flooding (looping thoughts, decision paralysis), global insomnia with agitation, abrupt withdrawal, and anhedonia under pressure (Halari et al., 2009; Katz et al., 2011; Treadway & Zald, 2011; Wong et al., 2011; Yaseen et al., 2013). These features may crescendo rapidly; without interruption, capability, planning, and access to highly lethal means can convert crisis into an attempt—the "last mile" where practical factors often determine outcomes (Smith & Cukrowicz, 2010; Cai et al., 2022).

Assessment, therefore, must "see the state," not only the story of risk. A sole focus on suicidal ideation misses a substantial share of those who will attempt or die; widely used ideation-anchored tools (e.g., C-SSRS) have modest sensitivity and specificity in routine care (Hubers et al., 2016; Steeg et al., 2018; Salvi, 2019). Brief, SCS-informed questions target entrapment, fear of dying, ruminative flooding, global insomnia/agitation, and acute withdrawal, saving explicit suicide questions for last to reduce defensive responding (Yaseen et al., 2014; Galynker, 2017, 2023).

The immediate response playbook emphasized a clinically agnostic, human-first sequence: stabilize arousal (co-regulate), build a safety plan now, secure the means, send caring contacts with fast follow-up, and treat the state (sleep, agitation, cognitive overload, sudden isolation) rather than only retelling the story behind it (Wong et al., 2011; Ballard et al., 2016; Jobes, 2023). Where imminent danger is present, do not leave the person alone; activate emergency supports and give a structured handoff that names observed SCS features and completed means safety steps (Galynker, 2017, 2023; Karsen et al., 2023).

Finally, we noted that clinician emotions are data. Strong countertransference—dread, urgent rescue impulses, irritation, unusual relief—can co-vary with near-term risk and, if unaddressed, erode alliance. Brief consultation, explicit co-regulation, and shared safety planning protect patients and clinicians alike (Yaseen et al., 2017; Barzilay et al., 2018, 2019; Soulié et al., 2018).

Taken together, this chapter's through-line is practical: name the state, interrupt the arousal–cognition–withdrawal loop, reduce lethal access, and keep connection alive through the peak of risk. This lens preserves clinical nuance while providing simple, actionable steps that any trained helper can implement across settings.

CONCLUSION

Acute suicidal states are time-sensitive, state-driven, and often quiet about intent. The path to prevention runs through recognition and rapid, concrete action: slow the body and room, co-author a same-day safety plan, change the lethal environment, and ensure brief, reliable contact in the next 24–72 hours. Because capability, planning, and access shape the "last mile," changing what is reachable can be as lifesaving as changing how someone feels (Smith & Cukrowicz, 2010; Cai et al., 2022). Evidence continues to show that we improve near-term prediction and care by assessing the syndrome itself (e.g., SCI-2; STS-3) and by treating the state—sleep, agitation, ruminations, and isolation—rather than relying on distal profiles or contracts against self-harm (Bloch-Elkouby et al., 2021; Galynker, 2017, 2023; Jobes, 2023).

This approach is humane and scalable. It does not require specialized settings to begin helping; it requires clear language, shared plans, safer environments, and dependable follow-up. When we teach teams to notice SCS features, ask high-yield questions, and act on means and connection, we move care from ideation-only screeningtoward state-informed prevention.

KEY TAKEAWAYS

- **Imminent risk is a state.** Look for a short-lived cluster—entrapment, affective turmoil, ruminative flooding, global insomnia/agitation, acute withdrawal—rather than relying only on stated intent (Galynker, 2017, 2023; Bloch-Elkouby et al., 2021).
- **Time narrows fast**. Rapid shifts in affect, arousal, cognition, and connection mark the transition from background vulnerability to immediate danger (Fawcett et al., 1990; Ballard et al., 2016).
- **Red flags cluster**. Fear of dying during panic, relentless looping thoughts, and near-global insomnia with agitation commonly co-occur before attempts—even when ideation is denied (Katz et al., 2011; Wong et al., 2011; Yaseen et al., 2013).
- **The "last mile" is practical**. Capability, planning, and access to lethal means strongly shape outcomes in short windows; change the environment to change the risk (Smith & Cukrowicz, 2010; Cai et al., 2022).
- **Assess the state, not just ideation**. Ideation alone has modest predictive value; use SCS-informed questions and, when feasible, brief tools with prospective validity (Yaseen et al., 2014; Hubers et al., 2016; Salvi, 2019).
- **Act now, concretely**. Co-regulate; co-write a safety plan; secure means; send caring contacts; schedule fast follow-up; treat sleep, agitation, and ruminations today (Wong et al., 2011; Jobes, 2023).
- **Name clinician emotions**. Your feelings are signals; consult quickly and use shared safety planning to protect the alliance (Yaseen et al., 2017; Barzilay et al., 2018, 2019).
- **Document what matters**. Record observed SCS features (with quotes), means safety steps, concrete follow-up, supporter involvement, and disposition rationale linked to the state.

RECOMMENDED READINGS

IGOR GALYNKER—*THE SUICIDAL CRISIS: CLINICAL GUIDE TO THE ASSESSMENT OF IMMINENT SUICIDE RISK* (1ST ED., 2017)

We intentionally include the first edition in this chapter because it is where Galynker most clearly introduces the core conceptual architecture of acute suicidal states, including entrapment, affective storm, cognitive dyscontrol, and hyperarousal. This chapter is concerned with *what an acute suicidal state is*, not yet with updated instruments, refinements, or implementation guidance. We recommend the first edition here because it foregrounds theory-building and phenomenology, which aligns directly with this chapter's task of helping readers recognize crisis as a distinct mental state.

THOMAS JOINER—*SUICIDE SCIENCE: EXPANDING THE BOUNDARIES* (2000)

Joiner's volume synthesizes decades of empirical suicide research with a strong focus on mechanisms that govern transitions from ideation to action. This book fits this chapter because it clarifies how desire, capability, impulsivity, and context converge in moments of acute danger. We recommend it here because it grounds the phenomenology of crisis states in a rigorous empirical framework without reducing them to checklists.

NORMAN L. FARBEROW AND EDWIN S. SHNEIDMAN—*THE CRY FOR HELP* (1961)

This early and foundational work is one of the first book-length clinical examinations of suicidal crises as urgent communications rather than fixed intentions. Farberow and Shneidman describe suicide attempts as expressions of acute psychological emergency, marked by desperation, ambivalence, and a narrowing of perceived options. We recommend this book here because it provides the historical and conceptual roots of modern understandings of suicidal crisis as a time-limited, intervention-sensitive state.

KEY REFERENCES

Bloch-Elkouby, S., Barzilay, S., Gorman, B. S., Lawrence, O. C., Rogers, M. L., Richards, J., Cohen, L. J., Johnson, B. N., & Galynker, I. (2021). The revised suicide crisis inventory (SCI-2): Validation and assessment of prospective suicidal outcomes at one-month follow-up. *Journal of Affective Disorders, 295*, 1280–1291. https://doi.org/10.1016/j.jad.2021.08.048

Fawcett, J., Scheftner, W. A., Fogg, L., Clark, D. C., Young, M. A., Hedeker, D., & Gibbons, R. (1990). Time-related predictors of suicide in major affective disorder. *The American Journal of Psychiatry, 147*(9), 1189–1194. https://doi.org/10.1176/ajp.147.9.1189

Galynker, I. (2023). *The suicidal crisis: Clinical guide to the assessment of imminent suicide risk* (2nd ed.). Oxford University Press. (Print ISBN: 9780197582718)

Melzer, L., Forkmann, T., & Teismann, T. (2024). Suicide Crisis Syndrome: A systematic review. *Suicide and Life-Threatening Behavior, 54*(3), 494–507. https://doi.org/10.1111/sltb.13065

Rogers, M. L., Richards, J., Cao, E., Krumerman, M., Barzilay, S., Blum, Y., Chistopolskaya, K., Çinka, E., Dudeck, M., Husain, M. I., Yilmaz, F., Kravtsova, N. A., Kuśmirek, O., Menon, V., Peper-Nascimento, J., Pilecka, B., Titze, L., Valvassori, S. S., You, S., & Galynker, I. (2023). Associations between long-term and near-term stressful life events, suicide crisis syndrome, and suicidal ideation. *International Journal of Stress Management, 30*(2), 209–221. https://doi.org/10.1037/str0000272

8

AFTER THE STORM

Suicide, Attempts, and Their Aftermath

WHAT SUICIDE LEAVES BEHIND

Suicide does not end a story; it fractures many. The break runs outward in concentric rings—family, peers, classrooms, teams, clinics, neighborhoods—each ring with its own physics of shock, rumor, silence, and sudden expertise (Jordan & McIntosh, 2001; Mitchell et al., 2004; Pitman et al., 2014). Contrary to the old

DOI: 10.4324/9781003758792-8

shorthand of "six survivors," population data suggest that dozens—often over a hundred—of people register consequential exposure to a single death (Cerel et al., 2019). Postvention, then, is not an afterthought; it is the coordinated clinical, communicative, and communal care of those rings so that grief is held, risk is contained, and daily life can resume without turning the deceased into a template (Campbell, 2003; Andriessen, 2009). Done well, postvention reduces contagion, restores a workable sense of safety and coordination, and helps communities tell more truthful, livable stories about the person who died and those who remain (Campbell, 2003; Andriessen, 2009).

WHAT CHANGES AFTER A SUICIDE

Bereavement after suicide differs in both temperature and texture. Survivors often report an almost gravitational pull toward explanation: a need to reconstruct a timeline, to interrogate last conversations, and to litigate who knew what when (Jordan & McIntosh, 2001). Alongside love and sorrow sit emotions that many find harder to admit—anger (sometimes at the decedent), shame, social stigma, and a reflexive self-indictment that sounds like "What did I miss?" (Cvinar, 2005; Tal Young et al., 2012; Hanschmidt et al., 2016). Somatic and cognitive sequelae—sleep fragmentation, intrusive images of the death, attentional narrowing—complicate ordinary grieving and can lengthen it (Mitchell et al., 2004; Sveen & Walby, 2008). For first-degree relatives, intimate partners, and close friends, the risk signal is not theoretical; rates of depression, posttraumatic stress symptoms, complicated grief, and even suicidal behavior rise in the months that follow (Sveen & Walby, 2008; Bolton et al., 2013; Pitman et al., 2014).

In schools and workplaces, the effects are social as much as individual. Routines stutter; classes go off-script; managers and teachers—people used to having answers—now have to hold questions without glamorizing the act or scapegoating the dead (Clark, 2001; Wilson & Clark, 2004). Risk concentrates in predictable "hot spots": peers who strongly identified with the deceased, students already struggling with mood or substance use, coworkers who shared role stressors or recent conflicts, and those with prior self-harm (Clark, 2001; Wilson & Clark, 2004;

Pitman et al., 2014). Social media accelerates everything—memorial pages, speculation, sanctification—making clear, timely, nonsensational messaging and active moderation not optional but part of care (Sudak & Sudak, 2005).

From a narrative suicidology lens, suicide is an abrupt, unwanted rewrite that destabilizes three coordinates at once: identity ("Who am I now, without them?"), role ("Where do I belong if the old pattern is gone?"), and plot ("What does this mean for us, and what happens next?"). These questions are not literary flourishes; they are the daily scaffolding of meaning-making, and their collapse is why otherwise functional systems wobble after a death. Immediate postvention goals, therefore, are deliberately modest and human-scaled: steady people and places long enough for safer stories to re-form (Campbell, 2003; Worden, 2009). In practice, this looks like acknowledging the death as a suicide once confirmed but refusing method details, naming the person as more than their manner of dying, and giving the bereaved language and logistics for the next few days (and then the next few weeks), including how to sleep, how to talk to children, and how to approach the firsts—first workday, first practice, first family meal (Campbell, 2003; Worden, 2009). It also looks like taking care with commemorations: honoring the person's life without idealizing the death, choosing time-limited or service-oriented memorials over permanent iconography, and ensuring that every public message couples remembrance with explicit routes to help (Clark & Goldney, 1995; Wilson & Clark, 2004).

Two final clarifications matter for tone and ethics. First, causality is almost always plural. Reducing a suicide to a single stressor ("exams," "a breakup," "discipline at work") offers quick relief but poor prevention; it invites imitation among those who share that one feature while obscuring the layered vulnerabilities and short-term states that made the act possible (Sudak & Sudak, 2005; Pitman et al., 2014). Second, the audience includes those already at risk. The same cognitive and interpersonal processes implicated in suicidal crises—constriction, perceived burdensomeness, hopelessness—can be activated in grief; postvention that widens perspective, restores belonging, and reopens future-tense language is therefore not merely compassionate—it is preventive (Jordan & McIntosh, 2001; Worden, 2009; Pitman et al., 2014).

CONTAGION, IMITATION, AND THE MEDIA (WERTHER AND PAPAGENO)

After a suicide, behavior can cluster—not because people are empty vessels waiting to be filled by headlines, but because grief, identification, and availability interact with pre-existing vulnerabilities. Mechanistically, three forces matter. First, **identification**: the more someone sees themselves in the deceased (age, gender, role, context, perceived shame), the lower their threshold to consider the act as a possible script. Second, **modeling**: when a death is narrated as a solution—clean, coherent, redemptive—it becomes cognitively available as a response template. Third, **opportunity + detail**: explicit method/location information shortcuts planning and increases capability through vicarious familiarity (Sudak & Sudak, 2005).

The media ecology is therefore not neutral. Sensational or repetitive reporting, especially with method specifics, locations, and iconographic images (e.g., yearbook glamour shots framed as martyrdom), correlates with short-term spikes in suicidal behavior—the so-called Werther effect (Sudak & Sudak, 2005). Conversely, coverage that emphasizes help-seeking, interrupted crises, and reasons to live—the Papageno effect—is associated with protective patterns, particularly when stories name ambivalence, show credible barriers to acting, and link to concrete supports (Sudak & Sudak, 2005). The same principles apply to school announcements, workplace emails, and social media memorial pages: say the least necessary about the method, avoid single-cause explanations, foreground help and recovery pathways, and actively moderate harmful posts (Sudak & Sudak, 2005).

History and culture give us cautionary exhibits. In Japan, widely publicized deaths at Kegon Falls following the poet Misao Fujimura's suicide and carved farewell were followed by imitative acts over subsequent years, illustrating how romanticized narratives can travel and sediment.

Similarly, the Mihara Mountain episodes—so persistent that authorities banned one-way tickets—show how place + publicity can behave like a magnet when story and logistics align.

Even earlier, the Werther episode—bans notwithstanding—signals what happens when a death is packaged as romance and destiny.

Contemporary syntheses of contagion, imitation, and cultural diffusion (Kral, 2016) remind us that ideas of suicide circulate through networks and norms, not just newspaper columns).

PRACTICE, TRANSLATED

- **Name, don't narrate.** Acknowledge the death as a suicide once confirmed, omit method/location, and avoid causal oversimplifications ("because of exams"). Pair every message with specific supports (crisis lines, walk-in times, school/work contacts) (Sudak & Sudak, 2005).
- **Lead with life and help.** Highlight interrupted attempt stories, coping, and recovery. Use quotes that model seeking help and tolerating ambivalence (Sudak & Sudak, 2005).
- **Moderate actively.** Memorial pages should remove method talk, blame, or glamorization, and add resource links; designate moderators for the first weeks, then at anniversaries (Sudak & Sudak, 2005).

MEMORIALIZATION AND COMMEMORATIONS

Memorials carry consequences. Permanent, highly public honors (e.g., retiring a jersey "for" the death, dedicating a trophy, installing plaques in central corridors) can unintentionally romanticize suicide and invite identification among vulnerable peers. Blanket prohibition, however, deepens stigma, isolates survivors, and erases the person's life. What works is the middle path: remembrance that is time-limited, person-centered, and oriented toward living legacies (Clark & Goldney, 1995; Wilson & Clark, 2004).

In practice, this looks like (1) private or small-group rituals facilitated by trained staff; (2) spaces for grief that do not center the method (e.g., memory books, drop-in rooms with counselors, closed-door moments for the team); and (3) service-oriented tributes—scholarships that fund mental health access, volunteer days that strengthen connection, or classroom/library collections on coping and help-seeking (Clark & Goldney, 1995; Campbell, 2003; Wilson & Clark, 2004). Communications should name the person's full identity—their humor, music, friendships, effort—without attributing the death to a single cause or implying destiny (Campbell, 2003).

Culture and history reinforce the stakes. How a community remembers its dead shapes what becomes thinkable for the living. Highly aestheticized or honor-laden narratives have, in some contexts, amplified imitation; policy responses that modified access + narrative (e.g., ticket restrictions to suicide sites, reframed public messaging) reduced clustering.

This is not to pathologize grief; it is to design it—so remembrance supports belonging and recovery while not turning the manner of death into a model (Clark & Goldney, 1995; Wilson & Clark, 2004).

PRACTICE, TRANSLATED

- **Prefer time-limited rituals** (weeks to months) over permanent markers tied to the death; route permanent philanthropy toward life-affirming goals (access to care, peer connection) (Clark & Goldney, 1995; Wilson & Clark, 2004).
- **Write memorial statements that balance truth and care.** Acknowledge suicide without method detail; avoid heroization or single-cause claims; include supports; and, where relevant, note the decedent's struggles in language that invites help-seeking among readers (Campbell, 2003).
- **Plan for anniversaries.** Calendar the 1-, 3-, and 12-month marks; anticipate renewed posts and media interest; reissue help information; and monitor at-risk groups (Wilson & Clark, 2004).

CORE POSTVENTION PRINCIPLES (FOR ANY SETTING)

Do the basics fast, then keep going. In the first hours, precision beats poetry. Confirm the death and the family's wishes; designate a response lead with authority to coordinate; identify a small cross-functional team (communications, clinical/HR, legal/privacy, operations); map the first-degree circle (family, intimate partners, close friends/teammates, recent points of conflict) and assign outreach; draft a brief, accurate statement; list supports with real hours/locations; and set a huddle cadence (daily for the first week, then taper). The point is to restore workable order and prevent rumor from becoming policy (Wilson & Clark, 2004). Practical note: a family liaison prevents well-meant chaos; a documentation lead ensures decisions, scripts, and outreach lists do not live only in someone's head (Wilson & Clark, 2004; Dyregrov & Dyregrov, 2008).

Name the death without details. Once confirmed and with family awareness, acknowledge suicide plainly while omitting method and location; avoid single-cause explanations ("because of exams"), glamorizing adjectives, and iconography that turns the person into a symbol. Pair every message (email, staff memo, school letter, social post) with concrete help options and next steps (walk-in times, crisis lines, on-site supports) (Sudak & Sudak, 2005). This is not euphemism; it is designing the narrative so it does not function as a tutorial or a template (Sudak & Sudak, 2005).

Support survivors' grief and practical needs. Bereavement after suicide often carries shame, anger, and an exhausting need to "reconstruct" the days before the death. Normalize this texture, offer flexible attendance/workload adjustments, and route people to survivor groups (local and online) where stigma is lower and meaning-making is shared (Clark, 2001; McMenamy et al., 2008; Worden, 2009). Expect somatic and cognitive sequelae (sleep disturbance, intrusive imagery, attentional narrowing), and plan care pathways that include trauma-informed supports (Mitchell et al., 2004; Worden, 2009).

Proactive risk management. Identify and monitor those at elevated risk: intimates, people with recent conflict or rupture, peers who strongly identified with the deceased, those with prior attempts/self-harm, and individuals who share method access or role stressors (Owens et al., 2005; Pitman et al., 2014). Increase caring contacts (brief, nondemanding outreach by text/phone/email), expedite appointments, and ensure means safety counseling where relevant (Owens et al., 2005; Pitman et al., 2014). Classic postvention guidance emphasizes early outreach (ideally within 72 hours), reality testing without platitudes, medical/mental health monitoring of survivors, and a horizon that extends beyond a handful of sessions—grief takes months, not meetings.

Sustain the response. Risk does not end after the funeral. Calendar check-ins at one month, three months, and one year; add dates that matter locally (birthdays, exam periods, performance reviews, seasonal transitions). Anticipate **anniversary reactions** and renewed social media activity, reissue help information, and refresh the risk map as relationships and disclosures evolve (Wilson & Clark, 2004; Dyregrov & Dyregrov, 2008).

Coordinate across systems. Fragmented care amplifies harm. Align leadership, communications, counseling/HR, operations, union/benefits, and community partners (employee assistance program [EAP], primary care, survivor organizations) to avoid mixed messages and duplicative outreach (Wilson & Clark, 2004; Dyregrov & Dyregrov, 2008). In practice, think ***incident command for humans***: a single lead, clear roles (family liaison, communications lead, clinical/risk lead, documentation lead), and daily briefings that end with "Who owns what, by when?"

PRACTICE, TRANSLATED (ONE-PAGE CHECKLIST)

- **Today:** Confirm facts; appoint lead + team; contact family; map close contacts; send a short factual notice with resources; stand up onsite/virtual supports; begin outreach to the risk map.
- **This week:** Small-group processing with trained facilitators; targeted screening of high-risk contacts; caring contacts; EAP access; supervisor/teacher support scripts.
- **This month and beyond:** Preplanned check-ins; anniversary calendar; moderated memorial spaces; living legacy options aligned with recovery (service/scholarship vs. permanent iconography).
- Adapted from school/workplace postvention summaries and classic postvention principles.

SCHOOLS, CAMPUSES, AND YOUTH PROGRAMS

Adolescents and emerging adults live inside dense peer ecologies and fast media loops; identification, modeling, and availability can converge quickly. Postvention here blends trauma-informed care with contagion prevention: small groups over assemblies; scripts over improvisation; moderation over mythmaking (Wilson & Clark, 2004; Miller, 2011).

CORE MOVES, TRANSLATED TO SCHOOLS/CAMPUSES

1. **Classroom-level communication:** Provide teachers/instructors with a short script: acknowledge the death, avoid method details and single-cause claims, normalize grief and mixed emotions, and list where help is available on campus **today** and **this week**. Invite students to talk after class or in drop-in rooms staffed by counseling (Wilson & Clark, 2004).
2. **Targeted screening and follow-up:** Proactively reach close friends, teammates, roommates, recent romantic partners, students with prior self-harm, and those flagged by staff/peers. Offer same-week appointments and caring contact nudges (texts/emails) for those who decline (Wilson & Clark, 2004; Pitman et al., 2014).
3. **Small-group processing, not large assemblies:** If a gathering is necessary (e.g., a team or residence floor), keep it facilitated, brief, and focused on coping and help-seeking—not biography, speculation, or public tribute (Miller, 2011).
4. **Gatekeeper activation:** Brief staff, coaches, resident assistants, and student leaders on warning signs, referral pathways, and language that avoids glamorization or blame; renew gatekeeper training and ensure same-day referral acceptance during the acute window (Centers for Disease Control and Prevention (CDC)-style recommendations for school gatekeepers and postvention).
5. **Memorials that don't make a model:** Prefer time-limited, person-centered remembrances; route "permanent" energy into living legacies (scholarships for access to counseling, peer connection projects). Moderated online memorial pages should remove method talk/blame and add resource links; assign moderators for the first 30 days and for key anniversaries (Clark & Goldney, 1995; Wilson & Clark, 2004).

6. **Care pathways that actually work:** Publish a one-pager with (1) how to access walk-in care today; (2) how to book follow-up this week; (3) after-hours crisis lines; (4) identity-affirming options (2SLGBTQ+, international students, Indigenous services); and (5) means safety counseling where relevant (Wilson & Clark, 2004; Dyregrov & Dyregrov, 2008).
7. **Build buffers on purpose:** Youth protective factors include positive peer modeling, feeling school is relevant, belonging to a community, and at least one reliable adult—make these visible and easy to access in the aftermath (advisory periods, clubs, peer connectors, faculty office-hour invites).

WHAT TO AVOID (AND WHY)

- **Large memorial assemblies** that center the decedent's story and imagery can fuel identification and clustering; design smaller, staff-facilitated spaces that emphasize coping and help-seeking (Miller, 2011).
- **Detailed method/location discussion** in classrooms, emails, or posts functions as inadvertent instruction (Sudak & Sudak, 2005).
- **"Single-cause" Narratives** ("it was the breakup/exams/discipline") miseducate and invite imitation among students who share that one feature (Sudak & Sudak, 2005).
- **Unmoderated memorial pages** rapidly accrete myth and misinformation; plan moderation and add resources from day one (Wilson & Clark, 2004).

ONE-PAGE CAMPUS CHECKLIST (DROP-IN READY):

- **Today:** Verify facts; notify staff with a short script; open staffed drop-in rooms; message students with supports; begin targeted outreach to the risk map.
- **This week:** Gatekeeper refreshers; same-week counseling slots; caring contacts; small-group sessions for affected teams/floors/classes; moderation protocols for memorial pages.

- **This term:** Standing check-ins at weeks 4 and 8; advisor outreach to students who disengage; anniversary calendar with planned communications and supports (Wilson & Clark, 2004; Dyregrov & Dyregrov, 2008; Miller, 2011).
- Youth-specific recommendations align with CDC-style guidance on school gatekeepers and postvention.

WORKPLACES, CLINICS, AND EMERGENCY SERVICES

Teams that cared for the person—emergency department, inpatient, emergency medical services (EMS), crisis lines, outpatient clinics—often carry a different weight: the counterfactuals feel louder ("If only we had...") and the professional identity piece can sting (Pompili et al., 2005). Moral distress and anger are common and not mutually exclusive. Postvention here is not about exoneration or prosecution; it is about containment, learning, and support. Structured debriefings that avoid blame, surface what was known/unknown, and reinforce real help pathways for staff reduce shame and burnout (Pompili et al., 2005; Dyregrov & Dyregrov, 2008).

Practical protocol—what "good" looks like in clinical/work settings: (1) communicate factual information to the team once family notification is confirmed; (2) acknowledge the loss plainly (without method details); (3) offer specific benefits and supports (EAP, protected time, peer support, flexible scheduling); (4) run a nonpunitive debrief that separates case review (facts, timelines, transitions) from self-attack; (5) identify secondary risk among staff (recent bereavement, prior attempts in family, vicarious trauma), and provide confidential outreach; (6) avoid permanent memorials tied to the death in the workplace while supporting private grieving (quiet room, time-limited book of memories circulating through a staff lounge); and (7) capture system lessons without scapegoating—handoff reliability, after-hours coverage, means safety counseling routines—and assign owners for fixes (Wilson & Clark, 2004; Dyregrov & Dyregrov, 2008). Timeliness matters: early contact in the first 72 hours helps steady both people and processes.

PSYCHOLOGICAL AUTOPSIES AND MEANING-MAKING

Used judiciously, a psychological autopsy (PA) synthesizes records and interviews to clarify proximal circumstances, stressors, protective factors, and the likely mode of death—primarily to improve prevention and care, not to fix blame (Isometsä, 2001; Cavanagh et al., 2003; Pouliot & De Leo, 2006). Contemporary PA practice integrates nomothetic patterns (clinical history, demographics, service use) and idiographic story (lived meanings, role disruptions, identity scripts) and typically seeks multiple informants (four to five) to reduce blind spots (Leenaars, 2017).

A helpful first page of any PA report answers three questions: Why this death, why now, and by what most probable mode?

Because grief invites mythmaking, PA work should hold complexity. Recurrent features in notes/diaries align with classic phenomenology: cognitive constriction (tunnel vision, absolutist terms like "only" and "never"), ambivalence (love and anger co-present), intense relationship themes (rejection, dependency, "loss of face"), instructions to survivors, and a present-tense focus with diminished future language (Leenaars, 1988; Shneidman, 1996).

PA protocols such as the Thematic Guide for Suicide Prediction (TGSP) explicitly include clusters like unbearable psychological pain, cognitive constriction, and interpersonal rejection/aggression—useful as a coding spine but never a substitute for context (Leenaars, 2017).

Ethics and limits. PAs are retrospective and susceptible to hindsight bias; they should avoid single-cause attributions, respect family preferences, and frame conclusions probabilistically. Findings should be translated into system learning (e.g., improving transitions, means safety routines, outreach cadence) and survivor care, not public spectacle (Cavanagh et al., 2003; Pouliot & De Leo, 2006). Where notes exist, remember their dual edge: they can humanize a life, and they can also reflect momentary constriction rather than stable identity; communicate that nuance in any feedback to families or teams (Shneidman, 1996; Leenaars, 2017).

EQUITY, CULTURE, AND STIGMA

Not all communities grieve—or can access help—the same way. Stigma around suicide survivorship can silence families and worsen outcomes; for some, honor/shame dynamics, immigration stressors, or distrust of services constrain help-seeking (Dyregrov & Dyregrov, 2008; Feigelman et al., 2009; Hanschmidt et al., 2016). Postvention should respect religious and cultural practices without reproducing punitive traditions (e.g., exclusion from rites), and partner early with faith and community leaders who can reduce isolation and shame (Dyregrov & Dyregrov, 2008; Ozawa-de Silva, 2008).

History and culture are not footnotes; they are levers. Narrative and practice shape what becomes thinkable: from romanticized deaths that spurred imitation at Kegon Falls to policy moves (e.g., one-way ticket bans to Mount Mihara) that changed behavior by altering logistics and story (Di Marco, 2016).

It also flags how community integration and religious belonging can buffer risk, while particular groups (e.g., Inuit youth) face structural and historical burdens that require tailored approaches rather than generic scripts (Kral, 2016).

Design postvention so that language access, identity-affirming services, transportation/childcare supports, and trusted messengers are part of the plan from day one.

MEDIA, MESSAGING, AND INTERNAL COMMUNICATIONS

Whether external (press, social media) or internal (all-staff emails, school letters), the rules are consistent: acknowledge the death as a suicide once confirmed; omit method and location; avoid single-cause explanations; include concrete supports and next steps; and, where possible, highlight recovery/help-seeking narratives to invoke the Papageno effect (Sudak & Sudak, 2005). For organizations, send an initial short factual notice with supports, then a follow-up that explains available services, how to access them today and this week, and how memorial spaces (if any) will be moderated. For social media, designate moderators for the first month and for anniversaries; remove method talk, blame, and glamorization; and add resource links on every thread (Sudak & Sudak, 2005).

Timeliness is protective—plan your first internal message and supervisor scripts within 72 hours and keep updates brief, non-speculative, and consistently branded across channels (align communications/HR/clinical) (Wilson & Clark, 2004)

Two writing moves that help: (1) Name, don't narrate—"We are saddened to share that [Name] died by suicide" (no details); and (2) Pair truth with routes to care—"Here is where to go today; here is who will follow up this week." This is not euphemism; it is designing the narrative so it does not function as a tutorial or a template (Sudak & Sudak, 2005).

LINKING POSTVENTION TO PREVENTION

Postvention and prevention form a loop: each safe message, caring contact, moderated memorial, and identity-affirming support reduces the likelihood of another death (Campbell, 2003; Andriessen, 2009). The mechanism is not mysterious. The same cognitive and interpersonal processes implicated in suicidal crises—psychache, cognitive constriction, defeat/entrapment, availability of suicidal self-associations—can be activated by grief and destabilization; postvention that widens perspective, restores belonging, and reopens the future is thus preventive (Shneidman, 1996; Joiner, 2005)

Concretely:

- **Caring contacts** (letters, texts) and outreach to those with close identification or recent conflict—small, nondemanding signals that someone is there—counter isolation and burdensomeness (Motto & Bostrom, 2001; Andriessen, 2009).
- **Means safety counseling** for those newly activated by the death reduces the gap between ideation and action by interrupting capability and opportunity (Hawton & van Heeringen, 2009).
- **Expedited access to care** and scheduled check-ins at 1, 3, and 12 months target the windows when constriction and anniversaries retighten the plot (Wilson & Clark, 2004).
- **Identity-affirming routines**—peer connectors, community groups, culturally specific supports—rebuild belonging where it was frayed (Dyregrov & Dyregrov, 2008; Ozawa-de Silva, 2008).

- **Leadership modeling** of nonstigmatizing language and visible help-seeking reframes the story at the top of the organization (Campbell, 2003).

Williams's **defeat → entrapment** sequence explains why survivors can feel suddenly more at risk and why practical, near-term help plus future-tense language matters.

And Nock and Banaji's (2007) finding that thoughts of suicide become more available—more tightly associated with the self—after attempts clarifies why memorial messaging must avoid method detail and must pair truth with routes.

CHAPTER SUMMARY

Suicide ripples outward. It affects families, peers, classrooms, teams, and services—and those ripples look different across places and people. Good postvention (care after a suicide or attempt) does three things at once: (1) supports grief with dignity; (2) reduces contagion by how we talk, remember, and report; and (3) rebuilds safety and belonging so the next death is less likely. This chapter explains why suicide bereavement can feel different, how media shape risk (Werther vs. Papageno), what balanced memorials look like, and which core practices help any school, workplace, or clinic respond well. It outlines what a PA can (and cannot) do, why equity and culture matter, and how postvention loops back into prevention through caring contacts, means safety, and practical access to help. The through-line is narrative: we steady people and places so safer stories can be told again—truthful, non-glamorizing, future-opening.

- **What changes after a suicide.** Grief is mixed—love, anger, shame, searching for "why." Risks rise for close contacts. Systems wobble; rumors rush in. The task is to steady people and routines while naming the death without method details and pairing every message with real supports.
- **Contagion and media.** Sensational coverage and method details raise risk (Werther); stories of help-seeking and recovery lower it (Papageno). Same rules for school/work emails

and memorial pages: say less about the "how" and more about "where to get help."

- **Memorialization.** Avoid permanent, public honors tied to the death; avoid banning remembrance altogether. Choose time-limited, person-centered, service-oriented memorials that honor the whole life and point to care.
- **Core principles for any setting.** Act fast and keep going; name without details; support grief + logistics; map and follow high-risk contacts; calendar check-ins; coordinate like "incident command for humans."
- **Schools/campuses.** Prefer small, staff-led groups over assemblies; targeted outreach to close friends/roommates/teammates; visible, identity-affirming pathways to help; and active moderation of online spaces.
- **Workplaces/clinics/EMS.** Run nonpunitive debriefs; acknowledge moral distress; offer protected time/EAP; capture system lessons without scapegoating; avoid permanent workplace memorials.
- **Psychological autopsies.** Use to learn, not blame. Combine patterns with the person's story, communicate probabilistically, and translate findings into prevention and survivor care.
- **Equity, culture, stigma.** Partner with trusted community/faith leaders; ensure language access and identity-affirming services; design around barriers (transport, childcare, documentation fears).
- **Media and internal communications.** Short, factual, consistent messages with supports today/this week; remove method talk and glamorization online; plan for anniversaries.
- **Linking to prevention.** Caring contacts, means safety, expedited care, and leadership modeling reduce the next-death probability; widening perspective and restoring belonging are prevention.

KEY TAKEAWAYS

- **Name the death, not the method.** Pair every message with concrete supports available *today* and *this week.*
- **Act fast, then keep going.** First 72 hours: facts, lead, team, outreach map, brief statement, supports. Then planned check-ins at 1, 3, and 12 months.

- **Design memorials to reduce risk.** Time-limited, person-centered, service-oriented—no permanent honors tied to the manner of death.
- **Targeted care beats blanket gestures.** Proactive outreach to close contacts and identified high-risk peers; caring contacts for those who decline.
- **Moderate the media environment.** No method/location details; remove glamorization/blame; amplify help-seeking and recovery.
- **Coordinate like "incident command."** Clear roles: family liaison, communications lead, clinical/risk lead, and documentation lead; daily huddles early on.
- **Workplaces/clinics need nonpunitive debriefs.** Support staff, protect time, and learn system lessons without scapegoating.
- **Equity is not an appendix.** Build language access, identity-affirming options, transportation/childcare, and trusted messengers into the plan.
- **PAs are for learning.** Integrate patterns with the person's story; avoid single-cause conclusions; translate into prevention and survivor support.
- **Postvention = prevention.** Caring contacts, means safety, expedited access, and belonging reduce the next-death probability.

For practical implementation tools, role assignment templates, communication scripts, outreach maps, moderation plans, and anniversary checklists, see the appendix tables that accompany the end of the book. These resources translate this chapter's principles into coordinated postvention actions that can be adapted to local context while preserving the core aims of safety, clarity, and prevention.

RECOMMENDED READINGS

ANDREA WALRAVEN-THISSEN—*RESPONDING AFTER SUICIDE: A PRACTICAL GUIDE TO IMMEDIATE POSTVENTION* (2019)

This book is one of the clearest, most operational guides to the first hours and days following a suicide. It focuses on immediate coordination, communication, role clarity, and risk containment rather than retrospective meaning-making alone. We recommend it here because this chapter emphasizes *what happens next*, and this text provides concrete structure for preventing further harm during the most volatile period after a death.

KARL ANDRIESSEN, KAROLINA KRYSINSKA, AND YOSSI LEVI-BELZ (EDS.)—*SUICIDE BEREAVEMENT AND POSTVENTION: ADVANCES IN RESEARCH, PRACTICE AND POLICY* (2023)

This contemporary volume integrates postvention research, clinical practice, and public policy into a single prevention-oriented framework. It is especially valuable for showing how postvention reduces contagion, supports exposed individuals, and strengthens systems rather than merely treating grief in isolation. We recommend it here because it positions postvention as a core pillar of suicide prevention at community, institutional, and population levels.

TERRI A. ERBACHER, JONATHAN B. SINGER, AND SCOTT POLAND—*SUICIDE IN SCHOOLS: A PRACTITIONER'S GUIDE TO MULTI-LEVEL PREVENTION, ASSESSMENT, INTERVENTION, AND POSTVENTION* (2015; REVISED ED. 2018)

This widely used practitioner text addresses postvention in one of the highest-risk environments for contagion: schools. It provides concrete guidance on communication, memorialization, staff support, student monitoring, and coordinated response following a suicide. We recommend it here because it exemplifies how postvention functions as prevention when it is structured, timely, and developmentally informed.

KEY REFERENCES

Andriessen, K. (2009). Can postvention be prevention? *Crisis, 30*(1), 43–47.

Bolton, J. M., Au, W., Leslie, W. D., Martens, P. J., Enns, M. W., Roos, L. L., & Sareen, J. (2013). Parents bereaved by offspring suicide: A population-based longitudinal case-control study. *JAMA Psychiatry, 70*(2), 158–167.

Cerel, J., Brown, M. M., Maple, M., Singleton, M., van de Venne, J., Moore, M., & Flaherty, C. (2019). How many people are exposed to suicide? Not six. *Suicide and Life-Threatening Behavior, 49*(2), 529–534.

Clark, S. E., & Goldney, R. D. (1995). Grief reactions and recovery in a support group for people bereaved by suicide. *Crisis, 16*(1), 27–33. https://doi.org/10.1027/0227-5910.16.1.27

Cvinar, J. G. (2005). Do suicide survivors suffer social stigma? A review of the literature. *Perspectives in Psychiatric Care, 41*(1), 14–21.

Dyregrov, K., & Dyregrov, A. (2008). *Effective grief and bereavement support: The role of family, friends, colleagues, schools and support professionals.* Jessica Kingsley. Feigelman, W., Gorman, B. S., Chastain Beal, K., & Jordan, J. R. (2008). Internet support groups for suicide survivors: A new mode for gaining bereavement assistance. *Omega, 57*(3), 217–243.

Feigelman, W., Gorman, B. S., & Jordan, J. R. (2009). Stigmatization and suicide bereavement. *Death Studies, 33*(7), 591–608.

9

SUPPORT AS PREVENTION

Working Together in Suicide Care

PREVENTION AS A SHARED RESPONSIBILITY

Suicide prevention is a team sport, not a referral slip. Families, friends, peers, teachers, and coaches shape the everyday perimeter around a person at risk; when their roles, words, and boundaries are clear, the ambient danger drops in ways as real as any single

DOI: 10.4324/9781003758792-9

clinic visit. The assignment is humble and repeatable: notice early, ask directly, respond without drama, connect to help, and hold confidentiality with care.

WHY SUPPORT MATTERS

Support works because it changes both the story and the situation. On the story side, feeling known by at least one dependable adult, belonging to a peer group that doesn't roll its eyes at distress, and living in a school or workplace where rules are clear and fair all widen a person's future tense. On the situation side, communities that pair everyday gatekeeping with pragmatic steps—safe media practices, safer storage of lethal means, simple routes into care—shift the baseline so that crises are fewer, shorter, and less likely to end in tragedy. None of this denies clinical complexity; psychiatric comorbidity is common and matters. It's simply that risk is multidetermined, and social architecture either amplifies or dampens it. Which means prevention cannot be clinic-centric. It has to be distributed: in homes and locker rooms, classrooms and group chats, break rooms and bus stops—any place where someone can notice a change, ask a plain question, and bridge to help without turning the moment into theater.

Mini-takeaway: Connection is not a vibe; it's a measurable buffer we can design into daily life.

ROLE CLARITY FOR HELPERS (FAMILY, FRIENDS, TEACHERS, COACHES)

Think of this as a set of "role cards," but written in paragraphs rather than laminated plastic. Each helper has three recurring tasks: know your scope (what you actually do), know your boundary (where you stop), and know your handoff (where the support goes next). When these three are clear, the ambient temperature drops; people feel held without being cornered, and the next safe step becomes obvious rather than theatrical (Mann et al., 2005; Stone et al., 2017a; Suicide Prevention Resource Center [SPRC], 2023).

FAMILY OR PARTNER

At home, prevention looks like noticing small shifts and treating them as data rather than drama. Sleep is suddenly ragged, meals are skipped, conversations shrink or bristle, substances edge forward—all of that is signal. The move is to ask plainly, in private, without euphemism: "Are you thinking about suicide?" If the answer is yes, the next move is mechanical and kind rather than philosophical: "Thank you for telling me. Let's lock up anything risky and go together to get help—would you rather call, text, or go in person?" Direct asking removes guesswork; pairing it with an immediate connection to care is the protective part (World Health Organization [WHO], 2014; Stone et al., 2017a). Families are uniquely positioned to reduce access to lethal means—locking firearms and medications, removing stockpiles, securing sharps—and to make the boring things possible: a ride to clinic, a reminder about the appointment, a sandwich set on the counter at noon (Mann et al., 2005; Sarchiapone et al., 2011; WHO, 2014). The boundary matters just as much. You are not the therapist; you are the bridge. Your job is to keep the person company in the immediate term, share the load with professionals and trusted others, and refuse the seductive idea that you alone are the plan (Stone et al., 2017a; SPRC, 2023). If the person refuses help, the script is honest and firm: "I hear you don't want that right now. Because I care about your safety, I'm going to involve [name/role] so we can keep you safe tonight." Safety outranks secrecy; name that and act accordingly (SPRC, 2023). Imminent risk—specific plan, access, intent—triggers a simple sentence and an action: "I'm staying with you and calling for help now," followed by means restriction and immediate contact with crisis or emergency services (WHO, 2014; Stone et al., 2017a).

FRIEND OR PEER

Peers often hear the truth before adults do, which is both an honor and a weight. The useful posture is simple: ask directly, stay with, and connect upward. You do not promise secrecy; you promise company. The line that threads the needle is something like "I'm really glad you told me. I can't keep this to myself because I care about you—let's text or call together, or I'll walk with you right now." The overnight babysitter fantasy—keeping someone safe by sheer proximity—burns people out and sometimes fails; friends are not meant to supervise through the night, manage medications, or take custody of lethal means (SPRC, 2023). The handoff is the point: a warm transfer to a trusted adult, a residence advisor, a coach, a school counselor, or a crisis service, made in real time while you stay on the line or in the room (Stone et al., 2017a). When a friend resists, you can keep the relationship intact and safety intact by naming both: "I hear you. I'm still going to bring in an adult so we can keep you safe." Peer programs work best when they are trained, supervised, and plugged into clear escalation pathways—credibility plus structure (Durlak et al., 2010; Wyman et al., 2010).

TEACHER OR PROFESSOR

In classrooms, prevention is mostly about tone and logistics. You notice changes—the student who was steady now misses seminars, the lab partner whose work has thinned to a sentence, and the athlete who sits far from her teammates. You invite a conversation in private, and, once there, you ask the same unadorned question: "Are you thinking about suicide?" If the answer is yes, you pivot from concern to connection: "I can walk with you to counselling now, or we can call together from my office." Your role is not to conduct therapy by the whiteboard or to coax out an origin story; it is to make a same-day referral, document the concern and the handoff, and offer appropriate flexibility on deadlines or attendance while the student engages care (Ayer & Colpe, 2023; Stone et al., 2017a). Privacy laws and school policies are real; share the minimum necessary to protect life and to activate the support system that exists precisely for this moment (SPRC, 2023). If the student refuses help and you still believe risk is high, you name your responsibility and act: "Because I'm concerned for your safety, I'm going to notify our student support team so we can help today" (Stone et al., 2017a).

COACH, MENTOR, OR SUPERVISOR

Teams and workplaces run on performance, which is why leaders in these spaces have to say the quiet part out loud: safety outranks output. The mentor's job is to create a channel—"See me after practice," "Drop by before your shift"—and then to use that small privacy to ask directly and respond without grandstanding: "I'm concerned about you. Are you thinking about suicide?" If yes, the sequence is predictable by design: step out, connect with support, and sit with the person while the call is made or the walk is taken. Accommodation follows—adjusted practice loads, altered shifts, deferred deliverables—because no one thrives under threat (Knox et al., 2004; Stone et al., 2017a). The boundary is bright: you do not interrogate motives or debrief the team; you do not turn a person's crisis into a locker room lesson (Stone et al., 2017a). The handoff is to Employee Assistance or occupational health in a workplace, to student services or the athletic department liaison in a school, or to crisis services if risk is acute (Knox et al., 2004; WHO, 2014). When communicating with the broader group, you keep it minimal and humane: support is available, privacy is respected, and accommodations are possible—see me privately (Stone et al., 2017a).

UNIVERSAL MOVES THAT TRAVEL ACROSS ROLES

There are three cross-cutting habits worth making boring. First, when someone says yes to suicidal thoughts, you do not leave them alone until there is a connection to help; you also address means safety in the same breath (Sarchiapone et al., 2011; WHO, 2014). Second, when someone says no but looks and sounds unwell, you co-author a 24-hour plan that names where they will be tonight, who checks in, what number to call if the floor drops out, and what happens tomorrow before noon (SPRC, 2023). Third, you document the essentials—who asked and when, what was said, what action you took, and where the person was handed off—because memory is bad under stress and continuity is protective (Stone et al., 2017a; SPRC, 2023). Finally, helpers themselves need care; a quiet debrief with a supervisor or peer, a boundary reset, a walk, and a meal are not luxuries. They are how you stay able to do the simple, brave work again tomorrow (Mental Health Commission of Canada [MHCC], 2018; SPRC, 2023).

ASKING AND RESPONDING (SCRIPTS YOU CAN ACTUALLY SAY)

The shortest distance between worry and help is a plain question asked without theatrics. You make enough privacy to be decent, and then you ask, "Are you thinking about suicide?"—not because you enjoy bluntness, but because direct language lowers ambiguity and, paradoxically, fear (WHO, 2014; Stone et al., 2017a). Then you stop talking. The pause is part of the intervention; it gives the person a place to land. If the answer is yes, you thank them and move immediately from explanation to logistics: "Thank you for telling me. Let's reduce risk here and get support—would you prefer we call, text 988, or go in person together?" You are choosing a door—phone, text, or walk-in—and you are going through it with them, not pointing from the sidewalk (WHO, 2014; Stone et al., 2017a).

If the answer is no but the distress is visible, you treat the "no" as a data point rather than a dismissal. You follow with curiosity that has a steering wheel: "Okay. What's hurting most right now? Let's make a plan for tonight and one for tomorrow—with names, times, and places." Plans beat pep talks because they create near-term structure—a location for the night, a person who checks in, a number to call if the floor drops out, and an action tomorrow before noon (SPRC, 2023).

Refusal is common. When someone declines help, you hold care and responsibility in the same breath: "I hear you don't want that now. Because I care and I'm worried about your safety, I'm going to involve [name/role] so we can keep you safe tonight." Safety outranks secrecy; you say so, and you act accordingly (SPRC, 2023). Imminent risk—method, intent, and access in the same sentence—collapses the decision tree: "We're going to keep you safe. I'm staying with you and calling for help now." You remove or lock lethal means within reach, and you connect to crisis or emergency services, staying until the handoff is real, not hypothetical (WHO, 2014; Stone et al., 2017a). The tone matters as much as the script: sit, do not hover; keep the phone face down unless you are using it to connect; document after, not during; and on telehealth or text, do not disconnect until you can name who is taking over (Stone et al., 2017a; SPRC, 2023).

CONFIDENTIALITY AND CONSENT

Confidentiality is not a force field; it is a practice that protects dignity while keeping people alive. The workable rule is simple: share the minimum necessary to protect life, seek consent whenever possible, and document what you shared and why (SPRC, 2023). When consent is given, widen the circle on purpose and by name: who will drive, who will lock the medications, who will adjust a shift or deadline. Use a teach-back so you are not imagining permission you do not have: "Tell me who you're comfortable with me updating today—what feels okay to share, and what doesn't?" (SPRC, 2023).

When consent is withheld and risk remains high, you disclose to the appropriate party—crisis services, emergency responders, or the designated campus/workplace contact—sharing only what is required to mobilize safety (Stone et al., 2017a; SPRC, 2023). Minors add a layer of law and policy: follow jurisdictional rules on caregiver notification and mature minor capacity, and, when safe, include caregivers because buffers multiply when families know what to do (Stone et al., 2017a). This chapter offers principles rather than legal advice; local policy governs, which means you consult it promptly and then act in favor of life (SPRC, 2023).

PEER SUPPORT AND LIVED EXPERIENCE

Peer support works because credibility is audible: the voice that says, "I've been in dark places too. You don't have to do this alone—can we text 988 together or meet the counsellor now?" often lowers both shame and threshold in the same moment (Wyman et al., 2010; SPRC, 2023). But effective peer work is structured, not heroic. Peers are trained and supervised; they know the edge between support and therapy; they can walk a safety plan; they understand how to discuss lethal means without euphemism or instruction; they never manage acute situations solo; and they track light-touch data—contacts, handoffs, whether the connection held—because systems forget what people need most (Durlak et al., 2010; MHCC, 2018; SPRC, 2023). Done well, peer programs increase belonging and help-seeking in the very hours when people tend to disappear; done poorly, they slide into unsupervised counseling and burnout. Structure is the difference: clear scope, escalation pathways that answer on the first try, and compensation that signals this is skilled labor, not invisible emotional volunteerism (Wyman et al., 2010; MHCC, 2018).

COORDINATING SCHOOLS AND WORKPLACES (THE TRIAD MODEL)

Coordination is easiest to picture as a triangle you could draw on the back of a receipt: the person at risk at one corner, natural supports at the second (family, friends, peers, coaches), and professional supports at the third (counselor, primary care, and employee assistance). The goal is steady movement around the triangle without flooding any one corner (Stone et al., 2017a). In schools, this looks like staff trained to ask directly and hand off the same day; classroom scripts that normalize help without rehearsing details; small-group processing led by trained adults rather than large assemblies; counselling slots reserved for this week rather than next month; identity-affirming routes to care so LGBTQ2S+, Indigenous, newcomer, and international students can use what exists; and a living risk map updated as information changes (Stone et al., 2017a; Ayer & Colpe, 2023; SPRC, 2023). In workplaces, it looks like fast-track access to employee assistance program or occupational health, supervisors who can say the words without spectacle, accommodations that buy time for care to work, and a culture where "nonpunitive" is not a slogan but a habit (Knox et al., 2004; Stone et al., 2017a).

A micro-standard operating procedure keeps the whole thing boring—in the good way. Name a single-point person rather than a committee so someone can actually move things; share only what each corner needs to play its part; book the next thing while you are with the person (an appointment with a time and a door); and treat means safety as a standing item on the checklist, not a garnish (Sarchiapone et al., 2011; Stone et al., 2017a). When the triangle hums, no one is carrying the entire load, and the person at risk is not being asked to bootstrap their way out of a crisis while simultaneously persuading a system to see them (SPRC, 2023).

MEANS SAFETY IN EVERYDAY SUPPORT

Means reduction is the least literary and most powerful part of this work. It does not argue with despair; it builds a fence around opportunity while the despair changes (Mann et al., 2005; WHO, 2014). Helpers can ask neutrally and act practically: "While you're feeling this bad, let's lock up or remove [firearms/medications/sharps]. I can pick up lockboxes or hold meds for a few days if you'd like." The neutrality matters because this is not a political speech; it is the design of the next 48 hours so that impulse cannot meet instrument in one unbroken motion (Sarchiapone et al., 2011; WHO, 2014). In homes, that often means a quick audit of drawers and closets and a decision about temporary storage; in dorms and shared apartments, it means securing what can be secured and removing what cannot; in workplaces, it means knowing how to connect someone to a clinician who can do a fuller means safety conversation without turning the break room into a clinic (Stone et al., 2017a). You pair the change with a time horizon—"for now," "until the next appointment," "through the weekend"—and you check back, because locks drift and promises evaporate. The point is not perfection; it is friction, enough of it at the right moment that a life can make it to morning (Mann et al., 2005; WHO, 2014).

EQUITY AND CONTEXT (KEEP PREVENTION FROM BECOMING PRIVILEGE)

Risk and access are uneven, which means a one-size plan quietly fits the people who already fit. The work is to build pathways that match real lives: language access that lets someone describe pain in the words they actually use; transportation and childcare that make a 3 pm appointment more than theoretical; partnerships with community and faith leaders who are trusted messengers; and care that is responsive to gender, culture, and history so that help does not require a performance of sameness (Caine, 2013; MHCC, 2018; SPRC, 2023). Centering groups that have been underserved or over-policed is not charity; it is calibration. Effective systems create multiple entry points—text, phone, walk-in—keep after-hours options real; recruit and pay peers from the communities being served; and bake explicit anti-stigma language into every script so people do not have to guess whether they are welcome (Stone et al., 2017a). Equity is not a paragraph at the end; it is the design spec at the start.

EVALUATION (HOW WE KNOW SUPPORT IS HAPPENING)

If we do not measure, we drift back to vibes. A practical evaluation spine has three vertebrae. Process tells you whether the system moves: the proportion of cases with a documented warm handoff, the median time from concern to first clinical contact, and the share with a recorded means safety action. These are the "are we doing what we said we would do?" metrics, and they respond quickly to better scripts and clearer ownership (Stone et al., 2017a; SPRC, 2023). Outcomes tell you whether the person's life is actually getting easier in the short term: return to class or work, fewer acute crises, satisfaction with care, and rising confidence among peers and teachers or supervisors that they know what to do—changes that comprehensive approaches tend to produce more reliably than single tactics (Mann et al., 2005; Zalsman et al., 2016). Equity asks whether success is shared: uptakes and outcomes by subgroup, requests for translation, and the use of transportation or childcare supports. When those numbers move in parallel rather than diverge, prevention has stopped being a privilege and started being a system (Caine, 2013; MHCC, 2018).

CHAPTER SUMMARY

This chapter argues that suicide prevention is shared work. Families, peers, teachers, coaches, and supervisors all matter because they shape the everyday perimeter around a person at risk. The most protective moves are deliberately simple: ask directly, respond without drama, reduce access to lethal means, and connect to help in real time. Schools and workplaces coordinate by naming a point person, booking the next step before the conversation ends, and practicing confidentiality as "minimum necessary" rather than silence. Equity is a design requirement—multiple entry points, after-hours options, language access, and identity-affirming care keep prevention from becoming a privilege (Caine, 2013; WHO, 2014; Stone et al., 2017a; MHCC, 2018; SPRC, 2023).

Support is not extra—it is the fabric that keeps tomorrow available. The practices here are small on purpose: clear roles, direct questions, unglamorous logistics, and handoffs that actually hand off. If we do these things on boring Tuesdays, we change the base rate (Mann et al., 2005; WHO, 2014; Stone et al., 2017a).

KEY TAKEAWAYS

- **Role clarity lowers risk.** Know your scope, boundary, and handoff.
- **Direct questions save time and lives.** Ask plainly, then pause and listen.
- **Connection beats instruction.** Accompany the person through a warm handoff, don't just advise.
- **Means safety is essential.** Reduce access now; let treatment do its work over time.
- **Confidentiality serves safety.** Share the minimum necessary, seek consent when you can, and document why.
- **Coordination is a triangle.** Person at risk, natural supports, professional supports—keep the energy moving.
- **Equity is the plan, not a paragraph.** Build language access, after-hours routes, and identity-affirming options into every step.
- **Measure what matters.** Warm handoffs completed, time to first contact, means safety actions, and whether gains are shared across groups (Mann et al., 2005; Caine, 2013; Zalsman et al., 2016; Stone et al., 2017a; MHCC, 2018; SPRC, 2023)

RECOMMENDED READINGS

IGOR GALYNKER—*TALKING TO FAMILIES ABOUT MENTAL ILLNESS* (2018)

This book addresses one of the most overlooked dimensions of suicide prevention: how clinicians communicate with families during periods of high risk, crisis, and uncertainty. Galynker offers concrete guidance on honesty, containment, boundary-setting, and alliance-building without inducing panic or false reassurance.

We recommend it here because effective family communication is itself a preventive intervention and a core element of shared suicide care.

STACEY FREEDENTHAL—*HELPING THE SUICIDAL PERSON: TIPS AND TECHNIQUES FOR PROFESSIONALS*

Freedenthal provides a practical guide for clinicians on how to work effectively and compassionately with suicidal individuals. This book focuses on core skills such as engagement, suicide risk assessment, safety planning, and treatment planning. This book emphasizes direct, empathic communication and encourages clinicians to reflect on their own fears and assumptions about suicide. Overall, it translates suicide theory and intervention principles into clear, usable strategies for everyday professional practice.

RORY C. O'CONNOR—*WHEN IT IS DARKEST: WHY PEOPLE DIE BY SUICIDE AND WHAT WE CAN DO TO PREVENT IT* (2021)

O'Connor integrates decades of research with practical prevention strategies spanning families, schools, workplaces, and health systems. This book belongs in this chapter because it explicitly frames suicide prevention as a shared societal responsibility rather than a specialty activity. We recommend it here for its clear articulation of how coordinated support reduces risk across contexts.

KEY REFERENCES

Ayer, L., & Colpe, L. J. (2023). The key role of schools in youth suicide prevention. *Journal of the American Academy of Child and Adolescent Psychiatry, 62*(1), 19–21. https://doi.org/10.1016/j.jaac.2022.06.022

Caine E. D. (2013). Forging an agenda for suicide prevention in the United States. *American Journal of Public Health, 103*(5), 822–829. https://doi.org/10.2105/AJPH.2012.301078

Cochrane, J., Duffy, C., & Sheehan, M. (2017). The role of schools in early suicide prevention: New evidence from the United States. *American Journal of Public Health, 107*(6), 947–948.

Durlak, J. A., Weissberg, R. P., & Pachan, M. (2010). A meta-analysis of after-school programs that seek to promote personal and social skills in children and adolescents. *American Journal of Community Psychology, 45* (3–4), 294–309. https://doi.org/10.1007/s10464-010-9300-6

Knox, K. L., Conwell, Y., & Caine, E. D. (2004). If suicide is a public health problem, what are we doing to prevent it? *American Journal of Public Health, 94*(1), 37–45. https://doi.org/10.2105/AJPH.94.1.37

Sarchiapone, M., Mandelli, L., Iosue, M., Andrisano, C., & Roy, A. (2011). Controlling access to suicide means. *International Journal of Environmental Research and Public Health, 8*(12), 4550–4562. https://doi.org/10.3390/ijerph8124550

10

MAKING MEANING

Bringing It All Together

RESTORING MEANING, CONNECTION, AND FUTURE

A book about suicide is, inevitably, a book about being human. The earlier chapters tracked risk and recovery across families, classrooms, clinics, and teams; this last chapter turns toward meaning—how people make sense of danger and loss, how communities

DOI: 10.4324/9781003758792-10

recover their voice, and how a life becomes livable again. The lens is deliberately ontological and people-centered. Death is not only an outcome but a given—something cultures narrate, resist, ritualize, and sometimes seek; meaning is the counterweight that lets a person move within that given without being crushed by it (Baumeister, 1991; Bowker, 1993). Shneidman named the engine of suicidal states *psychache*, the felt intolerability of mental pain; antidote here was never a single insight but relief plus purpose, the reduction of torment alongside the return of reasons (Shneidman, 1974, 2008). Frankl's wager is similar and stubborn: people can bear almost any *how* with a sufficiently honest *why*, a claim that survives not because it is neat, but because it is testable in ordinary time—appointments kept, laundry folded, a text returned because someone is waiting (Frankl, 2014). Even Hillman's unsettling meditation on suicide and the soul is useful: not an endorsement but a demand that we speak to identity and longing in their deepest registers rather than only to symptom counts (Hillman, 2014). If Chapter 9 made support practical, this chapter roots that practicality in meaning, grief, and culture—the textures by which people live their days and make it to morning (Berger & Perry, 1989; Staudacher, 1994; Fenwick & Fenwick, 2008; Kübler-Ross, 2008; Soper, 2021).

CHAPTERS 1–9: FROM DANGER TO DIRECTION

Across the book, prevention has been a team sport. We learned that direct questions cut through fog; that means safety lowers the odds that impulse meets instrument; that coordinated handoffs are better than referrals clipped to hope; and that postvention *is* prevention, because communities either glamorize or humanize the story that follows a death (Mann et al., 2005; Stone et al., 2017a; World Health Organization [WHO], 2014). Meaning threads these tactics together. When people can name what still matters—children who need breakfast, work worth doing, faith practices that scaffold a week, a team that expects them at practice, the dog who will not walk himself—risk narrows because the future fills back in (Baumeister, 1991; Frankl, 2014). Culture is not wallpaper; it is the script people are permitted to use when asking for help or declining it, the set of metaphors that either opens a door or bars it (Berger & Perry, 1989; Bowker, 1993).

CASE WALK-THROUGHS THAT BRAID MEANING AND METHOD

MAYA, AGE 17, AFTER AN ATTEMPT AND A HALL FULL OF RUMOR

The counselor does the basics first: privacy enough for honesty, a plain question, and a same-day connection to care. Then the conversation shifts from *why did this happen?* to *what keeps you here?* Maya writes down three anchors—finishing two commissioned drawings, tutoring a friend in algebra, and her grandmother's Friday dinners—and each becomes logistics: a schedule that protects time, a ride that makes attendance real, a text check-in that is more than sentiment. Lethal means at home are locked without drama. A teacher receives a short script and offers flexible deadlines while the first sessions begin. The school moderates memorial talk online, not to police grief but to avoid tutorials disguised as tribute. The narrative pivots from spectacle to stewardship—of Maya's time, her privacy, and her emerging future (WHO, 2014; Frankl, 2014; Stone et al., 2017a).

LUIS, 28, AN EMERGENCY MEDICAL TECHNICIAN AFTER A FIELD FATALITY

Debriefing happens quickly and without blame. The team reviews facts, names moral distress aloud, and points—specifically, not vaguely—to supports. For Luis, meaning work is concrete: pride in skill and service without quietly adopting omnipotence as a job requirement. He writes a short night plan, dials back alcohol for a month, and returns to Wednesday soccer—the ordinary rituals that keep him plural rather than reduced to one catastrophic scene (Staudacher, 1994; Fenwick & Fenwick, 2008; Shneidman, 2008).

ASHA, 42, DISCHARGED FROM THE EMERGENCY DEPARTMENT AFTER A SUICIDAL CRISIS

Two items are scheduled before discharge, not suggested: a follow-up within 72 hours and a phone check-in the next day. At home, medications are blister-packed; a supporter stores them for the weekend. Asha lists reasons to live that aren't poster-sized slogans: her daughter's morning routine, the art class she abandoned mid-semester, and the manager who said, "we can adjust your workload." These reasons are entered on a calendar with times and doors. The care transition becomes a walked bridge rather than a wish (Mann et al., 2005; Frankl, 2014; WHO, 2014).

CONVERSATION, SAFETY PLANNING, AND FOLLOW-UP—CHECKLISTS WITHOUT BULLETS

Every serious conversation has a beginning, a middle, and an end. The beginning is privacy and purpose—somewhere quiet enough for honesty and a sentence that sets the terms: *I'm concerned and I want to understand how to help you stay safe.* The middle is the direct ask and the deliberate silence that follows—*Are you thinking about suicide?*—a question that works precisely because it refuses code and gives the person room to tell the truth. The end is action with names, times, and places—*tonight you'll be at your sister's; tomorrow at 10:30 we meet Dr. K; I'll text at 9 p.m. to confirm the ride.* Nothing florid, just specificity, because specificity is how intent becomes a plan rather than a wish (WHO, 2014; Stone et al., 2017a).

Safety planning is where meaning meets method. You translate the person's early warning signs into ordinary language they recognize, pair coping steps with actual environments they can access, and list people to contact in the order they themselves would want to call them. Professional options and crisis numbers sit alongside those personal contacts, not above them, and the conversation addresses means safety in the same breath—what will be removed, locked, or stored elsewhere, and for how long. The plan is written, not remembered, because memory is bad under stress; it lives on a phone and on a fridge, and it is reviewed when the person is well, not only when they are in the tunnel (Shneidman, 1974; WHO, 2014).

Follow-up, by design, is unglamorous. Someone sends a brief caring message that expects nothing in return, confirms the next appointment, and checks whether the plan still fits the week the person is actually living. Communities practice anniversary awareness without turning remembrance into spectacle; families learn proximity without surveillance; and peers are trained and supervised so that credibility travels with structure rather than exhausting itself in unscripted heroics (Staudacher, 1994; Durlak et al., 2010; Wyman et al., 2010).

SYSTEM LEVERS THAT MOVE THE NEEDLE

Three levers show up in every setting. The first is means safety. Cultures disagree about metaphysics; they do not disagree about physics. When lethal means are less available during acute states, more people live to have different days, which is the whole point of prevention (Mann et al., 2005; WHO, 2014). The second is access. "Soon" is not a time frame; it is a deferral. Systems lower risk when text, phone, and walk-in doors remain open after hours and when near-term slots are reserved for acute need so that help is not an abstraction but a doorway with a handle (Stone et al., 2017a). The third is care transitions. Warm handoffs—staying with the person until another human answers—turn intent into connection; discharges with dates, addresses, and a ride outperform "follow up as needed" every time because friction, not bad faith, is often what kills appointments (Mann et al., 2005; WHO, 2014). Around these levers, culture and meaning do their quieter work: rituals that honor the dead without modeling the act; classrooms and teams that say the words without glamor; families that practice love as logistics—rides, meals, check-ins—rather than only as sentiments (Berger & Perry, 1989; Bowker, 1993; Kübler-Ross, 2008).

WHERE EVIDENCE IS THIN, AND WHERE TO KEEP LEARNING

We know a great deal about population-level levers; we know less about how to sustain peer programs at scale without burnout, how to tailor safety planning across languages and traditions without exporting a script that does not fit, and how to design online memorial spaces that comfort without contagion. We also need better longitudinal data on the ripple effects of postvention in schools and workplaces, sharper measures of belonging as a clinical buffer rather than an afterthought, and more trials that test identity-affirming care as a mechanism of change, not merely a courtesy (Caine, 2013; Mental Health Commission of Canada [MHCC], 2018). Readers can keep learning in practice communities that mix scholarship with lived testimony—survivor-of-attempt and survivor-of-loss groups, clinician learning collaboratives, and public health resources that update guidance as evidence accrues (WHO, 2014; Suicide Prevention Resource Center [SPRC], 2023). For the existential spine, the shelves remain good teachers: Shneidman on *psychache* and the relief-plus-purpose antidote; Frankl on reasons sturdy enough for ordinary time; Hillman on the soul's stakes; Baumeister on life's projects; Bowker on theologies of death; Kübler-Ross and the Fenwicks on dying and care; Staudacher on grief as a daily practice; and Soper on why, against odds, people choose to live (Shneidman, 1974, 2008; Baumeister, 1991; Bowker, 1993; Staudacher, 1994; Fenwick & Fenwick, 2008; Kübler-Ross, 2008; Frankl, 2014; Hillman, 2014; Soper, 2021).

CLOSING

Prevention, when you get close to it, stops looking like a capital-P Program and starts looking like a hundred small fidelities kept in sequence. It is not the heroic midnight insight so much as the 3 pm text that says, *I'm outside—ready when you are*; the soup that shows up at the right hour; the practical sentence—*we can adjust your shift, starting now*—that returns a person to human time. It is the teacher who asks the unadorned question and then refuses to hurry the answer; the coach who walks, literally walks, with a student to the counseling office; the clinician who does not merely advise but books the ride, writes the appointment on a card, and makes sure the card has a pocket to live in (WHO, 2014); Stone et al., 2017a). None of this is glamorous; all of it is causal.

To close a book like this, we owe an honest accounting of what moves the needle and why. Direct questions cut through fog; warm handoffs convert intent into connection; means safety changes physics at the crucial moment; near-term access makes tomorrow an address rather than a promise (Mann et al., 2005; WHO, 2014; Stone et al., 2017a). But technique, alone, has the half-life of a pep talk. What sustains technique is stance: a way of regarding the other that is curious without prying, steady without stone, tender without theater. Stance is the decision to build meaning *with* rather than *for* the person in pain—what Frankl would call a usable *why* that can survive the weather of an ordinary week (Frankl, 2014).

If there is a single thread running from our first chapter to this one, it is Shneidman's stubborn premise that suicidal states are powered by *psychache*—the felt intolerability of mental pain—and that relief plus purpose is the antidote, not enlightenment on demand (Shneidman, 2008). Relief is logistical: locked cabinets, blister packs, rides arranged, hours trimmed, sleep made possible. Purpose is particular: the kid who needs breakfast, the Wednesday night soccer, the commission due Friday, the grandmother's table at six. Put plainly, meaning is not an epiphany; it is a calendar entry with a door and a time (Baumeister, 1991; Frankl, 2014).

Culture, meanwhile, is the operating system underneath our scripts. It is not wallpaper; it is grammar—what can be said, to whom, and with what consequences (Berger & Perry, 1989; Bowker, 1993). In some communities, it is easy to ask for help and hard to confess ambivalence; in others, the opposite is true. Good prevention reads the room and edits the playbook: language access that lets people describe pain accurately; identity-affirming routes into care so that help does not require an audition; rituals that honor the dead without choreographing imitation; memorial spaces moderated like we mean it—compassion forward, method details absent (WHO, 2014). Equity, then, is not a footnote or a grant requirement; it is the difference between a plan that exists and a plan that fits.

We should linger on ordinariness, because that is where readers will live. The grandmother who locks the cabinet and ladles soup is, in that hour, a public health intervention disguised as dinner. The supervisor who says, "we can move you off nights this week," is practicing access—less wait, more tomorrow—without ever using the word *access*. The friend who texts at 9 pm *I'm still here if you want to talk; if not, I'll ping you at 9 am* is doing follow-up correctly: expectation-light, presence-heavy (Stone et al., 2017a). None of these people have solved The Problem; they have changed the base rate for one person on one Tuesday, which is how population-level change actually occurs—locally, repeatedly, at human scale (Mann et al., 2005).

There is also a way of being present that refuses to turn a person's pain into our project. Hillman's provocation—that talk about suicide must include the soul's stakes, the depth language of identity and longing—reminds us not to treat suffering as a customer service ticket to be closed (Hillman, 2014). The stance here is double: we take the person seriously in their metaphysics *and* we remain practical in our methods. We can ask about purpose and still check the locks. We can speak of grief and still book the ride. We can sit with a person's unsolved questions while making sure they have a sandwich and a plan for the night (Staudacher, 1994; Frankl, 2014).

Systems, for their part, do best when they behave like good neighbors rather than indifferent machines. A clinic that reserves near-term slots for acute need, a school that trains adults to ask directly and hand off the same day, an employer that treats accommodations as safety equipment instead of favors—these are not luxuries; they are the infrastructure of prevention (WHO, 2014; Stone et al., 2017a). Care transitions should feel like walked bridges, not scavenger hunts: someone stays until another human answers; the next appointment is a noun with an address, not a verb with a shrug (Mann et al., 2005). We measure what matters—warm handoffs completed, time to first contact, means safety actions taken—not to grade people but to see where the weave is loose and stitch there first.

And yet, for all the checklists and scripts, we end where we began: with meaning. People do not live by algorithms alone. They live by projects and promises, by belonging, and by the stubborn fact that someone expects them to arrive and has saved them a seat. The literature on dying and grieving is clear: the practices that carry us are often humble—prayer beads worn smooth, a teammate's knock on the door, the line of a poem remembered precisely because it is simple (Fenwick & Fenwick, 2008; Kübler-Ross, 2008). Even Soper's contemporary meditation on why we choose life lands in this neighborhood: we persist for reasons that are durable and personal, rarely cinematic (Staudacher, 1994; Soper, 2021).

So the closing argument is not grand but stubborn. Ask directly and pause long enough to hear the answer. Remove or lock the things that make bad moments irreversible. Book the next step now, while resolve and cell signals are both strong. Speak in the dialect of the community standing in front of you. Practice confidentiality as the minimum necessary to keep people alive, not as an excuse to stand back. And build meaning like a craftsman: slowly, with the materials at hand, in the company of the person whose life we are trying to help hold (Shneidman, 2008; Frankl, 2014; WHO, 2014; Stone et al., 2017a).

If earlier chapters taught technique, this one insists on posture: intelligent tenderness, an almost pedantic respect for logistics, and the humility to co-author a future rather than prescribe one. Support is not extra—it is the fabric that keeps tomorrow available, the quiet weave of rides and reminders and soup and check-ins, through which reasons to live can catch and hold (Shneidman, 2008; Frankl, 2014). And if tomorrow is available, then meaning can do its slow, unfashionable work; and if meaning can work, then people, being their stubborn and astonishing selves, will often choose to stay.

RECOMMENDED READINGS

EDWIN S. SHNEIDMAN—*A COMMONSENSE BOOK OF DEATH* (2008)

Shneidman's final reflections return suicidology to its ethical and human foundations: pain, dignity, ambivalence, and meaning. This book fits the closing chapter because it synthesizes a lifetime of thinking about why people suffer and how meaning tempers despair. We recommend it as a humane and fitting final voice for the book.

ROY F. BAUMEISTER—*MEANINGS OF LIFE* (1991)

Baumeister offers one of the most influential psychological accounts of how humans construct purpose, value, and coherence. This book belongs in this chapter because meaning loss is central to suicidal collapse, and meaning restoration is central to recovery. We recommend it here to ground existential prevention in rigorous psychological theory.

ANTOON A. LEENAARS (ED.)—*SUICIDOLOGY: ESSAYS IN HONOR OF EDWIN S. SHNEIDMAN* (2001)

This edited volume traces the intellectual legacy of Shneidman across clinical, theoretical, and ethical domains. It belongs in this chapter because it situates meaning-centered suicidology within a living scholarly tradition. We recommend it here to close the book by honoring the field's roots while pointing toward its future.

KEY REFERENCES

Baumeister, R. F. (1991). *Meanings of life*. Guilford Press. https://www.guilford.com/books/Meanings-of-Life/Roy-Baumeister/9780898625318

Frankl, V. E. (2014). *The will to meaning: Foundations and applications of logotherapy* (Expanded ed.). Plume. https://www.penguinrandomhouse.com/books/315814/the-will-to-meaning-by-viktor-e-frankl/

Hillman, J. (2014). *Suicide and the soul* (Rev. ed.). Spring Publications.

Kübler-Ross, E. (2008). *On life after death* (Rev. ed.). Celestial Arts. https://www.penguinrandomhouse.com/books/88306/on-life-after-death-by-elisabeth-kubler-ross/

Shneidman, E. S. (1974). *Deaths of man*. Quadrangle/The New York Times Book Co. https://catalog.hathitrust.org/Record/000221516

Shneidman, E. S. (2008). *A commonsense book of death: Reflections at ninety*. Rowman & Littlefield. https://rowman.com/ISBN/9780742563315/A-Commonsense-Book-of-Death-Reflections-at-Ninety

Staudacher, C. (1994). *A time to grieve: Meditations for healing after the death of a loved one*. HarperOne. https://www.harpercollins.com/products/a-time-to-grieve-carol-staudacher

REFERENCES

Adamiak, S., & Dohnalik, J. (2023). The prohibition of suicide and its theological rationale in Catholic Moral and Canonical tradition: Origins and development. *Journal of Religion and Health, 62*(6), 3820–3833. https://doi.org/10.1007/s10943-023-01900-w

Adam, K. S., Sheldon-Keller, A. E., & West, M. (1996). Attachment organization and history of suicidal behavior in clinical adolescents. *Journal of Consulting and Clinical Psychology, 64*(2), 264–272.

Afifi, T. O., Enns, M. W., Cox, B. J., Asmundson, G. J., Stein, M. B., & Sareen, J. (2008). Population attributable fractions of psychiatric disorders and suicide ideation and attempts associated with adverse childhood experiences. *American Journal of Public Health, 98*(5), 946–952. https://doi.org/10.2105/AJPH.2007.120253

Agerbo, E. (2005). Midlife suicide risk, mental health, illness and social adversity in a longitudinal study: A cohort analysis of 223,372 suicides in Denmark. *BMJ, 330*(7489), 347–354.

Aguinaldo, L. D., Sullivant, S., Lanzillo, E. C., Ross, A., He, J. P., Bradley-Ewing, A., Bridge, J. A., Horowitz, L. M., & Wharff, E. A. (2021). Validation of the ask suicide-screening questions (ASQ) with youth in outpatient specialty and primary care clinics. *General Hospital Psychiatry, 68*, 52–58. https://doi.org/10.1016/j.genhosppsych.2020.11.006

American Psychiatric Association. (2022). *Diagnostic and statistical manual of mental disorders* (5th ed., text rev.). https://doi.org/10.1176/appi.books.9780890425787

Apter, A., Kotler, M., Sevy, S., Plutchik, R., Brown, S. L., Foster, H., Hillbrand, M., Korn, M. L., & van Praag, H. M. (1991). Correlates of risk of suicide in violent and nonviolent psychiatric patients. *The American Journal of Psychiatry, 148*(7), 883–887. https://doi.org/10.1176/ajp.148.7.883

Ayer, L., & Colpe, L. J. (2023). The key role of schools in Youth Suicide prevention. *Journal of the American Academy of Child and Adolescent Psychiatry, 62*(1), 19–21. https://doi.org/10.1016/j.jaac.2022.06.022

Ballard, E. D., Vande Voort, J. L., Luckenbaugh, D. A., Machado-Vieira, R., Tohen, M., & Zarate, C. A. (2016). Acute risk factors for suicide attempts and death: Prospective findings from the STEP-BD study. *Bipolar Disorders, 18*(4), 363–372. https://doi.org/10.1111/bdi.12397

Barber, C. W., & Miller, M. J. (2014). Reducing a suicidal person's access to lethal means of suicide: A research agenda. *American Journal of Preventive Medicine, 47*(3 Suppl 2), S264–S272. https://doi.org/10.1016/j.amepre.2014.05.028

Barzilay, S., Yaseen, Z. S., Hawes, M., Gorman, B., Altman, R., Foster, A., Apter, A., Rosenfield, P., & Galynker, I. (2018). Emotional responses to suicidal patients: Factor structure, construct, and predictive validity of the Therapist Response Questionnaire–Suicide Form. *Frontiers in Psychiatry, 9*, 104. https://doi.org/10.3389/fpsyt.2018.00104

Barzilay, S., Schuck, A., Bloch-Elkouby, S., Yaseen, Z. S., Hawes, M., Rosenfield, P., Foster, A., & Galynker, I. (2019). Associations between clinicians' emotional responses, therapeutic alliance, and patient suicidal ideation. *Depression and Anxiety, 37*(3), 214–223. https://doi.org/10.1002/da.22973

Baumeister, R. F. (1990). Suicide as escape from self. *Psychological Review, 97*(1), 90–113. https://doi.org/10.1037/0033-295X.97.1.90

Baumeister, R. F. (1991). *Meanings of life.* Guilford Press. https://www.guilford.com/books/Meanings-of-Life/Roy-Baumeister/9780898625318

Beattie, D., & Devitt, P. (2015). *Suicide: A modern obsession.* Liberties Press.

Beautrais, A. L. (2000). Risk factors for suicide and attempted suicide among young people. *Australian & New Zealand Journal of Psychiatry, 34*(3), 420–436.

Beck, A. T., Kovacs, M., & Weissman, A. (1979). Assessment of suicidal intention: The scale for suicide ideation. *Journal of Consulting and Clinical Psychology, 47*(2), 343–352. https://doi.org/10.1037/0022-006X.47.2.343

Becker, E. S., Strohbach, D., & Rinck, M. (1999). A specific attentional bias in suicide attempters. *The Journal of Nervous and Mental Disease, 187*(12), 730–735. https://doi.org/10.1097/00005053-199912000-00004

Berger, A. A., & Perry, M. (Eds.). (1989). *Perspectives on death and dying: Cross-cultural and multi-disciplinary views.* Charles Press. https://books.google.com/books/about/Perspectives_on_Death_and_Dying.html?id=RuR-AAAAMAAJ

Blatt, S. J. (2004). *Experiences of depression: Theoretical, clinical, and research perspectives.* American Psychological Association.

Bloch-Elkouby, S., Barzilay, S., Gorman, B. S., Lawrence, O. C., Rogers, M. L., Richards, J., Cohen, L. J., Johnson, B. N., & Galynker, I. (2021). The revised suicide crisis inventory (SCI-2): Validation and assessment of prospective suicidal outcomes at one-month follow-up. *Journal of Affective Disorders, 295*, 1280–1291. https://doi.org/10.1016/j.jad.2021.08.048

Bolton, J. M., Au, W., Leslie, W. D., Martens, P. J., Enns, M. W., Roos, L. L., & Sareen, J. (2013). Parents bereaved by offspring suicide: A population-based longitudinal case-control study. *JAMA Psychiatry, 70*(2), 158–167.

Borenstein, J. (2020). *Stigma, prejudice and discrimination against people with mental illness*. American Psychiatric Association.

Borowsky, I. W., Ireland, M., & Resnick, M. D. (2001). Adolescent suicide attempts: Risks and protectors. *Pediatrics, 107*(3), 485–493.

Bowker, J. (1993). *The meanings of death*. Cambridge University Press.

Bridge, J. A., Goldstein, T. R., & Brent, D. A. (2006). Adolescent suicide and suicidal behavior. *Journal of Child Psychology and Psychiatry, 47*(3–4), 372–394.

Brown, G. K., Currier, G. W., Jager-Hyman, S., & Stanley, B. (2020). Detection and classification of suicidal behavior and nonsuicidal self-injury behavior in emergency departments. *Journal of Clinical Psychiatry, 81*(2), 19m12964. https://doi.org/10.4088/JCP.19m12964

Bryan, C. J., Hernandez, A. M., Allison, S., & Clemans, T. (2013). Combat exposure and suicide risk in two samples of military personnel. *Journal of Clinical Psychology, 69*(1), 64–77. https://doi.org/10.1002/jclp.21932

Cai, Z., Junus, A., Chang, Q., & Yip, P. S. F. (2022). The lethality of suicide methods: A systematic review and meta-analysis. *Journal of Affective Disorders, 300*, 121–129. https://doi.org/10.1016/j.jad.2021.12.054

Caine, E. D. (2013). Forging an agenda for suicide prevention in the United States. *American Journal of Public Health, 103*(5), 822–829. https://doi.org/10.2105/AJPH.2012.301078

Campbell, F. R. (2003). Changing the legacy of suicide. *Suicide and Life-Threatening Behavior, 33*(4), 407–418.

Canetto, S. S. (2008). Women and suicidal behavior: A cultural analysis. *The American Journal of Orthopsychiatry, 78*(2), 259–266. https://doi.org/10.1037/a0013973

Canetto, S. S., & Sakinofsky, I. (1998). The gender paradox in suicide. *Suicide and Life-Threatening Behavior, 28*(1), 1–23.

Cash, S. J., & Bridge, J. A. (2009). Epidemiology of youth suicide and suicidal behavior. *Current Opinion in Pediatrics, 21*(5), 613–619. https://doi.org/10.1097/MOP.0b013e32833063e1

Cavanagh, J. T., Carson, A. J., Sharpe, M., & Lawrie, S. M. (2003). Psychological autopsy studies of suicide: A systematic review. *Psychological Medicine, 33*(3), 395–405.

Centre for Addiction and Mental Health. (2020). *Words matter: Language guidelines for talking about* suicide. https://www.camh.ca/-/media/files/words-matter-suicide-language-guide.pdf

Cerel, J., Brown, M. M., Maple, M., Singleton, M., van de Venne, J., Moore, M., & Flaherty, C. (2019). How many people are exposed to suicide? Not six. *Suicide and Life-Threatening Behavior, 49*(2), 529–534.

Chambers, A. (2010, August 3). Japan: Ending the culture of the "honourable" suicide. *The Guardian.* https://www.theguardian.com/commentisfree/2010/aug/03/japan-honourable-suicide-rate

Chammas, F., Januel, D., & Bouaziz, N. (2022). Inpatient suicide in psychiatric settings: Evaluation of current prevention measures. *Frontiers in Psychiatry, 13*, 997974. https://doi.org/10.3389/fpsyt.2022.997974

Chandler, M. J., & Lalonde, C. E. (1998). Cultural continuity as a hedge against suicide. *Transcultural Psychiatry, 35*(2), 191–219.

Chang, S. S., Stuckler, D., Yip, P., & Gunnell, D. (2013). Impact of 2008 global economic crisis on suicide: Time trend study in 54 countries. *BMJ (Clinical Research ed.), 347*, f5239. https://doi.org/10.1136/bmj.f5239

Chen, Y. Y., Yip, P. S., Lee, C. K., Gunnell, D., & Wu, K. C. (2015). The diffusion of a new method of suicide: Charcoal-burning suicide in Hong Kong and Taiwan. *Social Psychiatry and Psychiatric Epidemiology, 50*(2), 227–236. https://doi.org/10.1007/s00127-014-0910-4

Chochinov, H. M. (2007). Dignity-conserving care. *BMJ, 335*(7612), 184–187.

Christodoulou, C., Douzenis, A., Papadopoulos, F. C., Papadopoulou, A., Bouras, G., Gournellis, R., & Lykouras, L. (2012). Suicide and seasonality. *Psychopathology, 45*(2), 89–96.Clark, S. (2001). Bereavement after suicide—How far have we come and where do we go from here? *Crisis, 22*(3), 102–108.

Clark, S. E., & Goldney, R. D. (1995). Grief reactions and recovery in a support group for people bereaved by suicide. *Crisis, 16*(1), 27–33. https://doi.org/10.1027/0227-5910.16.1.27

Cleary, A. (2012). Suicidal action, emotional expression, and the performance of masculinities. *Social Science & Medicine, 74*(4), 498–505.

Comtois, K. A., Jobes, D. A., O'Connor, S. S., Atkins, D. C., Janis, K., Chessen, C. E., Landes, S. J., Holen, A., & Yuodelis-Flores, C. (2011). Collaborative assessment and management of suicidality (CAMS): Feasibility trial for next-day appointment services. *Depression and Anxiety, 28*(11), 963–972. https://doi.org/10.1002/da.20895

Conwell, Y., & Brent, D. (1995). Suicide and aging I: Patterns of psychiatric diagnosis. *International Psychogeriatrics,* 7(2), 149–164.

Cook, C. R., Williams, K. R., Guerra, N. G., Kim, T. E., & Sadek, S. (2010). Predictors of bullying and victimization in childhood and adolescence: A meta-analytic investigation. *School Psychology Quarterly, 25*(2), 65–83. https://doi.org/10.1037/a0020149

Currier, G. W., Brown, G. K., Brenner, L. A., Chesin, M., Knox, K. L., Ghahramanlou-Holloway, M., & Stanley, B. (2015). Rationale and study protocol for a two-part intervention: Safety planning and structured follow-up among veterans at risk for suicide and discharged from the emergency department. *Contemporary Clinical Trials, 43*, 179–184. https://doi.org/10.1016/j.cct.2015.05.003

Cvinar, J. G. (2005). Do suicide survivors suffer social stigma? A review of the literature. *Perspectives in Psychiatric Care, 41*(1), 14–21.

Denning, D. G., Conwell, Y., King, D., & Cox, C. (2000). Method choice, intent, and gender in completed suicide. *Suicide and Life-Threatening Behavior, 30*(3), 282–288.

Dhingra, K., Boduszek, D., & O'Connor, R. C. (2016). A structural test of the integrated motivational-volitional model of suicidal behaviour. *Psychiatry Research, 239*, 169–178. https://doi.org/10.1016/j.psychres.2016.03.023

Di Marco, F. (2016). *Suicide in twentieth-century Japan* (1st ed.). Routledge. https://doi.org/10.4324/9781315676142

Diamond, G. S., Wintersteen, M. B., Brown, G. K., Diamond, G. M., Gallop, R., Shelef, K., & Levy, S. (2010). Attachment-based family therapy for adolescents with suicidal ideation: A randomized controlled trial. *Journal of the American Academy of Child and Adolescent Psychiatry, 49*(2), 122–131. https://doi.org/10.1097/00004583-201002000-00006

Dube, S. R., Anda, R. F., Felitti, V. J., Chapman, D. P., Williamson, D. F., & Giles, W. H. (2001). Childhood abuse, household dysfunction, and the risk of attempted suicide throughout the life span: Findings from the Adverse Childhood Experiences Study. *JAMA, 286*(24), 3089–3096.

Dundas, P. (2002). *The Jains* (2nd ed.). Routledge. Durkheim, É. (1951). *Suicide: A study in sociology* (J. A. Spaulding & G. Simpson, Trans.). Free Press. (Original work published 1897). https://doi.org/10.4324/9780203994320

Dyregrov, K., & Dyregrov, A. (2008). *Effective grief and bereavement support: The role of family, friends, colleagues, schools and support professionals*. Jessica Kingsley.

Ellis, T. E. (Ed.). (2006). *Cognition and suicide: Theory, research, and therapy*. American Psychological Association. https://doi.org/10.1037/11377-000

Farberow, N. L., & Shneidman, E. S. (1961). *The cry for help*. McGraw-Hill.

Fawcett, J., Scheftner, W. A., Fogg, L., Clark, D. C., Young, M. A., Hedeker, D., & Gibbons, R. (1990). Time-related predictors of suicide in major affective disorder. *The American Journal of Psychiatry, 147*(9), 1189–1194. https://doi.org/10.1176/ajp.147.9.1189

Feigelman, W., Gorman, B. S., & Jordan, J. R. (2009). Stigmatization and suicide bereavement. *Death Studies, 33*(7), 591–608.

Fenwick, P., & Fenwick, E. (2008). *The art of dying*. Bloomsbury/Continuum. https://www.bloomsbury.com/uk/art-of-dying-9780826499235/

Fontanella, C. A., Hiance-Stephens, A. R., Phillips, G. S., Bridge, J. A., Campo, J. V., & Sweeney, H. A. (2015). Widening rural–urban disparities in youth suicide. *JAMA Pediatrics, 169*(5), 466–473.

Frankl, V. E. (1959/2006). *Man's search for meaning.* Beacon Press.

Frankl, V. E. (2014). *The will to meaning: Foundations and applications of logotherapy* (Expanded ed.). Plume. https://www.penguinrandomhouse.com/books/315814/the-will-to-meaning-by-viktor-e-frankl/

Franklin, J. C., Ribeiro, J. D., Fox, K. R., Bentley, K. H., Kleiman, E. M., Huang, X., Musacchio, K. M., Jaroszewski, A. C., Chang, B. P., & Nock, M. K. (2017). Risk factors for suicidal thoughts and behaviors: A meta-analysis of 50 years of studies. *Psychological Bulletin, 143*(2), 187–232. https://doi.org/10.1037/bul0000084

Freuchen, A., Kjelsberg, E., & Grøholt, B. (2012). Differences between children and adolescents who commit suicide and their peers: A psychological autopsy of suicide victims compared to accident victims and a community sample. *Child and Adolescent Psychiatry and Mental Health, 6*(1), 1–12. https://doi.org/10.1186/1753-2000-6-1

Freud, S. (1917/1957). Mourning and melancholia. In J. Strachey (Ed. & Trans.), *The standard edition of the complete psychological works of Sigmund Freud* (Vol. 14, pp. 243–258). Hogarth Press.

Gabennesch, H. (1988). When promises fail: A theory of temporal fluctuations in suicide. *Social Forces, 67*(1), 129–145.

Galynker, I. (2017). *The suicidal crisis: Clinical guide to the assessment of imminent risk.* Oxford University Press.

Galynker, I. (2023). *The suicidal crisis: Clinical guide to the assessment of imminent suicide risk* (2nd ed.). Oxford University Press. (Print ISBN: 9780197582718)

Gay, M. (2025). The suicidal clock: Temporal constriction and the chronological collapse of narrative identity. *Illness, Crisis & Loss, 0*(0). https://doi.org/10.1177/10541373251350201

Gay, M. (2026). *Integrating narrative identity in suicidology: A clinical exploration of story, identity, and suicide* (1st ed.). Routledge. https://doi.org/10.4324/9781003639985

Geulayov, G., Gunnell, D., Holmen, T. L., & Metcalfe, C. (2012). The association of parental fatal and non-fatal suicidal behaviour with offspring suicidal behaviour and depression: A systematic review and meta-analysis. *Psychological Medicine, 42*(8), 1567–1580. https://doi.org/10.1017/S0033291711002753

Ghasemzadeh, N., Asghari, F., Shirazi, M., Faramarzi Razini, F., & Larijani, B. (2018). Islamic jurisprudential and ethical considerations of practicing medical procedures on nearly dead patients: Part I (The theoretical section). *Journal of Medical Ethics and History of Medicine, 11*, 14.

Gipson, P. Y., Agarwala, P., Opperman, K. J., Horwitz, A., & King, C. A. (2015). Columbia–suicide severity rating scale: Predictive validity with adolescent psychiatric emergency patients. *Pediatric Emergency Care, 31*(2), 88–94. https://doi.org/10.1097/PEC.0000000000000225

Goldstein, R. B., Black, D. W., Nasrallah, A., & Winokur, G. (1991). The prediction of suicide: Sensitivity, specificity, and predictive value of a multivariate model applied to suicide among 1,906 patients with affective disorders. *Archives of General Psychiatry, 48*(5), 418–422. https://doi.org/10.1001/archpsyc.1991.01810290030004\

Gone, J. P., Hartmann, W. E., Pomerville, A., Wendt, D. C., Klem, S. H., & Burrage, R. L. (2019). The impact of historical trauma on health outcomes for Indigenous populations in the USA and Canada: A systematic review. *American Psychologist, 74*(1), 20–35. https://doi.org/10.1037/amp0000338

Goschin, S., Briggs, J., Blanco-Lutzen, S., Cohen, L. J., & Galynker, I. (2013). Parental affectionless control and suicidality. *Journal of Affective Disorders, 151*(1), 1–6. https://doi.org/10.1016/j.jad.2013.05.096

Gould, M. S., & Kramer, R. A. (2001). Youth suicide prevention. *Suicide and Life-Threatening Behavior, 31*(Suppl 1), 6–31.

Gunnell, D., Bennewith, O., Hawton, K., Simkin, S., & Kapur, N. (2005). The epidemiology and prevention of suicide by hanging: A systematic review. *International Journal of Epidemiology, 34*(2), 433–442.

Halari, R., Premkumar, P., Farquharson, L., Fannon, D., Kuipers, E., & Kumari, V. (2009). Rumination and negative symptoms in schizophrenia. *The Journal of Nervous and Mental Disease, 197*(9), 703–706. https://doi.org/10.1097/NMD.0b013e3181b3af20

Hanschmidt, F., Lehnig, F., Riedel-Heller, S. G., & Kersting, A. (2016). The stigma of suicide survivorship and related consequences—A systematic review. *PLOS ONE, 11*(9), e0162688. https://doi.org/10.1371/journal.pone.0162688

Hawton, K., Casañas i Comabella, C., Haw, C., & Saunders, K. (2013). Risk factors for suicide in individuals with depression: A systematic review. *Journal of Affective Disorders, 147*(1–3), 17–28.

Hawton, K., Knipe, D., & Pirkis, J. (2024). Restriction of access to means used for suicide. *The Lancet. Public Health, 9*(10), e796–e801. https://doi.org/10.1016/S2468-2667(24)00157-9

Hawton, K., & van Heeringen, K. (2009). Suicide. *The Lancet, 373*(9672), 1372–1381.

Heckhausen, J., Wrosch, C., & Schulz, R. (2010). A motivational theory of life-span development. *Psychological Review, 117*(1), 32–60. https://doi.org/10.1037/a0017668

Hewitt, P. L., Flett, G. L., & Turnbull-Donovan, W. (1992). Perfectionism and suicide potential. *The British Journal of Clinical Psychology, 31*(2), 181–190. https://doi.org/10.1111/j.2044-8260.1992.tb00982.x

Hillman, J. (2014). *Suicide and the soul* (Rev. ed.). Spring Publications.

Hinsch, B. (2012). *Women in imperial China*. Rowman & Littlefield.

Hirsch, J. K. (2006). A review of the literature on rural suicide: Risk and protective factors, incidence, and prevention. *Crisis, 27*(4), 189–199. https://doi.org/10.1027/0227-5910.27.4.189

Hjern, A., & Allebeck, P. (2002). Suicide in first- and second-generation immigrants in Sweden. *Social Psychiatry and Psychiatric Epidemiology, 37*(9), 423–429.

Hochard, K. D., Heym, N., & Townsend, E. (2017). Investigating the interaction between sleep symptoms of arousal and acquired capability in predicting suicidality. *Suicide and Life-Threatening Behavior, 47*(3), 370–381. https://doi.org/10.1111/sltb.12285

Holden, R. R., Mehta, K., Cunningham, E. J., & McLeod, L. D. (2001). Development of the Psychache Scale. *Psychological Assessment, 13*(4), 435–443.

Horowitz, L. M., Snyder, D., Boudreaux, E. D., He, J. P., Harrington, C. J., Cai, J., Claassen, C., & Pao, M. (2020). Validation of the ask suicide-screening questions for adult medical inpatients. *Psychosomatics, 61*(6), 713–722. https://doi.org/10.1016/j.psym.2020.04.005

Hubers, A. A. M., Moaddine, S., Peersmann, S. H. M., Stijnen, T., van Duijn, E., van der Mast, R. C., Dekkers, O. M., & Giltay, E. J. (2016). Suicidal ideation and subsequent completed suicide in both psychiatric and non-psychiatric populations: A meta-analysis. *Epidemiology and Psychiatric Sciences, 27*(2), 186–198. https://doi.org/10.1017/S2045796016001049

Hume, D. (1987). Of suicide. In E. F. Miller (Ed.), *Essays, moral, political, and literary* (rev. ed., pp. 577–589). Liberty Classics. (Original work published 1757).

International Association for Suicide Prevention. (2022). *Language guidelines*. https://www.iasp.info/languageguidelines/

Isometsä, E. T. (2001). Psychological autopsy studies—A review. *European Psychiatry, 16*(7), 379–385.

Jobes, D. A. (2006). *Managing suicidal risk: A collaborative approach*. Guilford Press.

Jobes, D. A. (2023). *Managing suicidal risk: A collaborative approach* (3rd ed.). Guilford Press.

Joiner, T. (2005). *Why people die by suicide*. Harvard University Press.

Joiner, T. E., Pettit, J. W., Walker, R. L., Voelz, Z. R., Cruz, J., Rudd, M. D., & Lester, D. (2002). Perceived burdensomeness and suicidality: Two studies on the suicide notes of those attempting and those completing suicide. *Journal of Social and Clinical Psychology, 21*(5), 531–545. https://doi.org/10.1521/jscp.21.5.531.22624

Joiner, T. E., Van Orden, K. A., Witte, T. K., Selby, E. A., Ribeiro, J. D., Lewis, R., & Rudd, M. D. (2009). Main predictions of the interpersonal–

psychological theory of suicidal behavior: Empirical tests in two samples of young adults. *Journal of Abnormal Psychology, 118*(3), 634–646. https://doi.org/10.1037/a0016500

Jordan, J. R., & McIntosh, J. L. (2001). Is suicide bereavement different? A reassessment of the literature. In J. R. Jordan & J. L. McIntosh (Eds.), *Grief after suicide: Understanding the consequences and caring for the survivors* (pp. 3–17). Routledge.

Karsen, E., Cohen, L. J., White, B., De Goncearenco, I., Goncearenco, A., Galynker, I. I., & Miller, F. E. (2023). Impact of the abbreviated Suicide Crisis Syndrome Checklist on clinical decision making in the emergency department. *The Journal of Clinical Psychiatry, 84*(3), 22m14655. https://doi.org/10.4088/JCP.22m14655

Kessler, R. C., Borges, G., & Walters, E. E. (1999). Prevalence of and risk factors for lifetime suicide attempts in the National Comorbidity Survey. *Archives of General Psychiatry, 56*(7), 617–626.

King, C. A., & Merchant, C. R. (2008). Social and interpersonal factors relating to adolescent suicidality: A review of the literature. *Archives of Suicide Research, 12*(3), 181–196.

Kingsbury, M., Hammond, N., Colman, I., & Bulloch, A. (2022). Suicidality among sexual minority and transgender adolescents: A nationally representative population-based study of youth in Canada. *CMAJ, 194*(22), E767–E774. https://doi.org/10.1503/cmaj.212054

Kjølseth, I., Ekeberg, Ø., & Steihaug, S. (2010). Why suicide? Elderly people who committed suicide and their experience of life in the period before their death. *International Psychogeriatrics, 22*(2), 209–218.

Kleiman, E. M., & Liu, R. T. (2013). Social support as a protective factor in suicide: Findings from two nationally representative samples. *Journal of Affective Disorders, 150*(2), 540–545. https://doi.org/10.1016/j.jad.2013.01.033

Klein, M. (1940). Mourning and its relation to manic-depressive states. *International Journal of Psychoanalysis, 21*, 125–153.

Klonsky, E. D., & May, A. M. (2015). The three-step theory of suicide. *International Journal of Cognitive Therapy, 8*(2), 114–129.

Knipe, D., Gunnell, D., & Eddleston, M. (2017). Preventing deaths from pesticide self poisoning—learning from Sri Lanka's success. *Lancet Global Health, 5*(7), e651–e652. https://doi.org/10.1016/S2214-109X(17)30208-5

Knipe, D. W., Gunnell, D., Eddleston, M., Farmer, R., Konradsen, F., & Metcalfe, C. (2017). Association of pesticide regulation with suicide in Sri Lanka. *The Lancet Global Health, 5*(7), e651–e662.

Knox, K. L., Conwell, Y., & Caine, E. D. (2004). If suicide is a public health problem, what are we doing to prevent it? *American Journal of Public Health, 94*(1), 37–45. https://doi.org/10.2105/AJPH.94.1.37

Kposowa, A. J. (2000). Marital status and suicide in the National Longitudinal Mortality Study. *Journal of Epidemiology & Community Health, 54*(4), 254–261.

Kral, M. J. (2016). Suicide and suicide prevention among Inuit in Canada. *Canadian Journal of Psychiatry. Revue canadienne de psychiatrie, 61*(11), 688–695. https://doi.org/10.1177/0706743716661329

Kreitman N. (1976). The coal gas story. United Kingdom suicide rates, 1960-71. *British Journal of Preventive & Social Medicine, 30*(2), 86–93. https://doi.org/10.1136/jech.30.2.86

Kübler-Ross, E. (2008). *On life after death* (Rev. ed.). Celestial Arts. https://www.penguinrandomhouse.com/books/88306/on-life-after-death-by-elisabeth-kubler-ross/

Large, M., Kaneson, M., Myles, N., Myles, H., Gunaratne, P., & Ryan, C. (2016). Meta-analysis of longitudinal cohort studies of suicide risk assessment among psychiatric patients: Heterogeneity in results and lack of improvement over time. *PLoS One, 11*(6), e0156322. https://doi.org/10.1371/journal.pone.0156322

Large, M. M., Ryan, C. J., Carter, G., & Kapur, N. (2017). Can we usefully stratify patients according to suicide risk? *BMJ, 359*, j4627. https://doi.org/10.1136/bmj.j4627

Lawrence, R. E., Oquendo, M. A., & Stanley, B. (2015). Religion and suicide risk: A systematic review. *Archives of Suicide Research, 20*(1), 1–21. https://doi.org/10.1080/13811118.2015.1004494

Leenaars, A. A. (2017). *The psychological autopsy: A roadmap for uncovering the barren bones of the suicide's mind.* Routledge. https://doi.org/10.4324/9781315266213

Leenaars, A. A. (1988). *Suicide notes: Predictive clues and patterns.* Human Sciences Press.

Lester D. (1997). The role of shame in suicide. *Suicide & Life-Threatening Behavior, 27*(4), 352–361.

Linehan, M. M., Korslund, K. E., Harned, M. S., Gallop, R. J., Lungu, A., Neacsiu, A. D., McDavid, J., Comtois, K. A., & Murray-Gregory, A. M. (2015). Dialectical behavior therapy for high suicide risk in individuals with borderline personality disorder: A randomized clinical trial and component analysis. *JAMA Psychiatry, 72*(5), 475–482. https://doi.org/10.1001/jamapsychiatry.2014.3039

Litman, R. E., Curphey, T. J., Shneidman, E. S., Farberow, N. L., & Tabachnick, N. D. (1963). Investigations of equivocal suicides. *JAMA, 184*(12), 924–929. https://doi.org/10.1001/jama.1963.03700250060008

Liu, L., Capaldi, C. A., Orpana, H. M., Kaplan, M. S., & Tonmyr, L. (2021). Changes over time in means of suicide in Canada: An analysis of mortality data from 1981 to 2018. *CMAJ, 193*(10), E331–E338. https://doi.org/10.1503/cmaj.202378

Losey, B. (2011). *Bullying, suicide, and homicide: Understanding, assessment, and prevention*. Routledge.

Louzon, S. A., Bossarte, R., McCarthy, J. F., & Katz, I. R. (2016). Does suicidal ideation as measured by the PHQ-9 predict suicide among VA patients? *Psychiatric Services, 67*(5), 517–522. https://doi.org/10.1176/appi.ps.201500149

Martin, G., Bergen, H. A., Richardson, A. S., Roeger, L., & Allison, S. (2004). Sexual abuse and suicidality: Gender differences in a large community sample of adolescents. *Child Abuse & Neglect, 28*(5), 491–503. https://doi.org/10.1016/j.chiabu.2003.08.006

Mani, L. (1998). *Contentious traditions: The debate on sati in colonial India*. University of California Press.

Mann, J. J., Apter, A., Bertolote, J., Beautrais, A., Currier, D., Haas, A., Hegerl, U., Lönnqvist, J., Malone, K., Marusic, A., Mehlum, L., Patton, G., Phillips, M., Rutz, W., Rihmer, Z., Schmidtke, A., Shaffer, D., Silverman, M., Takahashi, Y., Värnik, A., … Hendin, H. (2005). Suicide prevention strategies: A systematic review. *JAMA, 294*(16), 2064–2074. https://doi.org/10.1001/jama.294.16.2064

Maris, R. W., Berman, A. L., & Silverman, M. M. (2000). *Comprehensive textbook of suicidology*. Guilford Press.

Marshal, M. P., Dietz, L. J., Friedman, M. S., Stall, R., Smith, H. A., McGinley, J., Thoma, B. C., Murray, P. J., D'Augelli, A. R., & Brent, D. A. (2011). Suicidality and depression disparities between sexual minority and heterosexual youth: A meta-analytic review. *The Journal of Adolescent Health: Official Publication of the Society for Adolescent Medicine, 49*(2), 115–123. https://doi.org/10.1016/j.jadohealth.2011.02.005

McIntire, M. S., & Angle, C. R. (1980). *Suicide attempts in children and youth*. HarperCollins.

McKean, A. J. S., Pabbati, C. P., Geske, J. R., & Bostwick, J. M. (2018). Rethinking lethality in youth suicide attempts: First suicide attempt outcomes in youth ages 10 to 24. *Journal of the American Academy of Child & Adolescent Psychiatry, 57*(10), 786–791. https://doi.org/10.1016/j.jaac.2018.04.021

McLaughlin, J., O'Carroll, R. E., & O'Connor, R. C. (2012). Intimate partner abuse and suicidality: A systematic review. *Clinical Psychology Review, 32*(8), 677–689.

McMenamy, J. M., Jordan, J. R., & Mitchell, A. M. (2008). What do suicide survivors tell us they need? Results of a pilot study. *Suicide and Life-Threatening Behavior, 38*(4), 375–389.

Melzer, L., Forkmann, T., & Teismann, T. (2024). Suicide crisis syndrome: A systematic review. *Suicide and Life-Threatening Behavior, 54*(3), 494–507. https://doi.org/10.1111/sltb.13065

Menninger, K. (1938). *Man against himself.* Harcourt, Brace.

Menon, V., Balasubramanian, I., Rogers, M. L., Grover, S., Lakdawala, B., Ranjan, R., Sarkhel, S., Nebhinani, N., Kallivayalil, R. A., Raghavan, V., Mishra, K. K., Aneja, J., Abhivant, N., Deep, R., Singh, L. K., De Sousa, A., Nongpiur, A., Subramanyam, A. A., Mohapatra, D., Kar, S. K., ... Praharaj, S. K. (2024). Factor structure, reliability, and validity of the revised Suicide Crisis Inventory in major depression: A multicentric Indian study. *Journal of Affective Disorders, 345*, 226–233. https://doi.org/10.1016/j.jad.2023.10.102

Mental Health Commission of Canada. (2018). *Research on suicide and its prevention: What the current evidence reveals and topics for future research.* https://mentalhealthcommission.ca/resource/research-on-suicide-and-its-prevention-what-the-current-evidence-reveals-and-topics-for-future-research/

Meyer, C. L. (2017). *Explaining suicide: Patterns, motivations, and what notes reveal.* Elsevier Academic Press.

Meyer, I. H. (2003). Prejudice, social stress, and mental health. *Psychological Bulletin, 129*(5), 674–697.

Miller, A. B., Esposito-Smythers, C., Weismoore, J. T., & Renshaw, K. D. (2013). The relation between child maltreatment and adolescent suicidal behavior: A systematic review and critical examination of the literature. *Clinical Child and Family Psychology Review, 16*(2), 146–172. https://doi.org/10.1007/s10567-013-0131-5

Miller, D. N. (2011). *Child and adolescent suicidal behavior: School-based prevention, assessment, and intervention.* Guilford Press.

Mina, E. E. S., & Gallop, R. M. (1998). Childhood sexual and physical abuse and adult self-harm and suicidal behaviour: A literature review. *The Canadian Journal of Psychiatry, 43*(8), 793–800. https://doi.org/10.1177/070674379804300803

Minois, G. (1999). *History of suicide: Voluntary death in Western culture* (L. G. Cochrane, Trans.). Johns Hopkins University Press.

Mitchell, A. M., Kim, Y., Prigerson, H. G., & Mortimer-Stephens, M. K. (2004). Complicated grief in survivors of suicide. *Crisis, 25*(1), 12–18.

Morrison, R., & O'Connor, R. C. (2008). A systematic review of the relationship between rumination and suicidality. *Suicide and Life-Threatening Behavior, 38*(5), 523–538. https://doi.org/10.1521/suli.2008.38.5.523

Motto, J. A., & Bostrom, A. G. (2001). A randomized controlled trial of postcrisis suicide prevention. *Psychiatric Services, 52*(6), 828–833. https://doi.org/10.1176/appi.ps.52.6.828

National Institute of Mental Health. (2017). *Ask Suicide-Screening Questions (ASQ) toolkit*. U.S. Department of Health and Human Services.

Neeleman J. (1996). Suicide as a crime in the UK: Legal history, international comparisons and present implications. *Acta Psychiatrica Scandinavica, 94*(4), 252–257. https://doi.org/10.1111/j.1600-0447.1996.tb09857.x

Neimeyer, R. A., Maltsberger, J. t., & Leenaars, A. A. (2013). *Treatment of suicidal people*. Taylor & Francis.

Niederkrotenthaler, T., Voracek, M., Herberth, A., Till, B., Strauss, M., Etzersdorfer, E., Eisenwort, B., & Sonneck, G. (2010). Role of media reports in completed and prevented suicide. *The British Journal of Psychiatry, 197*(3), 234–243.

Niehaus, I. (2001). *Witchcraft, power and politics: Exploring the occult in the South African Lowveld*. Pluto Press.

Nishimura, A., Shioiri, T., Nushida, H., Ueno, Y., Ushiyama, I., Tanegashima, A., Someya, T., & Nishi, K. (1999). Changes in choice of method and lethality between last attempted and completed suicides: How did suicide attempters carry out their desire? *Legal Medicine, 1*(3), 150–158. https://doi.org/10.1016/S1344-6223(99)80028-5

Nock, M. K. (2009). Why do people hurt themselves? New insights into the nature and functions of self-injury. *Current Directions in Psychological Science, 18*(2), 78–83. https://doi.org/10.1111/j.1467-8721.2009.01613.x

Nock, M. K., & Banaji, M. R. (2007). Assessment of self-injurious thoughts using a behavioral test. American Journal of Psychiatry, 164(5), 820–823. https://doi.org/10.1176/ajp.2007.164.5.820

Nock, M. K., Borges, G., Bromet, E. J., Alonso, J., Angermeyer, M., Beautrais, A., … Williams, D. R. (2008). Cross-national prevalence and risk factors for suicidal ideation, plans and attempts. *The British Journal of Psychiatry, 192*(2), 98–105. https://doi.org/10.1192/bjp.bp.107.040113

Nock, M. K., Hwang, I., Sampson, N. A., & Kessler, R. C. (2010). Mental disorders, comorbidity, and suicidal behavior: Results from the National Comorbidity Survey Replication. *Molecular Psychiatry, 15*(8), 868–876.

Nordentoft, M. (2011). Crucial elements in suicide prevention strategies. *Progress in Neuro-Psychopharmacology & Biological Psychiatry, 35*(4), 848–853. https://doi.org/10.1016/j.pnpbp.2010.11.038

O'Carroll, P. W., Berman, A. L., Maris, R. W., Moscicki, E., Tanney, B., & Silverman, M. M. (1996). Beyond the Tower of Babel: A nomenclature for suicidology. *Suicide and Life-Threatening Behavior, 26*(3), 237–252. https://doi.org/10.1111/j.1943-278X.1996.tb00609.x

O'Connor, R. C., Armitage, C. J., & Gray, L. (2006). The role of clinical and social cognitive variables in parasuicide. *The British Journal of Clinical Psychology, 45*(4), 465–481. https://doi.org/10.1348/014466505X82315

O'Connor, R. C., & Kirtley, O. J. (2010). The integrated motivational–volitional model of suicidal behaviour. *Philosophical Transactions of the Royal Society B, 373*(1754), 20170268.

O'Connor, R. C., & Pirkis, J. (2016). *The international handbook of suicide prevention* (2nd ed.). Wiley Blackwell.

Wenzel, A., Brown, G. K., & Beck, A. T. (2009). Cognitive therapy for suicidal patients: Scientific and clinical applications. *American Psychological Association*. https://doi.org/10.1037/11862-000

Öhman, A., & Mineka, S. (2001). Fears, phobias, and preparedness: Toward an evolved module of fear and fear learning. *Psychological Review, 108*(3), 483–522. https://doi.org/10.1037/0033-295X.108.3.483

Oliffe, J. L., Han, C. S., Ogrodniczuk, J. S., Phillips, J. C., & Roy, P. (2011). Suicide from the perspectives of older men who experience depression: A gender analysis. *American Journal of Men's Health, 5*(5), 444–454. https://doi.org/10.1177/1557988311408410

Orbach, I., Mikulincer, M., Sirota, P., & Gilboa-Schechtman, E. (2003). Mental pain and suicide. *Suicide and Life-Threatening Behavior, 33*(3), 231–241.

Owens, D., Horrocks, J., & House, A. (2002). Fatal and non-fatal repetition of self-harm: Systematic review. *British Journal of Psychiatry, 181*(3), 193–199. https://doi.org/10.1192/bjp.181.3.193

Owens, D., Wood, C., Greenwood, D. C., Hughes, T., & Dennis, M. (2005). Mortality and suicide after non-fatal self-poisoning: 16-year outcome study. *The British Journal of Psychiatry: The Journal of Mental Science, 187*, 470–475. https://doi.org/10.1192/bjp.187.5.470

Ozawa-de Silva, C. (2008). Too lonely to die alone: Internet suicide pacts and existential suffering in Japan. *Culture, Medicine and Psychiatry, 32*(4), 516–551. https://doi.org/10.1007/s11013-008-9108-0

Phillips, D. P. (1974). The influence of suggestion on suicide. *American Sociological Review, 39*(3), 340–354.

Phillips, D. P., & Wills, J. S. (1987). A drop in suicides around major national holidays. *Suicide and Life-Threatening Behavior, 17*(1), 1–12. https://doi.org/10.1111/j.1943-278X.1987.tb00057.x

Pirkis, J., Too, L. S., Spittal, M. J., Krysinska, K., Robinson, J., & Cheung, Y. T. D. (2015). Interventions to reduce suicides at locations. *The Lancet Psychiatry, 2*(11), 994–1001.

Pitman, A. L., Osborn, D. P., King, M. B., & Erlangsen, A. (2014). Effects of suicide bereavement on mental health and suicide risk. *The Lancet Psychiatry, 1*(1), 86–94.

Pompili, M., Girardi, P., Ruberto, A., Kotzalidis, G. D., & Tatarelli, R. (2005). Emergency staff reactions to suicidal and self-harming patients. *European Journal of Emergency Medicine, 12*(4), 169–178.

Posner, K., Brown, G. K., Stanley, B., et al. (2011). The Columbia–Suicide Severity Rating Scale (C-SSRS): Initial validity and internal consistency findings. *American Journal of Psychiatry, 168*(12), 1266–1277. https://doi.org/10.1176/appi.ajp.2011.10111704

Pouliot, L., & De Leo, D. (2006). Critical issues in psychological autopsy studies. *Suicide and Life-Threatening Behavior, 36*(5), 491–510.

Price, J., Sloman, L., Gardner, R., Gilbert, P., & Rohde, P. (1994). The social competition hypothesis of depression. *The British Journal of Psychiatry, 164*(3), 309–315. https://doi.org/10.1192/bjp.164.3.309

Province of Nova Scotia. (2022, May 25). *Preventing and reducing the risk of suicide.* https://novascotia.ca/preventing-and-reducing-the-risk-of-suicide/

Public Health Agency of Canada. (2019). *Suicide in Canada: Key statistics (infographic).* https://www.canada.ca/en/public-health/services/publications/healthy-living/suicide-canada-key-statistics-infographic.html

Public Health Agency of Canada. (2022). *Suicide-related behaviours: Help is available.* https://www.canada.ca/en/public-health/services/suicide-prevention.html

Qin, P., Agerbo, E., & Mortensen, P. B. (2003). Suicide risk in relation to socioeconomic, demographic, psychiatric, and familial factors: A national register-based study of all suicides in Denmark, 1981–1997. *American Journal of Psychiatry, 160*(4), 765–772.

Qin, P., & Nordentoft, M. (2005). Suicide risk in relation to psychiatric hospitalization: Evidence based on longitudinal registers. *Archives of General Psychiatry, 62*(4), 427–432.

Rankin, A. (2011). *Seppuku: A history of samurai suicide.* Kodansha.

Rasmussen, K. A., Slish, M. L., Wingate, L. R., Davidson, C. L., & Grant, D. M. (2012). Can perceived burdensomeness explain the relationship between suicide and perfectionism? *Suicide and Life-Threatening Behavior, 42*(2), 121–128. https://doi.org/10.1111/j.1943-278X.2011.00074.x

Rossom, R. C., Coleman, K. J., Ahmedani, B. K., Beck, A., Johnson, E., Oliver, M., Simon, G. E., & Lu, C. Y. (2017). Suicidal ideation reported on the PHQ-9 and risk of suicidal behavior across age groups. *Journal of Affective Disorders, 215*, 77–84. https://doi.org/10.1016/j.jad.2017.03.037

Rudd, M. D. (2006). Fluid vulnerability theory: A cognitive approach to understanding the process of acute and chronic suicide risk. In T. E. Ellis (Ed.), *Cognition and suicide: Theory, research, and therapy* (pp. 355–368). American Psychological Association. https://doi.org/10.1037/11377-016

Runeson, B., Tidemalm, D., Dahlin, M., Lichtenstein, P., & Långström, N. (2010). Method of attempted suicide as predictor of subsequent successful suicide: National long term cohort study. *BMJ, 341*, c3222. https://doi.org/10.1136/bmj.c3222

Rutz, W., & Rihmer, Z. (2007). Suicidality in men—Practical issues, challenges, solutions. *Journal of Men's Health & Gender, 4*(4), 393–401.

Sakinofsky, I. (2014). Preventing suicide among inpatients. *Canadian Journal of Psychiatry, 59*(3), 131–140.

Salvi, V. (2019). The role of risk assessment in suicide prevention. *BJPsych Advances, 25*(1), 25–32. https://doi.org/10.1192/bja.2018.31

Samaritans. (2020). *Media guidelines for reporting suicide.* https://media.samaritans.org/documents/Media_Guidelines_FINAL_v2_TABa8C6.pdf

Sarchiapone, M., Mandelli, L., Iosue, M., Andrisano, C., & Roy, A. (2011). Controlling access to suicide means. *International Journal of Environmental Research and Public Health, 8*(12), 4550–4562. https://doi.org/10.3390/ijerph8124550

Schaffer, A., Sinyor, M., Kurdyak, P., Vigod, S., Sareen, J., Reis, C., Green, D., Bolton, J., Rhodes, A., Grigoriadis, S., Cairney, J., Cheung, A. (2016). Population-based analysis of health care contacts among suicide decedents: Identifying opportunities for more targeted suicide prevention strategies. *World Psychiatry, 15*(2), 135–145. https://doi.org/10.1002/wps.20321

Schotte, D. E., & Clum, G. A. (1987). Problem-solving skills in suicidal psychiatric patients. *Journal of Consulting and Clinical Psychology, 55*(1), 49–54. https://doi.org/10.1037/0022-006X.55.1.49

Schrijvers, D. L., Bollen, J., & Sabbe, B. G. (2012). The gender paradox in suicidal behavior and its impact on the suicidal process. *Journal of Affective Disorders, 138*(1–2), 19–26.

Shaffer, D., & Craft, L. (1999). Methods of adolescent suicide prevention. *Journal of Clinical Psychiatry, 60*(Suppl 2), 70–74.

Shah, A., Bhat, R., Zarate-Escudero, S., De Leo, D., & Erlangsen, A. (2016). Suicide rates in five-year age-bands after the age of 60 years: The international landscape. *Aging & Mental Health, 20*(2), 131–138.

Shneidman, E. S. (1974). *Deaths of man.* Quadrangle/The New York Times Book Co. https://catalog.hathitrust.org/Record/000221516

Shneidman, E. S. (1985). *Definition of suicide.* Wiley.

Shneidman, E. S. (1993). Suicide as psychache. *Journal of Nervous and Mental Disease, 181*(3), 145–147. https://doi.org/10.1097/00005053-199303000-00001

Shneidman, E. S. (1997). The suicidal mind. In R. W. Maris, M. M. Silverman, & S. S. Canetto (Eds.), *Review of suicidology*, 1997 (pp. 22–41). Guilford Press. (Adapted from Shneidman, 1996, Oxford University Press).

Shneidman, E. S. (2008). *A commonsense book of death: Reflections at ninety.* Rowman & Littlefield. https://rowman.com/ISBN/9780742563315/A-Commonsense-Book-of-Death-Reflections-at-Ninety

Silverman, M. M., Berman, A. L., Sanddal, N. D, O'Carroll, P. W., & Joiner, T. E. (2007a). Rebuilding the Tower of Babel—Part 1: Background, rationale, and methodology. *Suicide and Life-Threatening Behavior, 37*(3), 248–263. https://doi.org/10.1521/suli.2007.37.3.248

Silverman, M. M., Berman, A. L., Sanddal, N. D., O'Carroll, P. W., & Joiner, T. E. (2007b). Rebuilding the Tower of Babel—Part 2: Suicide-related ideations, communications, and behaviors. *Suicide and Life-Threatening Behavior, 37*(3), 264–277. https://doi.org/10.1521/suli.2007.37.3.264

Simon, G. E., Rutter, C. M., Peterson, D., Oliver, M., Whiteside, U., Operskalski, B., & Ludman, E. J. (2013). Does response on the PHQ-9 Depression Questionnaire predict subsequent suicide attempt or suicide death? *Psychiatric Services (Washington, D.C.), 64*(12), 1195–1202. https://doi.org/10.1176/appi.ps.201200587

Smith, P. N., & Cukrowicz, K. C. (2010). Capable of suicide: A functional model of the acquired capability component of the interpersonal-psychological theory of suicide. *Suicide and Life-Threatening Behavior, 40*(3), 266–275. https://doi.org/10.1521/suli.2010.40.3.266

Solomon, R. L., & Corbit, J. D. (1973). An opponent-process theory of motivation. II. Cigarette addiction. *Journal of Abnormal Psychology, 81*(2), 158–171. https://doi.org/10.1037/h0034534

Soper, C. A. (2021). *The evolution of life worth living: Why we choose to live.* C. A. Soper. (Publisher page) https://www.malaprops.com/book/9781838343903 (eBook) https://www.barnesandnoble.com/w/the-evolution-of-life-worth-living-c-a-soper/1138692571

Soulié, T., Bell, E., Jenkin, G., Sim, D., & Collings, S. (2018). Systematic exploration of countertransference phenomena in the treatment of patients at risk for suicide. *Archives of Suicide Research, 24*(1), 96–118. https://doi.org/10.1080/13811118.2018.1506844

Spallek, J., Reeske, A., Norredam, M., & Razum, O. (2015). Suicide among immigrants in Europe. *European Journal of Public Health, 25*(1), 63–71.

Stack, S. (2000). Suicide: A 15-year review of the sociological literature. Part II: Modernization and social integration perspectives. *Suicide and Life-Threatening Behavior, 30*(2), 163–176.

Stanley, B., & Brown, G. K. (2012). Safety planning intervention. *Cognitive and Behavioral Practice, 19*(2), 256–264.

Staudacher, C. (1994). *A time to grieve: Meditations for healing after the death of a loved one.* HarperOne. https://www.harpercollins.com/products/a-time-to-grieve-carol-staudacher

Steeg, S., Quinlivan, L., Nowland, R., Carroll, R., Casey, D., Clements, C., Cooper, J., Davies, L., Knipe, D., Ness, J., O'Connor, R. C., Hawton, K., Gunnell, D., & Kapur, N. (2018). Accuracy of risk scales for predicting repeat self-harm and suicide: A multicentre, population-level cohort study using routine clinical data. *BMC Psychiatry, 18*, 113. https://doi.org/10.1186/s12888-018-1693-z

Stillion, J. M., & McDowell, E. E. (1996). *Suicide across the life span: Premature exits* (2nd ed.). Taylor & Francis. https://doi.org/10.4324/9781315783536

Stone, D. M., Holland, K. M., Bartholow, B., Logan, J. E., LiKamWa McIntosh, W., Trudeau, A., & Crosby, A. E. (2017a). *Preventing suicide: A technical package of policies, programs, and practices.* National Center for Injury Prevention and Control, CDC. https://stacks.cdc.gov/view/cdc/44283

Stone, D. M., Holland, K. M., Bartholow, B., Logan, J. E., LiKamWa McIntosh, W., Trudeau, A., & Rockett, I. R. H. (2017b). Deciphering suicide and other manners of death associated with drug intoxication: A Centers for Disease Control and Prevention Consultation meeting summary. *American Journal of Public Health, 107*(8), 1233–1239. https://doi.org/10.2105/AJPH.2017.303863

Sudak, H. S., & Sudak, D. M. (2005). The media and suicide. *Academic Psychiatry, 29*(5), 495–499.

Suicide Prevention Resource Center. (2023). *A comprehensive approach to suicide prevention.* https://sprc.org/a-comprehensive-approach-to-suicide-prevention/

Sveen, C. A., & Walby, F. A. (2008). Suicide survivors' mental health and grief reactions: A systematic review of controlled studies. *Suicide and Life-Threatening Behavior, 38*(1), 13–29.

Tal, I. B., Mauro, C., Reynolds, C. F., & Shear, M. K. (2017). Complicated grief after suicide bereavement and other losses. *American Journal of Geriatric Psychiatry, 25*(4), 433–442.

Tal Young, I., Iglewicz, A., Glorioso, D., Lanouette, N., Seay, K., Ilapakurti, M., & Zisook, S. (2012). Suicide bereavement and complicated grief. *Dialogues in Clinical Neuroscience, 14*(2), 177–186.

Taylor, P. J., Gooding, P., Wood, A. M., & Tarrier, N. (2011). The role of defeat and entrapment in depression, anxiety, and suicide. *Psychological Bulletin, 137*(3), 391–420. https://doi.org/10.1037/a0022935

Treadway, M. T., & Zald, D. H. (2011). Reconsidering anhedonia in depression: Lessons from translational neuroscience. *Neuroscience & Biobehavioral Reviews, 35*(3), 537–555. https://doi.org/10.1016/j.neubiorev.2010.06.006

Tsai, A. C., Lucas, M., & Kawachi, I. (2015). Association between social integration and suicide among women in the United States. *JAMA Psychiatry, 72*(10), 987–993. https://doi.org/10.1001/jamapsychiatry.2015.1002

Turecki, G., & Brent, D. A. (2016). Suicide and suicidal behaviour. *The Lancet, 387*(10024), 1227–1239. https://doi.org/10.1016/S0140-6736(15)00234-2

van Hooff, A. J. L. (2002). *From autothanasia to suicide: Self-killing in classical antiquity.* Routledge. (Original work published 1990). https://doi.org/10.4324/9780203032930

Van Orden, K. A., Witte, T. K., Cukrowicz, K. C., Braithwaite, S. R., Selby, E. A., & Joiner, T. E., Jr. (2010). The interpersonal theory of suicide. *Psychological Review, 117*(2), 575–600. https://doi.org/10.1037/a0018697

Van Os, J., & Kapur, S. (2009). Schizophrenia. *The Lancet, 374*(9690), 635–645. https://doi.org/10.1016/S0140-6736(09)60995-8

Värnik, P. (2012). Suicide in the world. *International Journal of Environmental Research and Public Health, 9*(3), 760–771.

Vijayakumar, L. (2005). Suicide and mental disorders in Asia. *International Review of Psychiatry, 17*(2), 109–114.

Wasserman, D., Cheng, Q., & Jiang, G. X. (2005). Global suicide rates among young people aged 15–19. *World Psychiatry, 4*(2), 114–120.

Wenzel, A., & Beck, A. T. (2008). A cognitive model of suicidal behavior: Theory and treatment. *Applied and Preventive Psychology, 12*(4), 189–201. https://doi.org/10.1016/j.appsy.2008.05.001

Williams, J. M. G. (2014). *Cry of pain: Understanding suicide and the suicidal mind.* Piatkus.

Williams, J. M. G. (1997). *Cry of pain: Understanding suicide and self-harm.* Penguin.

Williams, J. M. G., & Pollock, L. R. (2000). The psychology of suicidal behaviour. In K. Hawton & K. van Heeringen (Eds.), *The international handbook of suicide and attempted suicide* (pp. 79–93). Wiley. https://doi.org/10.1002/9780470698976.ch5

Wilson, A., & Clark, S. (2004). *South Australian suicide postvention project: Report.* Government of South Australia.

Witte, T. K., Merrill, K. A., Stellrecht, N. E., Bernert, R. A., Hollar, D. L., Schatschneider, C., & Joiner, T. E. (2008). "Impulsive" youth suicide attempters are not necessarily all that impulsive. *Journal of Affective Disorders, 107*(1–3), 107–116. https://doi.org/10.1016/j.jad.2007.08.010

Wong, M. M., Brower, K. J., & Zucker, R. A. (2011). Sleep problems, suicidal ideation, and self-harm behaviors in adolescence. *Journal of Psychiatric Research, 45*(4), 505–511. https://doi.org/10.1016/j.jpsychires.2010.09.005

Worden, J. W. (2009). *Grief counseling and grief therapy: A handbook for the mental health practitioner* (4th ed.). Springer Publishing.

World Health Organization. (2014). *Preventing suicide: A global imperative.* WHO Press. https://apps.who.int/iris/handle/10665/131056

World Health Organization. (2019). *International classification of diseases* (11th rev.). https://icd.who.int/

World Health Organization. (2021). *Suicide worldwide in 2019: Global health* estimates. https://www.who.int/publications/i/item/9789240026643

World Health Organization. (2025). *Suicide: Key facts.* https://www.who.int/news-room/fact-sheets/detail/suicide

Wrosch, C., Scheier, M. F., Miller, G. E., Schulz, R., & Carver, C. S. (2003). Adaptive self-regulation of unattainable goals: Goal disengagement, goal reengagement, and subjective well-being. *Personality and Social Psychology Bulletin, 29*(12), 1494–1508. https://doi.org/10.1177/0146167203256921

Wyman, P. A., Brown, C. H., LoMurray, M., Schmeelk-Cone, K., Petrova, M., Yu, Q., Walsh, E., Tu, X., & Wang, W. (2010). An outcome evaluation of the sources of strength suicide prevention program delivered by adolescent peer leaders in high schools. *American Journal of Public Health, 100*(9), 1653–1661. https://doi.org/10.2105/AJPH.2009.190025

Yaseen, Z. S., Chartrand, H., Mojtabai, R., Bolton, J., & Galynker, I. I. (2013). Fear of dying in panic attacks predicts suicide attempt in comorbid depressive illness: Prospective evidence from the National Epidemiological Survey on alcohol and related conditions. *Depression and Anxiety, 30*(10), 930–939. https://doi.org/10.1002/da.22039

Yaseen, Z. S., Galynker, I. I., Cohen, L. J., & Briggs, J. (2017). Clinicians' conflicting emotional responses to high suicide-risk patients—Association with short-term suicide behaviors: A prospective pilot study. *Comprehensive Psychiatry, 76*, 69–78. https://doi.org/10.1016/j.comppsych.2017.03.013

Yaseen, Z. S., Katz, C., Johnson, M. S., Eisenberg, D., Cohen, L. J., & Galynker, I. (2010). Construct development: The Suicide Trigger Scale (STS-2), a measure of a hypothesized suicide trigger state. *BMC Psychiatry, 10*, 110. https://doi.org/10.1186/1471-244X-10-110

Yaseen, Z. S., Kopeykina, I., Gutkovich, Z., Bassirnia, A., Cohen, L. J., & Galynker, I. I. (2014). Predictive validity of the Suicide Trigger Scale (STS-3) for post-discharge suicide attempt in high-risk psychiatric inpatients. *PLOS ONE, 9*(1), e86768. https://doi.org/10.1371/journal.pone.0086768

Yaseen, Z. S., Kopeykina, I., Farooqui, A. N., Fisher, R., Lehmann, M., & Galynker, I. (2012). Fear of dying in panic attacks predicts suicide attempt in comorbid depressive illness: Prospective evidence from the National Epidemiologic Survey on alcohol and related conditions. *Depression and Anxiety, 29*(11), 1021–1030. https://doi.org/10.1002/da.22039

Yip, P. S. F., Liu, K. Y., Lam, T. H., Stewart, S. M., Chen, E. Y. H., Fan, S., & Law, Y. W. (2004). Suicidality among high school students in Hong Kong, SAR. *Suicide and Life-Threatening Behavior, 35*(4), 491–502.

Zalsman, G., Hawton, K., Wasserman, D., van Heeringen, K., Arensman, E., Sarchiapone, M., … Zohar, J. (2016). Suicide prevention strategies revisited: 10-year systematic review. *The Lancet Psychiatry, 3*(7), 646–659. https://doi.org/10.1016/S2215-0366(16)30030-X

Zylstra R. G. (2002). Treating suicidal behavior: An effective, time-limited approach. *Primary Care Companion to The Journal of Clinical Psychiatry, 4*(6), 251.

GLOBAL SUICIDE PREVENTION AND CRISIS SUPPORT

GLOBAL DIRECTORIES

Resource	*Mission*	*Website*
Find a Helpline	Verified, country-by-country directory connecting people to free, confidential support (phone, text, chat, and WhatsApp).	findahelpline.com
Befrienders Worldwide	Global network of emotional support centers for people in distress.	befrienders.org

GLOBAL LEADERSHIP AND PREVENTION ORGANIZATIONS

Organization	*Mission (succinct)*	*Website*
World Health Organization (WHO)—LIVE LIFE	Supports countries to implement evidence-based suicide prevention as a public health response.	who.int/initiatives/live-life-initiative-for-suicide-prevention
International Association for Suicide Prevention (IASP)	Global collaboration to prevent suicide and suicidal behavior and reduce impacts.	iasp.info

NATIONAL CRISIS LINES

Region/ country	*Service*	*Mission*	*Website*
Canada	9-8-8 Suicide Crisis Helpline (988)	Connects people to trained crisis responders for nonjudgmental support.	988.ca
The United States	988 Suicide & Crisis Lifeline (988)	24/7 crisis support by call, text, or chat for emotional distress.	988lifeline.org
The UK and Ireland	Samaritans (116 123)	Confidential, 24/7 listening support for anyone struggling.	samaritans.org
Europe (varies by country)	Emotional Support Helpline (116 123)	Emotional support line; availability varies by country.	europa.eu/youreurope
Australia	Lifeline (13 11 14)	24/7 crisis support and suicide prevention services.	lifeline.org.au/131114
New Zealand	1737 (call or text 1737)	Free, confidential 24/7 brief support with trained counselors/peers.	1737.org.nz

APPENDIX

The appendix tables that follow operationalize Chapter 8's postvention guidance into practical tools that can be assigned, tracked, and revisited over time. Their intent is to reduce harmful improvisation in the aftermath of a suicide-related death, when emotion, urgency, and rumor can drive decisions faster than reflection. These tables are not meant to function as rigid rules, but as a coordinated response framework that supports safe communication, targeted outreach, careful memorialization, risk-aware follow-up, and clear accountability across roles. Together, they distill this chapter's core ethical commitments: name the death without teaching the method, support grief without glamorizing, and shape postvention responses in ways that protect the most vulnerable.

Table A1.1 functions as a rapid orientation "guardrail" after a suicide or serious attempt, contrasting actions that reliably stabilize people and systems with actions that unintentionally increase risk. Its intent is not to create rigid rules but to reduce harmful improvisation in the first hours and days, when emotion, urgency, and rumor can drive decisions faster than reflection. Read it as a practical distillation of this chapter's core ethics: name the death without teaching the method, support grief without glamorizing, and design communications and memorials to protect the most vulnerable readers.

Table A1.1 Postvention Do's and Don'ts

Domain	*Do*	*Don't*
Initial response	Confirm facts; appoint a response lead and small cross-functional team; map close contacts; start targeted outreach within 24–72 hours.	Rush to announce before facts are confirmed; leave roles ambiguous; let rumor set the agenda.
Communications (all channels)	State plainly that a death by suicide has occurred (once confirmed); keep messages brief, consistent, and aligned across teams.	Provide method/location details; speculate about causes; use euphemisms that breed rumor.
Language	Use "died by suicide"; validate mixed emotions; model non-stigmatizing tone.	Use glamorizing, sensational, or honorific framing tied to the manner of death; assign blame.
Resources in every message	Pair each message with concrete supports available **today** and **this week** (walk-ins, crisis lines, on-site rooms, EAP, contacts).	Announce the death without clear routes to help; bury supports at the bottom or in attachments only.
Social media and memorial pages	Actively moderate (remove method talk, blame, glamorization); pin help resources; assign moderators for 30 days and key anniversaries.	Leave pages unmoderated; allow detailed discussions of method/location; permit "how-to" comments.
Memorialization	Prefer time-limited, person-centered rituals and **living legacies** (scholarships, service projects, access-to-care funds).	Create permanent public honors tied to the death (plaques, jersey retirements "for" the suicide, trophies).

(*Continued*)

Table A1.1 (Continued)

Domain	*Do*	*Don't*
Classrooms/ teams/ workgroups	Offer small, staff-facilitated conversations that normalize grief and highlight help-seeking.	Hold large assemblies centered on biography, speculation, or iconography of the death.
Outreach and follow-up	Proactively contact high-risk groups (intimates, close friends/ teammates/roommates, prior self-harm, recent conflict); use caring contacts.	Wait for people to self-present; rely only on mass emails; stop outreach after the funeral.
Risk management	Provide means safety counseling when relevant; expedite appointments; track and revisit a living "risk map."	Ignore access to lethal means; allow long delays to care; treat risk as a one-time screen.
Timing and anniversaries	Schedule check-ins at ~1, 3, and 12 months; plan communications around birthdays, exams, seasons, and anniversaries.	Assume risk ends after the first week; be surprised by anniversary reactions.
Workplaces/ clinics/ emergency medical services	Run nonpunitive debriefs; offer protected time/EAP; capture system lessons (handoffs, after-hours coverage) and assign owners.	Conduct blame-oriented reviews; memorialize the death permanently at the workplace; skip staff supports.
Schools/ campuses	Provide teacher/resident assistant scripts; offer drop-in rooms; ensure identity-affirming pathways (2SLGBTQ+, international, Indigenous services).	Improvise classroom announcements; overlook subgroups facing barriers to access.

(*Continued*)

Table A1.1 (Continued)

Domain	*Do*	*Don't*
Psychological autopsy (PA)	Use PA to learn and improve prevention; integrate patterns with the person's story; communicate probabilistically.	Treat PA as blame assignment; reduce a life to a single cause; publicize sensitive details.
Equity and culture	Partner with faith/community leaders; ensure language access, transportation/childcare, and culturally safe options.	Apply a one-size-fits-all plan; exclude families from rituals due to punitive traditions.
Leadership and coordination	Operate "incident command for humans": clear roles (family liaison, communications, clinical/risk, documentation), and daily huddles early on.	Allow fragmented messaging; duplicate outreach; leave decisions undocumented.
Media relations	Use a short holding statement; avoid method; highlight help-seeking/recovery; provide a media contact.	Offer interviews that dramatize the death; provide scene details; speculate on motives.

CHECKLISTS—ORGANIZATIONAL/SCHOOL POSTVENTION (REFERENCE TABLES)

The following checklist tables that follow translate this chapter's principles into operational steps that can be assigned, tracked, and revisited over time. Their intent is to support coordination across roles (leadership, clinical/risk, communications, documentation, and community partners) so the response does not depend on memory, individual initiative, or inconsistent messaging. These are modular tools: an organization can use one table in isolation, but together they form a coherent response map that reduces fragmentation, duplication of outreach, and missed follow-up during the aftermath window when risk is elevated and systems are strained.

Table A1.2 outlines clarification of who holds coordination authority and who owns the essential functions of postvention. Its intent is to create a simple "incident command for humans" structure—family liaison, communications lead, clinical/risk lead, documentation lead, moderation lead, and anniversary coordinator—so decisions are consistent, families are protected from conflicting contacts, and the response remains accountable over weeks rather than days. Used well, it turns a collective intention to help into a coordinated plan with named owners and timelines.

Table A1.2 Leadership and Roles (Assign Today)

Item	*Key actions/notes*	*Assigned to*	*Due/status*
Response Lead	Overall coordination; convene team; run daily huddles (first week).		
Family Liaison	Single point of contact; confirm what can be shared publicly.		
Communications Lead	Draft/approve scripts; align internal/external messages; media contact.		
Clinical/Risk Lead	Map risk; arrange care pathways; track outreach/caring contacts.		
Documentation Lead	Decision log; copies of scripts; outreach ledger; version control.		
Memorial Page Moderator(s)	Moderate social + internal platforms; schedule shifts.		
Anniversary Coordinator	Build calendar; schedule check-ins and communications at 1, 3, and 12 months.		

Table A1.3 operationalizes proactive outreach by mapping who to contact, how, and when, emphasizing continuity and reattempted contact rather than passive "reach out if needed" messaging.

Table A1.3 Communication Scripts (Prepare and Use)

Item	*Key actions/notes*	*Assigned to*	*Due/status*
Initial factual notice	Acknowledge suicide once confirmed; **no method/ location**; list supports **today/this week**.		
Supervisor/ teacher script	Two to three sentences for small groups/classrooms; normalize grief; point to help.		
Family/ community letter	Plain language; what to expect; how to access supports.		
Media holding statement	Brief, nonspeculative; route press to media contact; include resources.		
Social post template	Resource-forward; pin moderation rules; link supports.		

Table A1.4 specifies near-term risk containment and care pathways (means safety, walk-ins, after-hours options, identity-affirming supports, escalation thresholds) so access to help is concrete and time-linked.

Table A1.4 Outreach Map (Who, How, when)

Item	*Key actions/notes*	*Assigned to*	*Due/status*
First-degree contacts	Family, intimates, roommates, teammates—assign outreach owner.		
High-risk peers	Prior self-harm, strong identification, recent conflict—assign outreach.		
Owner + due time	Set contact method/ time for each person; log outcomes.		
Same-week appointments	Offer priority slots; document accept/decline.		
Reattempt outreach	If declined/no answer, retry within **72 hours**; record follow-up.		

Table A1.5 focuses on staff supports (nonpunitive debriefing, protected time, employee assistance program (EAP) pathways, confidential outreach) to mitigate moral distress, secondary trauma, and silence in teams.

Table A1.5 Risk List and Care Pathways

Item	*Key actions/notes*	*Assigned to*	*Due/status*
Means safety counseling	Who provides it, when, and how (in-person/virtual).		
Walk-in slots	Publish times/locations/links; keep updated daily (first week).		
After-hours supports	Crisis lines, mobile crisis, 988—prominent in all communications.		
Identity-affirming options	2SLGBTQ+, Indigenous, international students, newcomers.		
Escalation rules	Clear thresholds for emergency services involvement.		

Table A1.6 frames documentation as a protective function (decision logs, script archives, outreach ledgers, evolving risk maps, lessons learned) that supports continuity, accountability, and system learning.

Table A1.6 Staff Supports

Item	*Key actions/notes*	*Assigned to*	*Due/status*
Nonpunitive debrief	Separate learning from blame; schedule within first week.		
EAP/benefits info	Include in all staff messages; easy access links/phones.		
Protected time/flex	Offer schedule adjustments where needed.		
Confidential outreach	Discreet check-ins for staff with known risk/ trauma exposure.		

Table A1.7 addresses moderated memorial spaces, especially online, specifying house rules and staffing to prevent method talk, blame, and glamorization while pinning resources and preserving safety.

Table A1.7 Documentation (Do Not Skip)

Item	*Key actions/notes*	*Assigned to*	*Due/status*
Decision log	Date/time-stamped record of key decisions.		
Script archive	Store all statements/ letters/posts used.		
Outreach ledger	Who contacted, by whom, outcome, next step.		
Risk map versions	Update as disclosures evolve; keep version history.		
Lessons learned	List fixes; assign owners and timelines.		

Table A1.8 builds a forward calendar for predictable vulnerability windows (1-, 3-, and 12-month check-ins, anniversaries, birthdays, exams/seasonal stressors), ensuring postvention is sustained rather than confined to the first week.

Table A1.8 Memorial Page Moderation Plan

Item	*Key actions/notes*	*Assigned to*	*Due/status*
Pin house rules	No method details/blame/ glamorization; resources linked.		
Daily moderation (×30 days)	Schedule moderators; reactivate for anniversaries.		
Archive harmful posts	Save and remove; document actions taken.		
Reporting channel	Provide easy way to flag concerning content.		

Table A1.9 condenses the entire postvention response into a time-sequenced quick start checklist, designed for immediate use under pressure; its intent is to help teams act decisively in the first hours, sustain coordinated follow-up over weeks and months, and ensure that postvention remains prevention-oriented rather than symbolic or reactive.

Table A1.9 Anniversary Calendar

Item	*Key actions/notes*	*Assigned to*	*Due/status*
Preschedule supports	Messages/check-ins at ~1, 3, and 12 months.		
Local meaningful dates	Birthdays, exams, playoffs, and seasonal stressors.		
Reissue help info	Refresh resources and moderation staffing for those windows.		

INDEX

Note: **Bold** page numbers refer to tables and *italic* page numbers refer to figures.

acute stressors 63, 69
acute suicidal states 109–120; access 112; affective disturbance 110; agitation 110–114, 116, 118–120; capability, planning, and access 112; cognitive dyscontrol 111, 116; entrapment 110; hyperarousal 110, 111; immediate response playbook 113–117; insomnia 110–114, 116, 118, 120; pair state-focused assessment 112–117; and social withdrawal 110, 112; Suicide Crisis Syndrome 110, 111, 113, 115–120, *117*
adolescence, of developmental patterns 61
adulthood, of developmental patterns 61–62
adverse childhood experiences (ACEs) 44, 58, 60, 67, 76
affective disturbance, of acute suicidal states 110
agitation 110–114, 116, 118–120
ambivalence 2, 3, 17, 18, 21, 22, 37, 80, 85–88, 104, 111, 126, 127, 134, 161
anniversary reactions 130
Ask Suicide-Screening Questions (ASQ) 50, 53
Attachment-Based Family Therapy (ABFT) 37
attachment disruption 42, 44

Baumeister, R. F. 94, 97–99, 106, 160
Beck, A. T. 26–28
belonging 12, 13, 18–21, 23, 24, 28, 30, 36, 38, 42, 43, 45, 58–60, 62, 63, 65–67, 69, 70, 76, 77, 87, 93–96, 98–102, 104, 106, 125, 128, 132, 135–139, 143, 148, 159, 162
biological theory 17, 18, 26
Bowker, J. 160
buffers, lifespan of 58
burdensomeness 18, 23, 28–31, 33, 36, 38, 45, 62, 78, 93, 96, 98–99, 103, 105–107, 125, 136

capability for suicide 59, 61, 64–68, 112
caring contacts 17, 37, 38, 46, 47, 54, 85–88, 115, 118, 120, 129–132, 136–139
childhood, of developmental patterns 60
coach/mentor/supervisor, of suicide prevention 145–146
cognitive-behavioral theories 17, 18, 26

Cognitive Behavioral Therapy for Suicide Prevention (CBT-SP) 37
cognitive constriction 25, 27, 134, 136
cognitive dyscontrol 111, 116
cognitive models 17, 95
Collaborative Assessment and Management of Suicidality (CAMS) 36
Columbia-Suicide Severity Rating Scale (C-SSRS) 3, 50–51, 53, 113, 118
communication: classroom-level 131; external 135–136; internal 135–136; media 130–131, 135–136, 138
confidentiality and consent 148, 151
contagion 7, 58, 61, 124, 126–127, 131, 137–138, 159; diffusion 126–127
Cry of Pain framework 25–26, 94

defeat 5, 17, 18, 23–26, 29–33, 36, 38, 42, 53, 74, 75, 77–79, 85–89, 93, 94, 96–102, 104–107, 136, 137
developmental patterns: adolescence 61; adulthood 61–62; childhood 60; cultural 62–64, 69; medical 59, 61, 63, 65, 66; minority stress 11–12, 42, 45, 52, 61, 62–63, 66–68, 70, 74, 88; psychiatric and medical conditions 63–64; relational 62–64, 69; social determinants 64; and social roots of vulnerability 58–60, 62–64, 67, 68, 70; trauma 63
Diagnostic and Statistical Manual of Mental Disorders 3
Dialectical Behavior Therapy (DBT) 36
distal risk factors 42, 44–45, **49**, 53, 58; Ask Suicide-Screening Questions (ASQ) 50; Columbia-Suicide Severity Rating Scale (C-SSRS) 50–51; and dynamic risk formulation 42, 44, 47, 53; interpretive errors 47–49; Patient Health Questionnaire-9 (PHQ-9) 51; protective factors 42–44, 46–49, **49**, 53; proximal warning signs 42–43, 45–46, 49, **49**; SCS 51–53; vulnerability 41–44
Durkheim, E. 7, 13, 18–21; *Le Suicide* 7

emergency departments (EDs) 50, 114, 116
entrapment 17, 18, 23–26, 29, 31–33, 36, 38, 42, 45, 47, 51, 53, 54, 67, 74–79, 83, 85–89, *89*, 93, 95–98, 100–107, 110–113, 116, 118, 136, 137
Existential Network of Suicidal Identity (ENSI) 17–18, 30–33, 38, 95, 97, 98, 106
existential theory 18, 21–22, 28, 32
external communications 135–136

family/partner, of suicide prevention 143–144
Farberow, N. L. 2
Fenwick, E. 160
Fenwick, P. 160
Fluid Vulnerability Theory (FVT) 26–28
follow-up care 17, 37, 59, 115, 118, 131–132, 135, 158–159
Frankl, V. E. 156, 160, 161
Freud, S. 21
friend/peer, of suicide prevention 144–145
Fujimura, M. 126

Galynker, I. 97
gatekeeping 143; gatekeeper activation 131
gendered patterns 79–80, 83
Goethe, J. W.: *The Sorrows of Young Werther* 7
guardrail orientation 187

help-seeking 7, 9, 12, 36, 42, 43, 52, 58, 63, 69, 77, 79, 126, 128, 131, 132, 135, 137, 139, 148
Hillman, J. 156, 160, 162
hopelessness 17, 18, 23, 24, 26, 28, 33, 37, 45, 46, 51, 78, 97, 101, 102, 104, 106, 110, 125
Hume, D.: *Of Suicide* 7
humiliation 73–75, 77, 83, 86, 87, 89
hyperarousal 110, 111

ideation-to-action models 17–18, 38
identity 8, 13, 17, 18, 30–33, 38, 46, 47, 58–60, 62–63, 65, 67, 70, 74, 78, 86–88, 97–99, 101, 105, 106, 125, 128, 133, 134, 156, 162
imitation diffusion 126–127
immediate response playbook, of acute suicidal states 113–117
insomnia 110–114, 116, 118, 120
Integrated Motivational-Volitional (IMV) model 18, 28–35, 96, 98–99, 106
intent 1–4, 7, 17, 18, 24, 25, 29, 34, 49, 50, 65, 83, 89, 96, 100, 101, 104, 110–112, 118, 119, 144, 147, 158–160, 187, 190, 191, 198
internal communications 135–136
interpersonal theory 17, 18, 28–36, 38, 93, 95, 98
Interpersonal Theory of Suicide (IPTS) 28–35

Klein, M. 21
Kübler-Ross, E. 160

left pan (vulnerabilities) 67
Le Suicide (Durkheim) 7
lethal means safety 10, 46, 66, 107, 148, 159
loss, role of 18, 20, 33, 66

Mann's stress–diathesis formulation 26–28
meaning-making 31–33, 125, 129, 134, 155–163; closing argument 160–163; connection 155–157, 159, 160; follow-up checklists 158–159; future orientation 155–157, 163; purpose 156, 158, 161, 162; and reasons for living 156, 158, 160, 162, 163; recovery 158; safety planning 158–159; sense of danger and loss 156–157; suicidal crisis 157–158; systems lower risk 159
means safety 10, 11, 17, 20, 23, 26, 46, 47, 53, 68, 74, 76, 78, 85, 95, 102, 107, 115–117, 119, 129, 132–134, 136–139, 146, 148, 150
media communication 130–131, 135–136, 138
memorialization 127–128, 138, 187
Mikulincer, M. 23
minority stress 11–12, 42, 45, 52, 61, 62–63, 66–68, 70, 74, 88
motivational phase 29, 96, 106

Narrative Crisis Model (NCM) 17–18, 30–33, 38, 95
narrative foreclosure 38, 45, 94, 98
narrative identity 17, 18, 32, 92, 97; belonging 93–96, 98–102, 104, 106; burdensomeness 93, 96, 98, 99, 103, 105–107; narrative foreclosure 94, 98; suicidal narratives 100–103; suicidal schemas 93, 95–96, 98, 102, 105; and suicidal scripts 94, 98, 99–100, 102–103; temporal constriction 93, 105, 106
nonsuicidal self-injury (NSSI) 3–4

Of Suicide (Hume) 7
Orbach, I. 23

Papageno effect 7, 126–127, 135, 137
Patient Health Questionnaire-9 (PHQ-9) 51, 53

peer support and lived experience 148–149
Phillips, D. P. 7
positive predictive value (PPV) 52, 54
postvention 8, 124, 125, 128–131, 133, 135, 136–137, 139, 156, 159, 187, **188–190**, 190–198; anniversary calendar **198**; checklist 190–198; communication scripts **192**; contagion 124, 126, 127, 131, 137, 159; documentation **196**; do's and don'ts 187, **188–190**; leadership and roles **191**; media communication 130–131, 135–136, 138; memorialization 127–128, 138, 187; memorial page moderation plan **197**; outreach map **193**; and Papageno effect 7, 126–127, 135, 137; and prevention 136–137; principles 128–131; risk list and care pathways **194**; staff supports **195**; suicide bereavement 137; Werther effect 7, 126, 127, 137
premotivational phase 29
proactive risk management 129–130
protective factors 42–44, 46–49, **49**, 53, 61, 68, 104, 132, 134
proximal warning signs 42–43, 45–46, 49, **49**
psychache 18, 22–24, 136, 156, 160, 161; ambivalence 18; and meaning 23; psychological pain 18, 23, 24, 28, 36
Psychache Scale 23
psychodynamic theory 18, 21–22
psychological autopsy (PA) 134, 137
psychological meaning 80, **81–82**, 83
public health: collaboration with clinical care 36; strategies 64

reasons for living 29, 43, 46, 58, 59, 65, 67, 69, 70, 77, 80, 85, 156, 158, 160, 162–163
relational environment 62–64, 69
right pan (buffers) 67–68
ruminative flooding 110–113, 116, 118, 120

safety planning 17, 24, 27, 33, 36–38, 47, 66, 69, 75, 85, 87, 94, 103, 117, 119, 120, 158–159; acute suicidal states 112; crisis response 127, 129, 132, 133; family and community support 129, 130, 133, 135–137; follow-up 131–132, 135; means safety 129, 132–134, 136–139; and role clarity for helpers 17, 143–146
Safety Planning Intervention 36
Scale for Suicide Ideation 3
schools/campuses: coordination 149; postvention 131–132
self/psychache, of suicide 22–24
semantic traps 5
Shneidman, E. S. 5, 23, 156, 160–161; influence 2
small-group processing 131
social connection 20
social determinants: of developmental patterns 64; of health 59, 64, 69, 70
social media 126–127, 135–136
social rank model 94
social roots of vulnerability 58–60, 62–64, 67, 68, 70
Soper, C. A. 160, 162
The Sorrows of Young Werther (Goethe) 7
state-dependent distortions 26
state-focused assessment 112–117
Staudacher, C. 160
stress 11, 25, 42, 43, 52, 57–61, 64, 67, 68, 70; lifespan 58; Mann's stress–diathesis formulation 26–28, 37; minority stress 11–12, 42, 45, 52, 61, 62–63, 66–68, 70, 74, 88; triggers of 73–74
stress-diathesis 18, 26–28, 30, 37

suicide: attempt 3, 4, 12, 44, 63, 111, 123–139; behavior 2, 3, 7, 9, 18, 21, 22, 24, 25, 27–31, 41, 42, 44, 58, 62, 63, 68, 69, 76, 97, 117, 118, 124, 126; bereavement 124–125, 137; changes 124–125; clinical/work settings 133; contagion diffusion 126–127; ideation 4, 28, 29, 37, 58, 60–62, 75, 77, 96, 100, 102, 118; memorialization 127–128; mode 18, 23, 26–28; postvention and prevention 136–137; postvention principles 128–131; psychological autopsy (PA) 134; safety planning *see* safety planning; schemas 92–107; schools/campuses 131–132; scripts 94, 98, 99–100, 102–103; social media 135–136; stigma 135
Suicide Act 1961 8
Suicide Crisis Inventory-2 (SCI-2) 110, 113, 119
Suicide Crisis Syndrome (SCS) 30, 31–33, 38, 46, 51–53, 93, 95, 97–99, 101, 102, 104, 105–107, 110–111, 113, 115–120, *117*
suicide definitions: and classification 1–9; durable prevention 9–13; intent 1–4, 7; terminology 3
suicide prevention 5, 11, 70, 142–143, 151, 185–186; coach/mentor/supervisor 145–146; confidentiality and consent 148; directories 185; equity and context 150–151; evaluation 151; family/partner 143–144; friend/peer 144–145; leadership and organizations 185; means safety 150; national crisis lines 186; peer support and lived experience 148–149; school coordination 149; scripts 147; support 143; teacher/professor 145; workplaces coordination 149
Suicide Semiotics Model 94
suicide theories 34, **34–35**; Attachment-Based Family Therapy (ABFT) 37; Beck, A. T. 26–28; biological 17, 18, 26; cognitive-behavioral 17, 18, 26; Cognitive Behavioral Therapy for Suicide Prevention (CBT-SP) 37; collaboration with clinical care and public health 36; Collaborative Assessment and Management of Suicidality (CAMS) 36; Cry of Pain framework 25–26; Dialectical Behavior Therapy (DBT) 36; Durkheim, E. 18–21; and ENSI frameworks 18, 33; ideation-to-action 17, 18, 38; interpersonal 17, 18, 28–36, 38; Interpersonal Theory of Suicide (IPTS) 28–35; Narrative Crisis Model 17, 18, 30–33, 38; psychodynamic 18, 21–22; self/psychache 22–24; sociological 17–21
Suicide Trigger Scale (STS-3) 113
suicidology, history of 5–9
systems lower risk 159

teacher/professor, of suicide prevention 145
temporal constriction 32, 33, 38, 45, 53, 74, 79, 83, 89, 93, 105, 106
Thematic Guide for Suicide Prediction (TGSP) 134
Three-Step Theory (3ST) 18, 28–35
thwarted belongingness 28, 31, 99
trait capability 64–68
trauma 11, 61, 69, 74, 77, 133, 194; developmental patterns 63
triggers and turning points across the lifespan 7, 26, 27, 51, 53, 60, 62, 63, 65, 68, 73–89, *89*, 144; and entrapment 74–79, 83, 85–89, *89*; gendered patterns

79–80, 83; humiliation 73–75, 77, 83, 86, 87, 89; illness 78, 86, 87; including rupture 74, 79, 87; legal or financial crisis 73–74, 78, 79, 87; practice 83–86; psychological meaning 80, **81–82**, 83; role loss 73, 74, 77, 78, 83, 86, 89; stress 73–74; vulnerability 74–75
Trigger → Trap → Turn 89, *89*

US Air Force program 20

Veterans Administration 2
volitional factors 18, 78, 79, 104
volitional phase 29, 30, 96, 98, 106
vulnerability 3, 9, 11, 13, 17, 20; distal risk factors 41–44; Fluid Vulnerability Theory (FVT) 26–28; lifespan of 58; social roots of 58–60, 62–64, 67, 68, 70; triggers 74–75; vulnerability–buffer balance 67, *67*

warning signs 9, 36, 41–54, 77, 85, 114, 131, 158
Werther effect 7, 126–127, 137
Williams, J. M. G. 97–99
workplace coordination 149

For Product Safety Concerns and Information please contact our EU representative GPSR@taylorandfrancis.com
Taylor & Francis Verlag GmbH, Kaufingerstraße 24, 80331 München, Germany

www.ingramcontent.com/pod-product-compliance
Lightning Source LLC
LaVergne TN
LVHW011957040926
847296LV00030B/345

9781041278443